THE MODERN PUSHTU INSTRUCTOR

THE MODERN PUSHTU INSTRUCTOR

QAZI RAHIMULLAH KHAN

EDITED BY
H. L. OGDEN

GYAN

Published by

Gyan Publishing House
5, Ansari Road
Daryaganj, New Delhi-110002
Phone: 011-47034999, 9811692060
E-mail: books@gyanbooks.com

Distribution Network
gyanbooks.com
India, USA, Canada, UK, Australia, France

ISBN : 978-81-212-4463-3 (PB)
First Published, Peshawar, 1938

2nd Impression 2020

Printed at: Gyan Press, Delhi.

The Modern Pushtu Instructor
Author: Qazi Rahimullah Khan

CONTENTS.

Part I.

GRAMMAR.

Part II.

PROSE COMPOSITION.

AUTHORS PREFACE.

The need for a new Pushtu hand-book has become imperative since the Board of Examiners has raised the standard of Military Examinations in this language and the N. W. F. P. has achieved the dignity of a province.

The previous manuals and grammars, good as they were in their day, do not fulfil modern requirements.

The grammar, syntax rules, and exercises in this Manual are entirely original and have been designed to ensure that the student should gain a knowledge of Pushtu as spoken by genuine Pathans.

In a work of this kind where for the first time a Pathan born and bred has attempted to codify his mother tongue, it is inevitable that some errors, or at least weaknesses, should occur.

I shall be most grateful to any of my brother Munshis who may point out to me such things or make suggestions for improvements in future editions.

I dedicate this work, which has largely been a labour of love, to all future students of Pushtu.

QAZI RAHIMULLAH, Khalil.

ACKNOWLEDGEMENT.

I am most grateful to the many friends who have helped me in compiling this Manual and in particular to Maulana Abdul Qadir Khan, M. A., LLB., B. T., (Honours in Arabic), Headmaster, Islamia Collegiate School, Peshawar, and member of the Text-book Committee, Department of Education, N. W. F. P.. Peshawar.

I should also like to mention Major F. J. Dillon M.C. R.I.A.S.C., and Captain A.H.W. Rowlandson S. Waziristan Scouts. who have helped me with suggestions and idiomatic translations.

QAZI RAHIMULLAH,

TESTIMONIALS.

I have read through the New Pushtu Instructor compiled by Qazi Rahimullah and find it extremely interesting and instructive. A real Pushtu Munshi, Qazi Rahimullah has brought the experience of years of teaching to bear on the subject he has so skilfully handled and I have not the slightest hesitation in stating that this "Instructor" has supplied the need which the existing Manuals on the market fail to supply. Comparisons are odious, but as it is, the Manuals referred to above were prepared, not with a view of bringing up Pushtu Grammar to a level with grammars written in other languages, but were simply attempts at organising a few facts of Pushtu Grammar to present them to students with scanty knowledge of the language. To a real student of the language, therefore, the need for properly organised facts of Grammar was imperative and Qazi Rahimullah has done well to undertake the work. About 150 Syntax Rules have been framed, which I am sure will be appreciated by those who have something to do with Pushtu and its Grammar.

It is very easy to understand, explain and even criticize rules but it is very difficult to frame rules where no rules are in existence. Besides these the author has left out nothing that a Pushtu Manual should contain and I hope and trust that students of Pushtu Grammar will find in it all that they require for the proper understanding of the idiom and the spirit of the people who use the language. The author has collected such proverbs as are commonly used by the Pathan as he sits in his Hujra (Club) and effort has been made to supply their equivalent where possible or at least their nearest translation where an equivalent proverb in English could not be found. Idioms and proverbs relating to the various parts of the body have been similarly incorporated and effort has been made to take the students into the very midst of the Pathans sitting in their Hujras and transacting their daily business. I am confident that the "Modern Pushtu Instructor" will be welcomed by all lovers of the Pathan and his language and it is to the attention of such that I would commend this book.

Every language has certain irregularities and peculiarities and Pushtu is not immune About 130 tricky sentences have been collected and translated in Section 13 and a student of Pushtu will find great help in mastering the language if he studies them. In Volume II are to be found a number of Examination Question papers of the various Military and Civil Examinations to give students a little practice and this I am sure will be welcomed by many students who burn midnight oil to get through their examinations. There is also one special feature of Volume II which must be mentioned, and it is that the author has collected and classified the vocabulary of the various Pathan tribes like the Afridis, the Mohmands and others and I am sure this could not be found anywhere in any book written on Pushtu Grammar.

In short the "Modern Pushtu Instructor" is a valuable contribution to Pushtu literature and I hope the Author's efforts will produce the result we all desire such a book to produce.

Maulana Abdul Qadir (Yousafzai)
M.A., LLB., B. T. (Honours in Arabic) Headmaster Islamia Collegiate School, Peshawar, and Member Text Book Committee Department of Education N.- W. F. P., Peshawar.

The greatest difficulty I found in learning Pushtu was that no two grammar books used the same rules and that the manuals of those days were very limited in scope. Each was compiled for one special group of learners, Civil, Militia or Army.

None of these by itself was sufficient for the modern Military Examinations, nor, if combined, would they cover the syllabus.

A new book was needed to put the study of Pushtu on a footing with the study of the other languages.

With his "Modern Pushtu Instructor" Munshi Qazi Rahimullah has produced what was required.

The new system of verb diagrams and the grammar sections are clear ; the papers and vocabularies useful.

But, for myself, I am particularly taken with the Syntax Rules (section 10 of Part I) the tricky sentences (section 13 of Part II) and the idioms and Proverbs in Volume II When a student has mastered these he should be able correctly to use Pushtu idiom, in other words, to be able to talk sense instead of nonsense or worse. For instance, what is meant by :—

هغه پهٔ سپين آس باندِ سوردےَ

compared with— هغه پهٔ سپين آس کښې سوردےَ

or again, which do you mean to say ?

هغه پهٔ مور باندِ تلیَ دےَ

or :— هغه مور ته تلیَ دےَ

A mistake here may easily be disastrous for the speaker !

I wish Qazi Sahib all good luck with his new book.

(Sd.) F. J. DILLON,
Major R. I. A. S. C.

I have read through Qazi Rahimullah's Pushtu Instructor and feel certain that it will be a success as it fills a much felt want. The book should be of great assistance to students of the language, as the author has taken great pains to be clear and concise in the explanation of the various Syntax Rules etc. The idioms and proverbs in Vol. II of the book should prove most useful as also should the various vocabularies especially the Afridi and Court vocabularies. I wish the author every success which he well deserves for taking the trouble to write a really up to date book on the language.

(Sd.) A. ROWLANDSON,
Captain.
South Waziristan Scouts.

۷۸۶

PART I.

Pushtu Alphabet.

1. The Pushtu Alphabet consists of forty letters :—

Form	Power.	Name.
ا	A	*Alif*
ب	B	*Bé*
پ	P	*Pé*
ت	T (Soft)	*Thé*
ټ	T (Hard)	*Té*
ث	S	*Sé*
ج	J	*Jim*
ح	H (Arabic)	*Hé*
خ	Kh	*Khé*
چ	Ch	*Ché*
ځ	S or Z	*Sim* or *Zim*
د	D (Soft)	*Dāl*
ډ	Ḍ (Hard)	*Dāl*
ذ	Z	*Zāl*
ر	R (Soft)	*Ré*
ړ	R (Hard)	*Ré*
ز	Z	*Zé*
ژ	Jh	*Jhé*
ږ	G	*Gé*

Form	Power.	Name.
س	S	*Sin*
ش	Sh	*Shin*
ښ	Kh	*Khin*
ص	S	*Swād*
ض	Z	*Zwād*
ط	T	*Twé*
ظ	Z	*Zwé*
ع	A or I	*Ain*
غ	Gh	*Ghain*
ف	F	*Fé*
ق	Q	*Qāf*
ک	K	*Kāf*
ګ	G	*Gāf*
ل	L	*Lām*
م	M	*Mim*
ن	N	*Nūn*
و	O, W, U	*Wāo*
ه	H (Round)	*Hé*
ھ	H (Butterfly)	*Hé*
ء	Á	*Hamza*
=ي	E, I, or Y.	Used generally in conjunction with ي = Y. broadening the sound. ئ = ai for example = جنئ = *Jinai* = Girl.

2. The following seven letter-forms are purely Pushtu viz:—

ټ	T (Hard)	*Té*
ځ	S or Z	*Sim* or *Zim*
ډ	D (Hard)	*Dāl*
ړ	R (Hard)	*Ré*
ږ	G	*Gay*
ښ	Kh	*Khin*
ګ	G	*Gaf*

The following eight letter-forms are Arabic viz:—

ث	S	*Sé*
ح	H	*Hé*
ص	S	*Swād*
ض	Z	*Zwād*
ط	T	*Twé*
ظ	Z	*Zwé*
ع	A	*Ain*
ق	Q	*Qāf*

The following three letter-forms are common to Pushtu. Hindustani and Persian, but not found in Arabic viz:—

پ	P	*Pé*
چ	Ch	*Ché*
ژ	Jh	*Jhé*

The remaining letter forms are common to Pushtu, Arabic, Persian, and Hindustani.

3. Pushtu Script is written from right to left.

4. When writing a word, all except the following letters are joined together from the right hand side and not from the left :—

ا	A	*Alif*
د	D	*Dāl*
ډ	D	*Dāl*
ذ	Z	*Zāl*
ر	R	*Ré*
ړ	R	*Ré*
ز	Z	*Zé*
ژ	Jh	*Jhé*
ږ	G	*Gé*
و	O, W	*Wao*
ه	H (Round)	*Hé*

See the shape of above letters in the middle of a word :—

ـاـ	A	ـوـ	O, W
ـدـ	D	ـهـ	H
ـرـ	R		

NOTE :—When writing a word in which any of the above letters occurs, a space is left between this letter and the next. See the position of the letter in the middle of the following words :—

خیال	*Khyāl*
عدالت	*Adālat*
صدر	*Sadar*
سړی	*Saray*
خراپ	*Kharāp*
خوار	*Khwār*

5. The following are initial, medial and final forms of the letters :—

NAME	FINAL	MEDIAL	INITIAL
Alif	...ـا	...ـا...	ا
Bé	...ـب	...ـبـ...	...بـ
Pé	...ـپ	...ـپـ...	...پـ
Thé	...ـت	...ـتـ...	...تـ
Té	...ـټ	...ـټـ...	...ټـ
Sé	...ـث	...ـثـ...	...ثـ
Jim	...ـج	...ـجـ...	...جـ
Hé	...ـح	...ـحـ...	...حـ
Khé	...ـخ	...ـخـ...	...خـ
Ché	...ـچ	...ـچـ...	...چـ
Sim or *Zim*	...ـځ	...ـځـ...	...ځـ
Dāl	...ـد	...ـد	د

NAME	FINAL	MEDIAL	INITIAL
Dal	...ډ	...ډ	ډ
Zal	...ذ	...ذ	ذ
Ré	...ر	...ر	ر
Ré	...ړ	...ړ	ړ
Zé	...ز	...ز	ز
Jhé	...ژ	...ژ	ژ
Gé	...ږ	...ږ	ږ
Sin	...س	...ـسـ...	...سـ
Shin	...ش	...ـشـ...	.. شـ
Khin	...ښ	...ـښـ...	...ښـ
Swād	...ص	...ـصـ...	...صـ
Zwād	...ض	...ـضـ...	.. ضـ
Twé	...ط	...ـطـ...	...طـ
Zwé	...ظ	...ـظـ...	.. ظـ
Ain	...ع	...ـعـ...	.. عـ
Ghain	...غ	...ـغـ...	...غـ
Fé	...ف	...ـفـ..	...فـ
Qāf	...ق	...ـقـ.	...قـ
Kāf	...ک	...ـکـ...	...کـ
Gāf	...گ	.. ـگـ...	...گـ
Lām	...ل	...ـلـ...	لـ
Mim	...م	...ـمـ...	.. مـ
Nūn	...ن	...ـنـ...	...نـ
Wāo	...و	...ـو...	...و
Hé	...ه	.. ـهـ ..	...هـ
Yé	...ی	...ـیـ ..	.. یـ

6. Vowels :—

SHORT.		LONG.
Zabar	= *a, u*	ا - ح - ع - ه - ۀ .
Zer	= *é,*	ی = *é* ي = *ee, i,* ئ = *ai*
Pésh	= o	و = ō, *w.* ؤ = *ū, oo*

EXAMPLES.

بَټ	*But*	جَل	*Jal*
بِټ	*Bét*	جِل	*Jél*
بُټ	*Bot*	جُل	*Jol*
کَل	*Kal*	دَر	*Dar*
کِل	*Kél*	دِر	*Dér*
کُل	*Kol*	دُر	*Dor*

يَ *ay*	i. e.	سړی	*Saray*	A man
ی *é* (like 'a' in English)	i. e.	ونی	*Wané*	Trees
ي *ee, i*	i. e	مالي	*Mali*	Gardener
ئ *ai*	i. e.	جنئ	*Jinai*	Girl
ه *a* (H. soft)	i. e.	ونه	*Wana*	Tree
ۀ *uh* (H. hard)	i. e.	نیکۀ	*Nikuh*	Grand father.

NOTE—The short vowels are not written explicitly, but they are understood and consequently pronounced.

(*a*) words ending in "ah" are pronounced as "a" = ۃ = *h* (Soft) i. e. تبه = *Taba* = Fever.

(*b*) *o*, or *u* (short) at the beginning or a word = اُ = *o* or *u* i. e. اُستاذ = *Ostāz* = Teacher.

(*c*) '*E*' (short) or '*I*' at the beginning of a word اِ = *é*, *ī* i. e., اِقرار = *Iqrār* = Agreement, promise.

7, In addition to the above vowels, there are certain signs used with consonants, to modify their sound ; they are :—

(i) ٓ *mad*, only used on the top of ا = *alif* to lengthen the sound, thus = آمین = *āmin* = so be it.

(ii) ّ *tashdid* ; an Arabic sign causing the consonant over which it is placed to sound double ; thus = اِتّفاق = *Ittefāq* = a chance, union.

(iii) ً *two zabars* on the top of alif sounds "*an*" as فوراً *fauran* At once.

تخمیناً *takhminan* Nearly.

Section 2.

(READING AND WRITING EXERCISES).

(I)

ںور - مور - خور - جوړ - کار - مار - لار - سَر - وَر - پَر - نَر - اَلم

رټ - غَر - لور - سور - سُور - پُل - چَپ - سَل - میخ - زېړه

وینس - رَنګ - بَر - حَق - پیِر - چَل - جال - مال - کال - میِل

ګز - تنګ - لږ - واک - خر - سیِند - بازار - تول - مَن - اوښ

آس - اسپه - کښه - اوز - چرګ - خوار - سردار - اِقرار - آختر

اُستاذ - اوبهٔ

Kōr. Mōr. Khōr. Jōr. Kār. Mār. Lār. Sar. War. Paṛ. Nar. Lām. Rag. Ghar. Lōr. Sōr. Sūr. Pul. Chuṗ. Sal. Maikh. Raig. Wikh. Ṛang. Bar. Haq. Pir. Chal. Jāl. Māl. Kāḷ. Miḷ. Gaẓ. Tang. Ḷag. Wāk Khar. Sind. Bāžār. Tōḷ. Mad. Ükh. Áss Áspa. Kat. Aor. Cẖarg. Khwār. Sardār. Iqrār. Akhtar. Ostāz. Obuh.

(II)

دَفتَر - چَرته - دوست - خراپ - دَلته - پلار - ورور - غریب - کوهاټ

لاهور - جلال آباد - کابل - نوکر - کتاب - ماښام - وړوکی

پېښور - چترال - مردان - ړوند - چرګه - زوړ - مَیز - کُرسي

ناوخته - ټوکري - جواب - جنګ - واښهٔ - کلی - سپَی - سړیَ

مالیان- هلته- راشه- کښه- فارسِي- پښتو- پُښتُون- هندوستانِي

انګریزی. بادشاه-

Daftar. Charta. Dōst. Kharāṗ. Dalta. Plār. Vrōr. Gharib. Kohāt. Lāhōr. Jalālabād. Kābal. Nōkar. Kitāb. Mākhām. Warūkay Pékhawar. Chatrāl. Mardān. Rūnd. Charga. Zōr. Maiz. Kursai. Nāwākhta. Tōkrai. Jawāb. Jang. Wākhuh. Kalay. Spay. Saray. Mālián. Halta. Rāsha. Kaina. Fārsi. Pukhtō. Pukhtūn. Hindustāni. Angrézi. Bādshāh.

(III)

زهٔ دَ صاحب نوکریم . دا هلک ځما وروړ دےَ - ځما کور پهٔ کوهاټ کښې
دےَ - دا لار چرته تلی دَه - ځما سپےَ ناجوړ دےَ - دننه راشه - ستا
پلار دلته راغلےَ نهٔ دے - ته دَ هغهٔ څهٔ کیږے ؟ اوس ناوخته دےَ
بیا راشه - دا څوک دےَ - دَ هغهٔ کور چرته دےَ - دَ هغې مور چرته وَه
سړے باهر وَه - ځما سلام ورکړه - ورته ووایه چه دلته راشی - زهٔ به ډاکټر
وبلم - مردان خراب ځای نهٔ دے - دا لار ښهر ته تلی دَه - ډیره ښه ده

Zuh da Sāhib naukar yam. Dā halak zamā vrōr day. Zmā kōr puh Kohāt ké day. Dā lār charta talé dah. Zamā spay nājōr day. Danana rāsha. Stā plār dalta rāghalay nuh day. Tuh da haghuh suh kége. Ôss nāwakhta day. Biā rāsha. Dā sōk day. Da haghuh kōr charta day. Da haghé mōr charta wah. Saray bāhar woh. Zamā salām warkra. Warta wo wāya chi dalta rāshi. Zuh ba dāktar wo balam. Mardān kharāp zāi nuh day. Dā lār khahar ta talé dah. Déra kha dah.

(*IV*)

دوه تنَ سړی ولاړ وو - یو بادشاه ځما مُلک ته راغےَ - دَ بادشاه څوی
ناجوړ شو - دوه کالَ پس هغه مړ شو - دَ کور پهٔ خواکښې یو جماعت
دےَ - دَ کلی خلق ډیر ښهٔ دی - هغوی ټول پهٔ کورونو کښې اوسیږی

ټول سپاهيان اوس آرام کوي - ځما طلب چرته دی - کمان افسر صاحب ښه سړی دی - ټول افسران ښه دي - دهغو پلټن اوس په کراچۍ کښې ده - زر لاړشه بيا دلته مه راځه - زر زر کار کوه - زه دفتر ته ځم - په څلور بجې به بيرته راځم -

Dawa tana sari walār woo. Yao bādshāh zamạ mulk ta rāghay. Da bādshāh zōi nājōr sho Dwa kāla pas hagha mar sho. Da kōr puh khwā ké yao jumait day. Da kali khalq dair khuh di Haghāi tōl puh kōrūno ké oségi. Tōl spāhyān oss arām kawi. Zamā talab charta day. Kamān afsar sāhib khuh saray day. Tōl afsarān khuh di. Da hagho paltan oss puh Karāchai kė dah. Zar lārsha biā dalta muh rāza. Zar zar kạr kawa. Zuh daftar ta zam. Puh salōr bajé ba biartā rāzam.

Section 3.

There is no article in Pushtu, corresponding to the "a" or "an" in English, the article being inherent in the noun itself.

يو = *Yau* = one, which is an indefinite numeral, is some times used as an article, as :—

يو بادشاه = *Yau bādshāh* = A king.

PERSONAL PRONOUNS.

زهٔ	*Zuh*	I	Singular.
تهٔ	*Tuh*	Thou	
هغه	*Hagha*	He, she, it or that	
مونږ	*Mūng*	We	Plural.
تاسو	*Tāso*	You	
هغوی	*Haghūi*	They (Masculine and Feminine)	

POSSESSIVE PRONOUNS.

زما	*Zamā*	My or mine	Singular.
ستا	*Stā*	Thy or thine	
دَ هغهٔ	*Da haghuh*	His	
دَ هغې	*Da haghé*	Her	
زمونږ	*Zamūng*	Our or ours	Plural.
ستاسو	*Stāso*	Your or yours	
دَ هغوی	*Da haghūi*	Their or theirs (m. or f.)	

THE VERB "TO BE."

Present Tense.

زهٔ یم	*Zuh yam*	I am	Singular.
تهٔ یې	*Tuh yé*	Thou art	
هغه دیَ	*Hagha day*	He is	
هغه ده	*Hagha dah*	She is	

مونږ یو	*Mūng yū*	We are	Plural
تاسو یئی	*Tāso yai*	You are	
هغوی دی	*Haghūi di*	They are (M. and F.)	

FUTURE TENSE.

زهٔ به یم	*Zuh ba yam*	I will be or I shall be	Singular
تهٔ به یی	*Tuh ba yé*	Thou wilt be	
هغه به یي	*Hagha ba yi* or	He, she, it will be	
هغه به وي	*Hagha ba wi*		
مونږ به یو	*Mūng ba yū*	We will be	Plural.
تاسو به یئ	*Tāso ba yai*	You will be	
هغوی به یي	*Haghūi ba yi* or	They will be (M. and F.)	
هغوی به وی	*Haghūi ba wi*		

PAST TENSE.

زهٔ وم	*Zuh wam*	I was	Singular
تهٔ وی	*Tuh wé*	Thou wast	
هغه وهٔ	*Hagha woh*	He was	
هغه وه	*Hagha wah*	She was	
مونږ وو	*Mūng woo*	We were	Plural.
تاسو وئ	*Tāso wai*	You were	
هغوی وو	*Haghūi woo*	They were	
هغوی وې	*Haghūi wé*	They were (Feminine)	

Section 4.

PREPOSITIONS AND POST-POSITIONS

A preposition is composed of two parts and the noun or pronoun qualified is placed in the middle, while a postposition is always placed after the noun or pronoun.

NOTE :—The inflected form of زه = *Zuh* is ما = *mā*; and ته = *tuh* is تا = tā, of هغه = *hagha* is هغهٔ = *haghuh* and in the case of feminine singular هغه = *hagha* becomes هغې = *haghé*; while in 1st 2nd and 3rd person plural the pronouns remain uninflected, as :—

لهٔ نه = *Luh-na* from

لهٔ ما نه	*Luh mā na*	from me	Singular
لهٔ تا نه	*Luh tā na*	from thee	
لهٔ هغهٔ نه	*Luh haghuh na*	from him	
لهٔ هغې نه	*Luh haghé na*	from her	
لهٔ موږ نه	*Luh mūng na*	from us	Plural
لهٔ تاسو نه	*Luh tāso na*	from you	
لهٔ هغوی نه	*Luh haghūi na*	from them	
لهٔ هغوی نه	*Luh haghūi na*	from them (Feminine)	

NOTE:—Either of the two parts can be used to express the same meaning as above, but the first part can only be used with nouns and pronouns ending in consonants, in which case

Zabar = *a*, should be put over the last consonant letter of the noun and pronoun, instead of نه = *na*, as :—

لهٔ پېښور نه	*Luh pekhawar na*	From Peshawar.
پېښور نه	*Pekhawar na*	
لهٔ پېښوره	*Luh pekhawara*	

ته = *ta* له = *la* لره = *lara* or وته = *wata* = to as :—

ماته	*mā ta*	to me	Singular.
تاته	*tā ta*	to thee	
هغهٔ ته	*haghuh ta*	to him	
هغې ته	*haghé ta*	to her	
مونږ ته	*mūng ta*	to us	Plural.
تاسو ته	*tāso ta*	to you	
هغوی ته	*haghūi ta*	to them	
هغوی ته	*haghūi ta*	to them (Feminine)	

NOTE :—Decline the personal pronouns with the following post or prepositions as above :—

پهٔ-کښې	*puh-ké*	In
پهٔ ماکښې	*puh mā ké*	In me etc.

NOTE :—The last part of above can also be used to express the same meaning as:—

پهٔ پېښور کښې	or *puh pekhawar ké*	In Peshawar.
یا	or	
پېښور کښې	*pekhawar ké*	
پهٔ-باندې	*puh-bāndé*	On.
پهٔ ما باندې	*puh mā bāndé*	On me etc.

NOTE :—Either of the two parts of above can be used to express the same meaning as :—

پۀ میز باندې	*Puh méz bāndé*	On the table.
پۀ میز	*Puh méz*	
میز باندې	*Méz bāndé*	
لاندې	*Lāndé*	Beneath, below, under.
مالاندې	*Mā lāndé*	Beneath, below or under me etc.

NOTE :—Certain post-positions can also be used with the noun or pronoun in the Genitive Case *e. g.* :—

دَ دَلاندې یا	*da-da lāndé* or	Beneath, below or under.
دَلاندې	*da-lāndé*	
ځما دلاندې	*zamā da lāndé*	Under me.
ځما لاندې	*Zamā lāndé*	Under me.
ځما میز دَلاندې	*Zamā méz da lāndé*	Under my table.
ځما میز لاندې	*Zamā méz lāndé*	Under my table.
سره	*Sara*	With.
ماسره	*Mā sara*	With me.
	or	
د سره	*da sara*	With.
ځما سره	*Zamā sara*	With me etc.
دپاره	*Dapāra*	For
دَ دَپاره	*Da dapāra*	
ما دَپاره	*Mā dapāra*	For me etc.
ځما دَپاره	*Zama da pāra*	

پشان	*Pashān*	Like
دَپشان	*Da pashān*	
ما پشان	*Mā pashān*	Like me
خما پشان	*Zamā pashān*	
کره	*Kara*	In the house of
دَکره	*Da kara*	
ما کره	*Mā kara*	In my house etc
خما کره	*Zamā kara*	
پوری	*Pōré*	Near or by
ما پوری	*Mā poré*	Near or by me etc.
ته نیزدی	*Ta nizdé*	Near
ما ته نیزدی	*Mā ta nizdé*	
سخه	*Sakha*	Near, it is also used for the possessive case in the verb to have.
دَسخه	*Da sakha*	

EXAMPLE I

ما سخه	*Mā sakha*	Near me etc:
یا	or	
خما سخه	*Zamā sakha*	

EXAMPLE II

ما سخه کتاب دیَ	*Mā sakha kitāb day*	lit, near me book is = I have a book.
یا	or	
خما سخه کتاب دیَ	*Zamā sakha kitāb day*	
تا سخه کتاب دیَ	*Tā sakha kitāb day*	lit near thee book is = thou hast a book.
	or	
ستا سخه کتاب دیَ	*Stā sakha kitāb day*	

هغهٔ سخه کتاب دیَ	*Haghuh sakha kitāb day*	lit near him book is = he has a book.
یا	or	
دَ هغهٔ سخه کتاب دیَ	*Da haghuh sakha kitab day*	

NOTE:—سخه *sakha,* can only be used when the object is light and moveable as well as to denote owner-ship otherwise the possessive case should be used as :—

ما سخه یو قلم دیَ	*Mā sakha yau qalam day*	I have a pen
ملک سخه یوه اسپه ده	*Malak sakha yawa aspa dah*	The malik owns a mare
ستا څو کورونه دي	*Stā so korūna dee*	How many houses have you?
ستا څو ورونړه دي	*Sta so vrūnra dee*	How many brothers have you ?

دَ پاسَ	*Da pāsa*	above.
دَ...دَ پاسَ	*da...da pāsa*	
ما دَ پاسَ	*Mā dapāsa*	above me etc.
ځما دَ پاسَ	*Zamā dapāsa*	
دَ...په مینځ کښې	*da...pa mianz ké*	in the middle of or through, among.
دَ باغ په مینځ کښې	*da bāgh pa mianz ké*	Through the garden.
لهٔ...نه وړاندې	*luh na varāndé*	before (in place)
دَ...دَ وړاندې	*da...da varāndé*	

لهٔ مانه وړاندِ خما دَوړاندِ	*luh mā na vrāndé* or *Zamā da vrāndé*	before me (etc).
لهٔ...نه وړمبی یا لهٔ-نه اول	*luh-na vrūmbay* or *awal*	before (in time.)
لهٔ ما نه وړمبی لهٔ ما نه اول	*luh mā na vrūmbay* *luh mā na awal*	before me
لهٔ...نه ورستو دَ...دَ ورستو	*luh-na vrosto* *da...da vrosto*	behind (in place)
لهٔ ما نه ورستو یا خما دَ ورستو	*Luh mā na vrosto* or *Ẑmā da vrosto*	behind me.
لهٔ...نه پس	*Luh-na pas*	after (in time).
لهٔ ما نه پس	*Luh mā na pas*	after me etc.

NOTE:—پس = *Pas*, does not inflect any noun of time.

پسی = *Pasé* = after (in the case of a person or business).

ما پسی	*Mā pasé*	after me.
څهٔ پسی	*suh pasé*	after what business).
لهٔ..نه دی خوا	*Luh-na dé khwā*	this side of.
لهٔ دفتر نه دی خوا	*Luh daftar na dé khwā*	this side of the office.
لهٔ...نه هغه خوا	*Luh-na hagha khwā*	beyond.
لهٔ دفتر نه هغه خوا	*Luh daftar na hagha khwa*	Beyond the office.
لهٔ..نه گیرچاپیره	*Luh-nā gér chāpéra*	around.
لهٔ ښهر نه گیر چاپیره	*Luh khahar na gér chāpéra*	Around the City.

دَ...پۀ باب کښې	*Da...puh bāb ké*	About, concerning.
زما پۀ باب کښې	*Zmā puh bāb ké*	About me etc.
دَ...پۀ سبب یا دَ...پۀ وجه	*Da...puh sabab* or *Da puh waja*	Owing to, on account of or by reason of
دَ باران پۀ سبب یا دَ باران پۀ وجه	*Da bārān puh sabab* or *Da bārān puh waja*	Owing to the rain
دَ...پۀ مؤجب	*Da...puh mūjeb*	According to
دَ حکم پۀ مؤجب	*Da hukam puh mūjeb*	According to order
بې لۀ.. نه	*bé luh...na*	Without, except, besides.
بې لۀ ما نه	*bé luh mā na*	Without me etc.
دَ...پۀ شا	*Da...puh shā*	At the back of
دَ کور پۀ شا	*Da kōr puh shā*	At the back of the house.
دَ	*Da*	Of
دَ میجر صاحب آس	*Da maijar sāhib ass*	The Major's horse.

The particles را = *Rā*, در = *Dar*, ور = *War* are used with post positions and with the 2nd part of prepositions as well as with some verbs denoting the singular and plural both numbers and they have the force of personal pronouns :—

را	*Rā*	For 1st person singular and plural.
در	*Dar*	For 2nd ,, ,, ,,

ور	*War*	For 3rd person singular and plural.

as :—

را نه	*Rā na*	From me or from us.
در نه	*Dar na*	From thee or from you.
ور نه	*War na*	From him or from them, her, or it.
را باندی	*Rā bāndė*	On me or on us.
در باندی	*Dar bāndė*	On thee or on you.
ور باندی	*War bandė*	On him or on them, her or it.
را ته	*Rā ta*	To me or to us.
در ته	*Dar ta*	To thee or to you.
ور ته	*War ta*	To him or to them.
را سره	*Rā sara*	With me or with us.
در سره	*Dar sara*	With thee or with you.
ور سره	*War sara*	With him or with them, her or it.
وتل	*Watal*	To go out.
را وتل	*Rā watal*	To come out towards me or us.
در وتل	*Dar watal*	To come out towards thee or you.
ور وتل	*War watal*	To come out towards him or them, her or it.

Section 5.

THE NOUN.

A noun is a word denoting a person, place or thing, and has two Genders—Masculine and

Feminine and two numbers—Singular and Plural :—

ENDINGS OF MASCULINE NOUNS.

I. Nouns ending in ی = *ay*. are masculine as :—

سړی *Saray* A man.

کلی *Kalay* Village.

پړی *Paray* Rope.

سپی *Spay* Dog.

مړی *Maray* Dead body.

کاڼړی *Kānray* Stone.

II. Nouns ending in consonants are masculine as :—

چرگ *Charg* Cock.

هلک *Halak* Boy.

میز *Méz* Table.

کور *Kōr* House.

دفتر *Daftar* Office.

مَلک *Malak* Head man.

EXCEPTIONS:—

لار *Lār* Road.

پلټن *Paltan* Regiment.

ورځ *Vraz* Day.

وریځ *Woriaz* Cloud.

میاشت *Miāsht* Month, half moon.
برستن *Brastan* Quilt.
څرمن *Sarman* Skin, leather.
څنګل *Sangal* Elbow.
دُرشل *Durshal* Frame of a door.
ږُمنز *Gumanz* Comb.
ستن *Stan* Needle. Pillar, Telegraph Post.
لمن *Lman* Skirt.
میچن *Mechan* Hand Mill.

III. Nouns ending in ي = *ī*, denoting profession are masculine as :—

مالي *Mālī* Gardener.
دوبي *Dōbī* Washerman.
نايي *Nāyī* Barber.
قاضي *Qāzī* Judge.
موچي *Mochi* Shoe Maker.

IV. Nouns ending in ه = *uh*. (Hard) are masculine as :—

واده *Wāduh* Marriage.
نیکه *Nikuh* Grand father.
کارغه *Kārghuh* Crow.
مارغه *Mārghuh* Bird.

EXCEPTIONS :—

چاړه *Chāruh* Knife (Fem).
تیاره *Tyāruh* Darkness (Fem).

ENDINGS OF FEMININE NOUNS.

I. Nouns ending in ہَ = *h* (soft) are feminine as :—

وَنَہ	*Wana*	Tree.
تَبَہ	*Taba*	Fever.
ښځَہ	*Khaza*	Woman or wife.
چغَہ	*Chagha*	Pursuit party.
مږَہ	*Maga*	Rat.
خټَہ	*Khata*	Mud.

II. Nouns ending in ئ = *ai* are feminine as:—

جنئ	*Janai*	Girl.
چټئ	*Chitai*	Letter.
ټوکرئ	*Tokrai*	Basket.
ګلئ	*Galai*	Hail-storm, Hail-stone.
نالئ	*Nālai*	Quilt.
سیلئ	*Silai*	Sand or dust-storm.
څپلئ	*Saplai*	Sandals.

III. Nouns ending in ی = *ī* denoting qualities are feminine as :—

دوستِی	*Dostī*	Friendship.
بدِی	*Badī*	Enmity, feud.
دُشمنِی	*Dushmanī*	Enmity.
غریبِی	*Gharibī*	Poverty.

نیکي	*Nekī*	Goodness.
نا مردي	*Nāmardī*	Cowardice.

IV. Nouns = ending in ا = ā (*alif*) are feminine as :—

بلا	*Balā*	Calamity.
قلا	*Qalā*	Fort.
سزا	*Sazā*	Punishment.
نیا	*Niā*	Grand-mother.
ژړا	*Jharā*	Crying, weeping.
خندا	*Khandā*	Laughter.

EXCEPTIONS —

ملا	*Mulā*	A priest	ملا یان	*Mulayan*	Priests.
گدا	*Gadā*	A beggar	گدایان	*Gadayan*	Beggars.
کاکا	*Kakā*	An uncle (Polite term of calling an old man	کاکا گان	*Kākāgān*	Uncles.

سنډا	*Sandā*	Male buffalo.
سنډ گان	*Sandgān*	Male Buffaloes.

V. Nouns ending in و = *o*, are feminine as :—

پیشو	*Pisho*	Cat.
بیزو	*Bizo*	Monkey.
ور شو	*Warsho*	Grazing ground.
لانبو	*Lānbo*	A swim.

FORMATION OF FEMININE FROM MASCULINE.

I. Nouns ending in ی = *ay,* form their feminine by changing this letter in ئ = *ai* as :—

سپی	*Spay*	Dog.	سپئ	*Spai*	Bitch
چیلی	*Chelay*	He goat.	چیلئ	*Chelai*	She goat.
نوسی	*Nwasay*	Grand son	نوسئ	*Nwasai*	Grand daughter.
اوسی	*Osay*	Antelope.	اوسئ	*Osai*	Female antelope

II. Nouns ending in consonants form their feminine by adding ه = *h* (soft) as :—

چرگ	*Charg*	Cock	چرگه	*Charga*	Hen
خر	*Khar*	He ass	خره	*Khara*	She ass
گډ	*Gad*	Male sheep	گډه	*Gada*	F. sheep
غل	*Ghal*	Thief	غله	*Ghla*	F. thief
آس	*Ass*	Horse	آسپه	*Aspa*	Mare.

(Persian = اسپ = *Asp* = horse)

III. Nouns ending in ي = *i* form their feminine by changing this letter into نړه = *nra* (or *narah*) as :—

دوبي	*Dobi*	Washerman.
دوبنړه	*Dōbanra*	Washer woman.
نائيي	*Nāi*	Barber.
نائينړه	*Nāyanra*	Barber's wife.

مالي	*Māli*	Gardener.
مالنړه	*Mālanra*	Gardener's wife, f. gardener.
بنګي	*Bangi*	Sweeper.
بنګنړه	*Banganra*	Sweeper's wife.

NUMBER OF MASCULINE NOUNS.

I. Nouns ending in ی = *ay* form their oblique singular and nominative plural by changing this letter into ي = *i* as:—

سړی *Saray* A man. سړي *Sari* Men.

سپی *Spay* A dog. سپي *Spi* Dogs.

له سړي نه *Luh Sari na* from a man (ob. s.)

II. Nouns ending in consonants denoting animate objects and those ending in ي = *ī* remain un-changed in the oblique singular and form their nominative plural by adding آن = *ān,* and those denoting time, measure, and weight, form their plural by adding ——*zabar* over the final letter as :—

هلک *Halak* Boy. هلکان *Halakān* Boys.

ملک *Malak* Head Man ملکان *Malakān* Head men.

د ملک *da malak* of the head man (remains un-changed).

Singular.			Plural.		
کال	*Kāl*	Year.	کالَ	*Kāla*	Years.
ګز	*Gaz*	Yard.	ګزَ	*Gaza*	Yards.

	Singular.			Plural.	
من	*Man*	Maund.	مَن	*Mana*	Maunds
سیر	*Sér*	Seer.	سیَر	*Séra*	Seers.
میل	*Mīl*	Mile.	میلَ	*Mīla*	Miles.
قدم	*Qadam*	Pace.	قدمَ	*Qadama*	Paces.
جیرب	*Jirub*	½ acre.	جیربَ	*Jiruba*	Jiribs.
ملیټ	*Mélat*	Minute.	ملیټَ	*Mẹlata*	Minutes

III. Nouns ending in consonants denoting in-animate objects remain unchanged in the oblique singular and form their nominative plurals by adding ونه = *ūna* as:–

کور	*Kōr*	House.	کورُونه	*Korūna*	Houses
کتاب	*Kitāb*	Book.	کتابُونه	*Kitābūna*	Books.
میز	*Méz*	Table.	میزُونه	*Mézūna*	Tables

پہ کور کښی *Pa kōr ké* In the house (ob.s.)

IV. Nouns ending in وُ = *ū*. They remain unchanged in the oblique singular and form their nominative plural by adding گان = *gān* as:––

بابُو	*Bābū*	Clerk.	بابُوگان	*Bābūgān*	Clerks.
میلُو	*Mélū*	Bear.	میلُوگان	*Mélūgān*	Bears.
پارُو	*Pārū*	Snake charmer.	پاروگان	*Pārūgān*	Snake charmers
تارُو	*Tārū*	Francolin.	تارُوگان	*Tārūgān*	Francolins.

دَ بابُو *Da bābū* of the clerk. (ob. s.)

V. Nouns having ۇ = *ū* in the last syllable, change the ۇ = *ū* into ا = *ā* = (alif) and ۀ = *H* (hard) after it to form their nominative plural and they remain unchanged in the oblique singular:—

پښتون	*Pukhtūn*	Pathan.	پښتانۀ	*Pukhtā-nuh*	Pathans
شپون	*Shpūn*	Shepherd,	شپانۀ	*Shpānuh*	Shepherds.
سور	*Sōr*	Horse man, rider.	سوارۀ	*Swāruh*	Riders.

دَ پښتون *Da pukhtūn* of the Pathan. (ob. s.)

VI. Some nouns form their nominative plural irregularly as :—

ورور	*Vrōr*	Brother	ورونړه	*Vrūnrah*	Brothers
ځوي	*Zōi*	Son	ځامن	*Zāman*	Sons.
ترۀ	*Truh*	Uncle	ترونه	*Trūna*	Uncles (Paternal)
ماما	*Mā mā*	Uncle	ماماګان	*Māmā gān*	Uncles. (Maternal)
اس	*Ass*	Horse	اسونه	*Assūna*	Horses.
غل	*Ghăl*	Thief	غلۀ	*Ghluh*	Thieves.
میلمه	*Mélma*	Guest	میلمانۀ	*Mèlmānuh*	Guests.
زړۀ	*Zruh*	Heart	زړونه	*Zrūna*	Hearts.

VII. Some nouns, are only used in the plural as :—

شراپ	*Sharāp*	Wine.
غنم	*Ghanam*	Wheat.
جوار	*Jowār*	Maize.

پئ	*Pai*	Milk.
ماستۀ	*Māstuh*	Curds.
کُچ	*Kuch*	Butter.
تیل	*Tail*	Oil.
اپیم	*Apim*	Opium.
ماغزۀ	*Māghzuh*	Brain.
زهر	*Zahar*	Poison.
بانړۀ	*Bānruh*	Eye-lashes
اوړۀ	*Oruh*	Flour.
سکارۀ	*Skāruh*	Charcoal.
ریښم	*Rékham*	Silk.

NUMBER OF FEMININE NOUNS.

1. Nouns ending in ۀ = *h* (soft) form their oblique singular and nominative plural by changing this letter into ي = *é* as :—

ونه	*Wana*	Tree	ونی	*Wané*	Trees.
تبه	*Taba*	Fever	تبی	*Tabé*	Fevers.

دَونی *Da wané* of the tree. (ob. s.)

NOTE :—In the locative case feminine singular they are not inflected.

پۀ ونه کښې	*Puh wana ké*	In the tree.
پۀ ونه باندې	*Puh wana bāndé*	On the tree.

EXCEPTION.

Feminine nouns ending in ي = *i*.

دوستی	*Dōsti*	Friendship.
پہ دوستئ کښې	*Puh dōstai ké*	In friendship.

II. Nouns ending in ی = ī form their oblique singular and nominative plural by changing this letter into ئ = *ai*, as :

دوستی *Dōsti* Friendship دوستئ *Dōstai* Friendships
دشمنی *Dushmanī* Enmity دشمنئ *Dushmanai* Enmities.
پهٔ دوستئ کښې *Puh dostai ké* In friendship (Ob. S.)

III. Nouns ending in consonants form their oblique singular and nominative plural by adding ے = *é*, or zer under the final letter.

یوه ورځ *Yawa vraz* One day دوه ورځے *Dwa vrazé* Two days.
پلټن *Paltan* Regiment پلټنے *Paltané* Regiments.
د ورځے *Da vrazé* of the day (idiomatic "in the day time") Ob. S.

IV. Nouns ending in ئ = *ai*, remain unchanged in the oblique singular and nominative plural as :—

جنئ *Jinai* Girl or girls جنکئ *Jinakai* Girls.
(In Khalil and Mohmand.)
درئ *Darai* Carpet or Carpets.
څپلئ *Saplai* Sandal or Sandals.
د جنئ *Da jinai* of the girl. (Ob. S.)

V. Nouns ending in ا = *ā* (alif) remain unchanged in the oblique singular and nominative plural in Yusafzai, but in Khalil and Mohmand add گانی = *gāné* as :—

قلا *Qalā* Fort or Forts.

(Khalil and Mohmand قلا گانی = *Qalā gāné* = Forts.)

نیا *Niā* Grand mother or Grand mothers.

(In Khalil and Mohmand نیا گانی = *Niā gāné* = Grand mothers)

په قلا کښې *Puh qalā ké* In the fort.

VI. Some nouns form their plural irregularly as :—

لوړ	*Lūr*	Daughter	لونړه	*Lūnra*	Daughters
مور	*Mōr*	Mother	میندی	*Méndé*	Mothers
خور	*Khōr*	Sister	خویندی	*Khwéndé*	Sisters.
ترور	*Trōr*	Aunt	تروریاني	*Trōryāné*	Aunts

VII. Some nouns are only used in the plural as :—

اوربشي	*Orbashé*	Barley
شوملی	*Shōmlé*	Butter milk.
وريژي	*Vrijhé*	Rice (in shop)
شولی	*Shōlé*	Rice (in field)
توکانړی	*Tukānré*	Spittle.
اوبهٔ	*Obuh*	Water.

OBLIQUE PLURAL.

All masculine and feminine plural nouns

form their oblique plural by adding و = "*o*" to the last consonant letter of the word as:—

لهٔ سړونه	*Luh sarō na*	From men.
پهٔ ښځو باندې	*Puh khazō bāndé*	On the women
مالیانو ته	*Māliāno ta*	To the gardeners
پهٔ کورونو کښې	*Puh korūno ké*	In the houses.

CASE OF NOUN.

There are eight cases of noun in Pushtu :—

1.	Nominative.	Subject always, but object in the past tenses of a transitive verb.
2.	Accusative	Object in the present and future.
3.	Agentive	Subject in past tenses of a transitive verb.
4.	Genitive	Possessive (دَ = *da* = of)
5.	Dative	In direct object (ته = *ta*, له = *la* or لره = *lara* = to)
6.	Ablative	Distance from a place (لهٔ-نه = *luh-na* = from)
7.	Locative	Remaining in a place: (په-کښې *pa-ké* in) (پهٔ-باندې *puh-bāndé* on)
8.	Vocative	Used in calling.

INFLECTION OF MASCULINE NOUNS.

I. Nouns ending in يَ = *ay* are thus inflected :—

Singular.	Plural.
1. Nominative :	
سَړی *Saray* A man	سړيِ *Sari* men
2. Accusative :	
سَړی *Saray* The man	سړيِ *Sari* The men
3. Agentive :	
سړيِ *Sari* By a man	سړو *Saro* by men
4. Genitive :	
د سړيِ *Da sari* Of a man	دَ سړو *da saro* of the men
5. Dative :	
سړي ته *Sari ta* To a man	سړو ته *Sarō ta* To men
6. Ablative :	
له سړيِ نه *Luh sarī na* From a man	له سړونه *Luh saro na* From men
7. Locative :	
په سړيِ کښې *Puh sari ké* In a man	په سړو کښې *Puh saro ké* In men
8. Vocative :	
ای سړيه *Ay sarīya* Oh man !	اي سړو *Ay saro* Oh men !

NOTE :—The nominative and accusative are the same in both Singular and plural, therefore if one knows nominative, then one will know the accusative, and if one knows the agentive one will also know all the rest.

II. Nouns ending in consonants denoting animate objects are thus inflected :—

	Singular.		Plural.	
Nominative	هلک	*Halak* Boy	هلکان	*Halakān* Boys
Agentive	هلک	*Halak* by boy	هلکانو	*Halakāno* by boys.

III. Nouns ending in consonants denoting in animate objects are thus inflected :—

	Singular.		Plural.	
Nominative	کور	*Kōr* House	کورونه	*Korūna* Houses
Agentive	کور	*Kōr* by house	کورونو	*Korūno* by houses.

INFLECTION OF FEMININE NOUNS.

I. Nouns ending in ه = *h*, are inflected thus:--

	Singular.		Plural.	
Nom	ونه	*Wana* Tree	ونې	*Wané* Trees.
Agent	ونې	*Wané* by tree	ونو	*Wanō* by trees

II. Nouns ending in ي = *ī*, are inflected thus:-

	Singular.		Plural.	
Nom	دوستي	*Dōstī* Friendship	دوستئ	*Dostai* Friendships.
Agent	دوستئ	*Dostai* by Friendship	دوستو	*Dōsto* by Friendships.

III. Nouns ending in consonants are inflected thus :—

	Singular.		Plural.	
Nom	ورځ *Vraz*	Day	ورځ یا ورځې *Vrazé*	Days.
Agent	ورځې *Vrazé*	by day	ورځو *Vrazō*	by days.

IV. Nouns ending in ۍ = *ai*, are declined thus :—

	Singular.		Plural.	
Nom	جنۍ *Jinai*	girl	جنۍ *Jinai* or جنکۍ *Jinakài*	girls.
Agent	جنۍ *Jinai*	by girl	جینو *Jino* or جنکو *Jinakō*	by girls.

V. Nouns ending in ا = a (*alif*) are declined thus :—

	Singular.		Plural.	
Nom	قلا *Qalā*	Fort	قلا *Qalā* or قلاګانې *qalāgāné*	forts.
Agent	قلا *Qalā*	by fort	قلاو *Qalāo* or قلاګانو *Qalāgānō*	by forts.

Section 6.

THE ADJECTIVE.

The adjective follows the rules of the noun for Gender, number and case. It is generally placed before its noun.

EXAMPLE :—

I. نرى سړى *Naray saray* A thin Man.
نري سړي *Nari sari* thin men.

دَ نرِی سڑِی *Da nari sari* of a thin man (m. ob. s)

دَ نرو سڑو *Da narō sarō* of thin men (mas. ob. plu).

نریٔ ښځه *narai khaza* thin woman.

نریٔ ښځی *narai khazé* thin women.

دَ نریٔ ښځی *da narai khazé* of a thin woman (f. ob. s.)

دَ نرو ښځو *da narō khazō* of thin women (f. ob. plu.)

II. But note:—Expressing sympathy.

سڑَی نرَی دَی *saray naray day* the man is thin.

ښځه نریٔ دَه *khaza narai dah* the woman is thin.

سڑَی نا جوړَ دَی *saray nā jora day* the man is (unfortunately) ill.

2. The following adjectives ending in ی = *ay* Change ي = *ay* into ی = *i*. in the nominative plural and form their feminine singular and plural by changing ی = *ay* into ي = *é* as:—

m. s.		f. s. & f. p.	
نوَي *naway*		نوي *nawé*	new.
تږَي *tagay*		تږي *tagé*	thirsty.
غلَي *ghalay*		غلي *ghalé*	silent.
خوشَي *khūshay*		خوشي *khushé*	useless
اوږَي *ogay*		اوږي *ogé*	hungry.

وړوکی	*warūkay*	وړوکي	*warūké*	small.
وړکوټی	*warkōtay*	وړکوټي	*warkōté*	small.
کمزوری	*kamzōray*		*kamzōré*	weak.

3. Adjectives ending in consonants do not change in the nominative plural and follow the rules of nouns for feminine singular and plural as:—

خراب سړی	*kharāp saray*	A bad man.
خراب سړي	*kharāp sari*	Bad men.
خرابه ښځه	*kharāpa khaza*	A bad woman.
خرابې ښځې	*kharāpé khazé*	Bad women.

4. The following adjectives remain unchanged except in the oblique plural :—

خائیسته	*Khāiesta*	beautiful or handsome.
ناکاره	*nā kāra*	bad, ugly.
خپه	*khapa*	unhappy.
دروغ	*darogh*	lie.
رښتیا	*rikhtiā*	true.
ځیني	*ziné or bāzé*	some.
پوره	*pūra*	complete.
بی حیا	*bé hayā*	shameless.
بی وفا	*bé wafā*	faithless.
وړیا	*wéryā*	free, gratis.
مفت	*muft*	free, gratis.
ټکړه	*takra*	strong.

5. The following adjectives are irregular as :—

M. S.	M. P.	F. S.	F. P.	
مړ *Mar*	مړهٔ *mruh*	مړه *mra*	مړی *mré*	dead
لُوند *lūnd*	لاوندهٔ *lāunduh*	لونده *launda*	لاوندی *laundé*	wet.
کوږ *kōg*	کاږهٔ *kāguh*	کږه *kaga*	کږی *kagé*	crooked.
درُوند *drūnd*	درانهٔ *drānuh*	درنه *drana*	درنی *drané*	heavy.
موړ *mōr*	ماړهٔ *māruh*	مړه *mara*	مړی *maré*	rich, replete.
پروت *prōt*	پراتهٔ *prātuh*	پرته *prata*	پرتی *prate*	prostrate.
زوړ *zōr*	زاړهٔ *zāruh*	زړه *zara*	زړی *zaré*	old.
تود *tōd*	تاودهٔ *tāuduh*	توده *tauda*	تودی *taudé*	hot.
تریو *triw*	تاروهٔ *tārwuh*	تروه *trawa*	تروی *tarwé*	sour
خوږ *khōg*	خواږهٔ *khwā-guh*	خوږه *khwaga*	خوږی *khwagé*	sweet.
ترینس *trikh*	تارخهٔ *tārkhuh*	ترخه *tārkha*	ترخی *tarkhé*	bitter
وروست *vrōst*	وراستهٔ *vrāstuh*	وروسته *vrasta*	وروستی *vrasté*	rotten.
شین *shin*	شنهٔ *shnuh*	شنه *shna*	شنی *shné*	green.

ړوند *rūnd* ړانده *rānduh* ړنده *randa* ړندې *randé* blind.

کوڼ *kūnr* کاڼه *kānruh* کڼه *kanra* کڼې *kanré* deaf.

پوښ *pōkh* پاښه *pākhuh* پښه *pakha* پښې *pakhé* cooked, ripe.

6. COMPARISON OF ADJECTIVE.

There is no special form for the Comparative Degree in Pushtu. Comparison is expressed by using the Positive Degree with the Ablative case as :—

آس لهٔ اوښ نه ګړندی دی = *Ass luh ūkh na garanday day* the horse is swifter than the Camel.

SUPERLATIVE.

There is no special form for the superlative degree in Pushtu. It is expressed by using the positive degree with the following phrases as :—

لهٔ ټولو نه	*luh tōlō na*	than all	Used by Khalils.
لهٔ واړو نه	*luh wārō na*		Yusafzais
لهٔ جمله ونه	*luh jumlaō na*		Afghans.

as :—

دا هلک لهٔ ټولو نه هوښيار دی *dā halak luh tōlo na hukhyār day*

This boy is the cleverest

Section 7.

THE NUMERAL CARDINAL NUMBERS.

1	—	١	یو	*Yau.*
2	—	٢	دوه	*dwa.*
3	—	٣	دري	*dré.*
4	—	۴	څلور	*salōr.*
5	—	۵	پنځه	*pinzuh.*
6	—	۶	شپږ	*shpag.*
7	—	٧	اوهٔ	*owuh.*
8	—	٨	اتهٔ	*atuh.*
9	—	٩	نههٔ	*nahuh.*
10	—	١٠	لس	*las.*
11	—	١١	یَو لس	*yaolas.*
12	—	١٢	دو لس	*dōlas.*
13	—	١٣	دیارلس	*diārlas.*
14	—	١۴	څوارلس	*swārlas.*
15	—	١۵	پنځهٔ لس	*pinzalas.*
16	—	١۶	شپاړس	*shpāras.*
17	—	١٧	اولس	*owalas.*
18	—	١٨	اتَلس	*atalas.*
19	—	١٩	نُولس	*nūlas.*
20	—	٢٠	شل	*shal.*
21	—	٢١	یو ویشت	*yau wīsht.*
22	—	٢٢	دوه ویشت	*dwa wīsht.*
23	—	٢٣	در ویشت	*dar wīsht.*
24	—	٢۴	څلیریشت	*salréīsht.*
25	—	٢۵	پنځهٔ ویشت	*pīnza wisht.*

26 — ۲۶ شپږ ویشت *shpag wisht.*
27 — ۲۷ اوهٔ ویشت *owuh wisht.*
28 — ۲۸ اتهٔ ویشت *atuh wisht.*
29 — ۲۹ نههٔ ویشت *nahuh wisht.*
30 — ۳۰ دیرش *dérsh.*
31 — ۳۱ یو دیرش *yau dérsh.*
32 — ۳۲ دوه دیرش *dwa dérsh.*
33 — ۳۳ دری دیرش *dré dérsh.*
34 — ۳۴ څلور دیرش *salōr dersh.*
35 — ۳۵ پنځهٔ دیرش *pinzuh dérsh.*
36 — ۳۶ شپږ دیرش *shpag dérsh.*
37 — ۳۷ اوهٔ دیرش *owuh dérsh.*
38 — ۳۸ اتهٔ دیرش *atuh dérsh.*
39 — ۳۹ نههٔ دیرش *nahuh dérsh.*
40 — ۴۰ څلویښت *salwékht.*
50 — ۵۰ پنځوس *panzōs.*
60 — ۶۰ شپیتهٔ *shpétuh*
70 — ۷۰ اویا *auyā.*
80 — ۸۰ اتیا *atyā.*
90 — ۹۰ نوي *navi.*
100 — ۱۰۰ سلَ *sal.*
200 — ۲۰۰ دوه سوَ *dwa swa.*
1000 — ۱۰۰۰ زر *zar.*
2000 — ۲۰۰۰ دوه زرَ *dwa zara.*
100000 ۱۰۰۰۰۰ لک *Lak.*

پهٔ سلګونو *Puh salgūnō* Hundreds of
په زر ګونو *Puh zargūnō* Thousands of.
په لکونو *Puh lakūnō* "Laks" of.

Numerals (both cardinal and ordinal) are used in Pushtu as adjectival nouns. When governed by any preposition and post position they are put into the Oblique Plural as :—

په خلورو سړو باندې *Puh salorō sarō bāndé* On four men.

يو = *Yau* becomes يوه = *Yawa* in the case of Feminine as :—

يوه ښځه *Yawa Khaza* One woman.

The Ordinal numbers are formed (with the exception of اول = *Awal* = 1st and دويم = *Dwém* = 2nd) by adding م = *m* to the Cardinals. They form the Feminine by the addition of ه = *h* (soft).

CARDINAL.

Masculine.	Feminine.
دري سړي *Dré sari* three men	درى ښځي *Dré khazé* three women

ORDINAL.

Masculine.	Feminine.
دريم سړى *Drém saray* 3rd man.	دريمه ښځه *Dréma khaza* 3rd woman

خلورم	*salōram*	4th
پنځم	*pinzam*	5th
شپږم	*shpagam*	6th

In Pushtu only the simpler fractions can be expressed :—

EXAMPLES.

1/4	پاؤ	*Pāw*
1/2	نیم	*Nim*
3/4	دری پاؤ	*Dré Pāwa*
1¼	پنځۀ پاؤ	*Pinzuh Pāwa*
1½	یو نیم	*Yau Nim*
1¾	پاؤ کم دوه	*Pāw kam dwa*
2¼	پاؤ باندِ دوه	*Pāw bāndé dwa*
2½	دوه نیم	*dwa nim*

Some times the villagers count by *Shal* = a score the plural of which is *Shalé* as

دوه شلی	*dwa shalé*	two scores 40.
دری شلي	*dré shalé*	three scores 60
پنځۀ دَا پاسَ دري شلي	*Pinzuh dapāsa dréshalé*	5 over 3 scores 65.
پنځۀ کم دری شلي	*Pinzuh kam dréshalé*	5 less of 3 scores 55.

واړۀ *Wāra* all. put after a cardinal number indicates universality.

دواړۀ	*dwāra*	both.
دری واړۀ	*dré wāra*	all three.
څلور واړۀ	*salōr wāra*	all four.

Multiplication by degree is expressed by using the particle پۀ = *Puh* between the cardinal یو = *yau* and any other cardinal as :—

یو پۀ دوه	*yau puh dwa*	twice as much.
یو پۀ دری	*yau puh dré*	thrice as much.
یو پۀ څلور	*yau puh salōr*	four times as much.

Some times the word چند = *chand* is used after any cardinal number to express the same meaning as above.

دو چند	*do chand*	twice as much.
درې چند	*dré chand*	thrice as much.
څلور چند	*salōr chand*	four times as much.

Section 8.

PRONOUNS.

1st Person.

	Singular.			Plural.	
Nom :	زه	*zuh* I.	مونږ	*mūng*	we.
Acc :	ما	*mā* me.	مونږ	*mūng*	us.
Agent :	ما	*mā* by me.	مونږ	*mūng*	by us.
Gent:	زما	*zamā* my.	زمونږ	*zamūng*	our.
Dat :	ما ته	*mā ta* to me.	مونږ ته	*mūng ta*	to us.
Abl:	له ما نه	*luh mā na* from me.	له مونږ نه	*luh mūng na*	from us.
Loc :—	په ما کښې	*puh mā ké* in me	په مونږ کښې	*puh mūng ké*	in us.
Voc :—	اې زه	*ay zuh* oh me!	اې مونږ	*ay mūng*	oh us!

2nd Person.

	Singular.			Plural.	
Nom :	ته	*tuh* thou.	تاسو	*tā so*	you.
Acc :	تا	*tā* thee.	تاسو	*tā so*	you.
Agent:	تا	*tā* by thee	تاسو	*tā so*	by you

	Singular.			Plural.		
Gent:	ستا	*stā*	thy.	ستاسو	*stā so*	your.
Dat :	تاته	*tā ta*	to thee.	تاسو ته	*tā so ta*	to you.
Abl:	له تا نه	*luh tā na*	from thee.	له تا سونه	*luh tā- so na*	from you.
Loc :—	په تا کښې	*puh tā ké*	in thee.	په تاسو کښې	*puh tāso ké*	in you.
Voc :—	اي تهٔ	*ay tuh*	oh thou	اى تا سو	*ay tāso*	oh you

3rd Person.

	Singular.			Plural.		
Nom :	هغه	*hagha*	he	هغوي	*haghūi*	they.
Acc :	هغه	*hagha*	him.	هغوي	*hughūi*	them.
Agent:	هغهٔ	*haghuh*	by him	هغوي	*haghūi*	by them.
Gent:	دَ هغهٔ	*da haghuh*	his.	دَ هغوي	*da haghūi*	their.
Dat :—	هغهٔ ته	*haghuh ta*	to him	هغوي ته	*haghūi ta*	to them.
Abl :—	له هغهٔ نه	*luh haghuh na*	from him.	له هغوي نه	*luh hughūi na*	from them.
Loc :—	په هغهٔ کښې	*puh haghuh ké*	in him.	په هغوي کښې	*puh haghūi ké*	in them.
Voc :—	اى هغهٔ	*ay haghuh*	oh him!	اي هغوي	*ay haghūi*	oh them.

NOTE:—A. Some times دی = *day* is used for هغه = *hagha*, when the object is close at hand and it is inflected thus :—

	Singular.			Plural.	
Nom:	دی *day*	he	دوی *dui*	they	
Agent:	دهٔ *duh*	by him	دوی *dui*	by them.	

B. The following particles are used as pronouns in three cases, accusative, agentive and genitive.

Singular.		Plural.	
مِ *mé*	me, by me or my	مو *mō*	us, by us or our.
دِ *dé*	thee, by thee or thy	مو *mō*	you, by you or yours
يې *yé*	him, by him or his	يې *yé*	them, by them or their

EXAMPLE :

Accus :	هغه مِ وهي	*hagha mé wahi*	He beats me
Agent :	هغه مِ ووهٔلو	*hagha mé wo wahalo*	I beat him
Geni :	كتاب مِ	*kitab mé*	My book

Ordinarily in Pushtu sentences the subject is placed first, the object second and the Verb last, but where the above particles are used, in the case of a transitive verb Past-Tense, the object is put first and the subject second.

هغه م و ليدلو *hagha mé wo lidalo* I saw him.

C. The following particles are used as prepositions and have the force of personal pronouns :—

پرې *pré* on him, on them, on her, or on it.

ترې *tré* from him, from them, from her or from it.

There was only one chair in the room and he himself was sitting on it.

پۀ کمره کښې خالي يوه کُرسيءَ وه اؤ هغه پخپله پرِناست وه "*puh kamra ké khāli yawa kursai wah aw hagha pakhpala pré nāst woh*".

DEMONSTRATIVE PRONOUNS.

There are only three Demonstrative Pronouns in Pushtu which are inflected thus :—

Nom	دا *dā* this or these		دغه *dagha* this or these.	
	هغه *hagha*		that or those.	
Agent	دې *dé* by this or these		دغې *daghé* by this or these.	
	هغې *haghé*		by that or by those.	

دا خما نوکر دی *dā zamā naukar day* this is my servant.

لۀ دې هلک نۀ *luh dé halak na* from this boy.

دغه څوک دی *dagha sōk day* who is this.

دَ دغې هلک پلارِ م نوکر دی *da daghé halak plār mé naukar day* this boy's father is my servant.

هغه زما کلی دی	*haghá zamā kalay day*	that is my village.
دَ هغی کلیِ نه هغه خوا	*da haghé kali na hagha khwā*	beyond that village.

THE INTERROGATIVE PRONOUNS.

څوک	*sok*	who.
څه	*suh*	what.
کوم	*kum*	which
کوم یو	*kum you*	which one.
څو یا څو مره	*sō or somra*	how many or how much.
څوک	*sōk*	is inflected thus :—

Nom	څوک	*sōk*	who	used in singular and plural both numbers.
Agent	چا	*chā*	by whom	

m. s.	m. p.	f. s.	f. p.	ob. p.
کوم سړی	کوم سړیِ	کومه ښځه	کومې ښځې	دَ کومو خلقو
kum saray	*kum sari*	*kuma khaza*	*kumé khazé*	*da kumo hhalqo*
which man.	which men	which woman	which women	of which people.

THE RELATIVE PRONOUNS.

There is only one relative pronoun in Pushtu چه = *Chi,* which is also used as a conjunction for joining two sentences. It also makes any interrogative word relative as :—

1.	هغه سړی راوبله چه پرون دلته وه	*hagha saray rā wōbala chi parūn dalta woh*	Call that man who was here yesterday.
2.	هغه و وِ چه نوم م احمد دی	*haguh wō wé chi nūm mé Ahmad day*	he said that my name is Ahmad (direct speech) he said his name was Ahmad.
3.	څوک چه	*sōk chi*	he who.
	هر څوک چه راشي	*har sōk chi rāshee*	whoever may come.
	کوم چه دِ خوښ وي	*kum chi dé khwakh wé*	whichever you like.
	کوم یو چه د خوښ وي	*kum yau chi dé khwakh wé*	which ever one you like.
	څهٔ چه کوې	*suh chi kawé*	whatever you do.

THE CORRELATIVE PRONOUNS.

Interrogative			Correlative		
کهٔ	*kuh*	if	نو	*no*	then.
چه	*chi*	when.	نو	*no*	then.
کله چه	*kala chi*	when.	نو	*no*	then.
څومره چه	*sōmra chi*	as much as	دومره	*dōmra*	that much.
څنګه چه	*sanga chi*	what ever	هسې	*hasé*	thus.

EXAMPLE.

کهٔ ستا خوښه	*kuh stā khwakha*	
وي نو لاړ شه	*wī nō lārsha*	go if you like.
چه یا کله چه	*chi or kala chi mā*	he also spoke
ما ووِ نو هغهٔ هم ووِ	*wo wé no haghuh hum wo wé*	when I spoke.
څومره چه غواړې دومره واخله	*sōmra chi ghwāré dōmra wākhla*	take as much as you want Literally: as much as you want take so much.
څنګه چه د خوښه وي هسې کوه	*sanga chi dé khwa-hha wi hasé kawa*	do as you like. Literally: whatever you wish, thus do.

INDEFINITE PRONOUNS.

In Pushtu the simple indefinite pronouns are :—

څوک	*sōk*	some one.
څهٔ	*suh*	some, something or anything.
څینې	*ziné*	some.
هیڅ	*hiss*	no, or nothing. anyone, anything which is followed by a negative *e. g.*
هیڅوک نشته	*hiss sōk nishta*	there is no body.
هیڅ نشته	*hiss nishta*	there is nothing.

څوک *sōk* beeomes چا *chā* in the oblique case *e. g.*

هیڅ چا ته مهٔ وایه یا	*hiss chā ta muh wāya*	Don't tell any one
هیچا ته مهٔ وایه	*hichā ka muh wāya*	" " " "

خینی = *ziné* takes the regular inflection and څهٔ = *suh* and هیڅ = *hiss* are indeclinable.

EXAMPLE.

څوک په دی کور کښی شته	*sōk puh dé kor ké shta*	is there anyone in this house?
څوک خو شته	*sōk kho shta*	there is someone (*Kho* = really.)
څهٔ شيَ راکړه	*suh shay rākra*	give me something.
خینی هوښیاردي خیني کم عقل	*ziné hukhyār di ziné kam akal*	some are clever, some foolish.
خینو خلقو ته	*zinō khalqō ta*	to some people.

Numerous compound indefinite pronouns are formed from the above thus :—

هر = *har* every, combining with څوک = *sōk*, څهٔ = *suh* and یو = *yau* makes:— هرڅوک = *har sōk* every one هرڅهٔ = *har suh* every thing

هر یو = *har yau* every one and similarly بل = *bal* another and نور = *nōr* more or others make:— بل څوک = *bal sōk* anyone else.

نور څوک = ***nōr sōk*** any others. بل څه = ***bal suh*** anything else. نور څه = ***nōr suh*** something more. نور هيڅ = ***nōr hiss*** nothing else. بل يو = ***bal yau*** another.

VERBAL NOUNS.

In Pushtu the verbal nouns can be formed in two ways Viz:—

1. By changing the final لَ = L of the infinitive into نه = ***na*** which is always feminine singular as :—

تړل ***taral***	to bind.	تړنه ***tarana***	binding
هيرول ***hérawal***	to forget	هيرونه ***herawana***	forgetting.
ښودل ***khodal***	to show.	ښودنه ***khōdana***	showing

2. The infinitive itself can be used as a verbal noun as :—

تړل ***taral***	to bind or binding.
هيرول ***hérawal***	to forget or forgetting.

NOTE :—This form of the verbal noun is always masculine plural. So when it is governed by a preposition or post position the oblique plural should be used as :—

په تړلو کښې	***puh taralo ké***	in binding.
په هيرولو باندې	***puh hérawalo bāndé***	on forgetting

The Noun of agency is formed by changing the final ل = ***l***, of the infinitive into ونکَی = ***ūnkay*** which is declinable as :—

ليکل *likal* to write ليکونکی *likūnkay* writer.

دَ ليکو نکي نوم *da likūnkī nūm* the name of the writer

In the case of an intransitive verb it also expresses the meaning of "to be about to" as:—

راتلل *rātlal* to come هغه راتلونکی دَی *hagha rātlūnkay day* He is about to come.

NOTE :—To express "to be about to" use the preposition *pa-ké* with verbal noun as :—

هغه پهٔ تلو کښی دي *hagha puh tlo ké day* he is about to go.

ABSTRACT OR DERIVED NOUNS.

(Substantive and Adjective.)

Secondary nouns are derived from primary by the following suffixes :— ا = *ā*, ي = *i*

ستيا = *stiā* توب = *tōb* والی = *wālay* گلي = *galī*.

تون = *tūn* تيا = *tiā* :—

غل *ghal* a thief becomes غلا *ghlā* theft.

خوښ *khwakh* pleased ,, خوښي *khwakhi* pleasure.

سپاهي *spāhi* soldier ,, سپاهي توب *spāhi tōb* soldiering.

شين *shin* green ,, شينوالي *shin wālay* green-ness

پیژندل	*péjhandal*	knowing becomes	پیژندګلي	*péjhandgali* acquaintance.
بیل	*bial*	separate ,,	بیلتون	*bīltūn* separation.
ناجوړ	*nājōr*	ill	ناجوړتیا	*nājōrtiā* illness.
میلمه	*mėlma*	guest	میلمستیا	*mélmastia* hospitality

Section 9.

THE VERB.

As regards their formation, the Pushtu verbs are devided into seven different classes: —

1. Regular transitive.
2. Regular intransitive.
3. Irregular transitive.
4. Irregular intransitive.
5. Compound transitive.
6. Compound intransitive.
7. Verbs which are irregular in the formation of the present Tense and Tenses derived from it.

Class I.

REGULAR TRANSITIVE.

All verbs in Pushtu end in ل = *l* :—

وهل *Wahal* to beat, strike.

تړل	*taral*	to bind, tie.
ليکل	*likal*	to write.
بلل	*balal*	to call.
خوړل	*khwaral*	to eat.
سکل	*skal*	to drink.
منل	*manal*	to obey, agree, accept.
ساتل	*sātal*	to keep, guard, cherish
استول يا ليږل	*astawal* or *légal*	to send.
کرل	*karal*	to sow.
ګندل	*gandal*	to sew.
خريل	*khrayal*	to shave.
ګڼړل	*ganral*	to consider.
چيچل	*chichal*	to bite.
ښيل	*khayal*	to show or direct.

THE PRESENT TENSE.

Change the final ل = L of the infinitive into:—

			Singular			Plu.
1st P.	م	*m*		ؤ	*oo*	
2nd P.	ی	*é*		ئ	*ai*	
3rd P.	يِ	*ee*		يِ	*ee*	

as

زۀ وهم	*zuh waham*	I beat	Sing.
تۀ وهی	*tūh wahé*	thou beatest	
هغه وهيِ	*hagha wahee*	he beats.	

مونږ وهو	*Mūng wahoo*	We beat	Plu.
تاسو وهئ	*tāso wahai*	you beat	
هغوی وهي	*haghūi wahee*	they beat	

THE FUTURE TENSE.

Prefix به = *Ba*, to the Present tense as :—

زه به وهم	*zuh ba waham*	I will beat	Sing.
ته به وهی	*tuh ba wahé*	thou wilt beat	
هغه به وهی	*hagha ba wahee*	he will beat	
مونږ به وهو	*Mūng ba wahoo*	we will beat	Plu.
تاسو به وهئ	*tāso ba wahai*	you will beat	
هغوی به وهي	*haghui ba wahee*	they will beat.	

THE AORIST (PRESENT SUBJUNCTIVE.)

Prefix :—و = *wo*, to the present tense as :—

زه و وهم	*zuh* wo *waham*	I may beat	Sing.
ته و وهی	*tuh wo wahé*	thou mayst beat	
هغه و وهي	*hagha wo wahee*	he may beat	
مونږ و وهو	*Mūng wo* wahoo	we may beat	Plu.
تاسو ووهئ	*tāso wo wahai*	you may beat.	
هغوي ووهي	*haghūi* wo *wahee*	they may beat.	

THE IMPERATIVE.

Is formed by changing the final م = *m* of the aorist into ه = *a* (H. soft) to form singular and into ئ = *ai* to form plural as :—

و وهه	*wo waha*	beat (thou)
و وهئ	*wo wahai*	beat (you)

THE PROHIBITIVE.

Is formed by changing the first و = *wo* of the imperative into مه = *muh* as :—

مه وهه	*muh waha*	don't beat (thou)
مه وهئ	*muh wahai*	don't beat (you)

THE IMPERFECT TENSE.

Add to the infinitive the following suffixes :—

1st P.	م *m*	Singular.	ؤ *oo*	Plural.
2nd P.	ي *é*		ئ *ai*	
3rd P.	و *ō*		infinitive	
3r P. F.	ه *h*		ي *é*	

NOTE :—(A) The verb agrees with the subject in the present and object in all past tenses.

(B) Object in the past tenses is always put into the nominative form as :—

هغه زه وهلم	*haghuh zuh wahulam*	he was beating me	Sing.
هغه ته وهلې	*haghuh tuh wahalé*	he was beating thee	
هغه هغه وهلو	*haghuh hagha wahalō*	he was beating him	
هغه هغه وهله	*haghuh hagha wahalō*	he was beating her	

هغهٔ موږ وهلوٌ	*haghuh mūng wahaloo*	he was beating us (Plu.)
هغهٔ تاسو وهلئ	*haghuh tāso wahalai*	he was beating you (Plu.)
هغهٔ هغوی وهل	*haghuh haghūi wahal*	he was beating them (Plu.)
هغهٔ هغوی وهلي	*haghuh haghūi wahalé*	he was beating them (fem.) (Plu.)
ما هغه وهلو	*mā hagha wahalō*	I was beating him.
موږ هغه وهله	*mūng hagha wahala*	We were beating her.

PAST HABITUAL.

Prefix به = *ba* to the imperfect tense as :—

Singular.

هغهٔ زه به وهلم	*haghuh zuh ba wahalam*	he used to beat me or he would beat me.	
هغهٔ تهٔ به وهلي	*haghuh tuh ba wahalé*	do.	thee
هغهٔ هغه به وهلو	*haghuh hagha ba wahalō*	do.	him
هغهٔ هغه به وهله	*haghuh hagha ba wahala*	do.	her

Plural.

هغهٔ موږ به وهلوٌ	*haghuh mūng ba wahaloo*	he used to beat us or he would beat us	
هغهٔ تاسو به وهلئ	*haghuh tāso ba wahalai*	do.	you
هغهٔ هغوي به وهل	*haghuh haghuī ba wahal*	do.	them

هغهٔ هغوي بِه وهلي	*haghuh haghui ba wahalé*	he used to beet them or he would beat them (fem.)
ما هغوي بِه وهل	*mā haghui ba wahal*	I used to beat them.

PAST DEFINITE.

Prefix و = *wo*, to the imperfect tense as :—

هغهٔ زه و وهلم	*haghuh zuh wō wahalam*	he beat me	Sing.
هغهٔ ته و وهلي	*haghuh tuh wō wahalé*	do. thee	
هغهٔ هغه و وهلو	*haghuh hagha wō wahalo*	do. him	
هغهٔ هغه و وهله	*haghuh hagha wō wahalah*	do. her	
هغهٔ مونږ و وهلو	*haghuh mūng wō wahaloo*	he beat us.	Plu.
هغهٔ تاسو و وهلئ	*haghuh tāso wō wahalai*	do you.	
هغهٔ هغوي و وهل	*haghuh haghū wō wahal*	do them.	
هغهٔ هغوي و وهلي	*haghuh haghui wō wahalé*	do them. (feminine).	

جنى هلک و وهلو	*jinai halak wō wahalo*	the girl beat the boy.
هلک جنئ و وهله	*halak jinai wō wahāla*	the boy beat the girl.

THE PAST PARTICIPLE.

Is formed by adding یَ = *ay*, to the infinitive as :—

وهلىَ *wahalay* beaten.

This is used as an adjective and is inflected as nouns ending in یَ = *ay* as :—

وهلَی سړَی	*wahalay saray*	beaten man.
وهلِي سړِي	*wahali sart*	beaten men:
دَ وهلو سړو	*da wahalo saro*	of the beaten men (Ob. Plu.)
وهلې جنئ ته	*wahalé jinai ta*	to the beaten girl (F. Ob. S.)
وهلو ښځو ته	*wahalo khazo ta*	to the beaten women (F. Ob. P.)

PERFECT TENSE.

Conjugate the present tense of the verb to be after the past participle as :—

هغهٔ زهٔ وهلَی یم	*haghuh zuh wahalay yam*	he has beaten me	Sing
هغهٔ تهٔ وهلَی یې	*haghuh tuh wahalay yé*	he has beaten thee	
هغهٔ هغه وهلَی دَی	*haghuh hagha wahalay day*	he has beaten him.	
هغهٔ هغه وهلې دَه	*haghuh hagha wahalé dah*	he has beaten her.	
هغهٔ مونږ وهلِي یوُ	*haghuh mūng wahali yū*	he has beaten us.	Plu.
هغهٔ تاسو وهلِي یئ	*haghuh tāso wahali yai*	he has beaten you.	
هغهٔ هغوِي وهلِي دِي	*haghuh haghui wahali dee*	he has beaten them.	
هغهٔ هغوی وهلې دِي	*haghuh haghui wahalé dee*	he has beaten them (Feminine.)	

ښځې سړی وهلی دی	*khazé saray wahalay day*	the woman has beaten the man.
سړي ښځه وهلې ده	*sari shaza wahalé dah*	the man has beaten the woman.
هلکانو هندو وهلی دی	*halakāno hindū wahalay day*	the boys have beaten a Hindu.

PLUPERFECT TENSE.

Conjugate the past tense of the verb to be after the past participle as :—

هغهٔ زهٔ وهلی وم	*hāghuh zuh wahalay wam*	he had beaten me.	Sing
هغهٔ تهٔ وهلی وې	*hāghuh tuh wahalay wé*	he had beaten thee.	
هغهٔ هغه وهلی وهٔ	*haghuh hagha wahalay woh*	he had beaten him.	
هغهٔ هغه وهلې وه	*haghuh hagha whalé wah*	he had beaten her.	
هغهٔ مونږ وهلي وو	*haghuh mūng wahali woo*	he had beaten us.	Plu.
هغهٔ تاسو وهلي وئ	*haghuh tāso wahali wai*	he had beaten you.	
هغهٔ هغوي وهلي وو	*haghuh haghui wahali woo*	he had beaten them.	
هغهٔ هغوي وهلې وې	*haghuh haghui wahalé wé*	he had beaten them (feminine).	

هلک ښځه وهلی وَه	*halak khaza wahalé wah*	The boy had beaten the woman.
ښځی هلک وهلی وَه	*khazé halak wahalay woh*	The woman had beaten a boy

PRESENT POTENTIAL.

Add ی = *ay* to the infinitive and conjugate the word شم = *sham* after it according to the present personal terminations as :—

زهٔ وهلیَ شم	*zuh wahalay sham*	I can beat.	Sing.
تهٔ وهلیَ شی	*tuh wahalay shé*	Thou canst beat.	
هغه وهلیَ شيِ	*hagha wahalay shee*	He or she can beat.	
مونږ وهلیَ شو	*mung wahalay shoo*	We can beat.	Plu.
تاسو وهلیَ شئ	*tāso wāhalay shai*	You can beat.	
هغوی وهلیَ شيِ	*haghui wahalay shee*	They can beat M. & F.	

هغه ما وهلیَ شيِ یا هغه مِ وهلیَ شيِ	*hagha mā wahalay shee* or *hagha mé wahalay shee*	He can beat me.
زهٔ هغه وهلیَ شم یا زهٔ یی وهلیَ شم	*zuh hagha wahalay sham* or *zuh yé wahalay sham*	I can beat him.

THE PAST POTENTIAL.

Add یَ = *ay* to the infinitive and conjugate the word شوم = *shwam* afrer it according to the past personal terminations :—

هغۀ زۀ وهلیَ شوم	*haghuh zuh wahalay shwam*	He could beat me or he was able to beat me.	Sing
هغۀ تۀ وهلی شوی	*haghuh tuh wahalay shwé*	He could beat thee.	
هغۀ هغه وهلیَ شو یا شۀ	*haghuh hagha wahalay sho* or *shuh*	He could beat him.	
هغۀ هغه وهلیَ شوه یا شوله	*haghuh hagha wahalay shwa* or *shwala*	He could beat her.	
هغۀ مونږ وهلیَ شوُو یا شوُ	*haghuh mūng wahaly shwoo* or *shoo*	He could beat us.	Plu.
هغۀ تاسو وهلیَ شوئ	*haghuh tāso wahalay shwai*	He could beat you.	
هغۀ هغوی وهلیَ شوُو یا شولَ	*haghuh haghūi wahalay shwoo* or *shwal*	He could beat them,	
هغۀ هغوی وهلیَ شوی یا شولی	*haghuh haghui wahalay shwé* or *shwalé*	He could beat them (Feminine.)	

خما نوکر هغه وهلیَ شو	*zamā naukar hagha wahalay sho*	My servant could beat him
هلک جنئ وهلیَ شوه	*halak jinai wahalay shwa*	The boy could beat the girl.

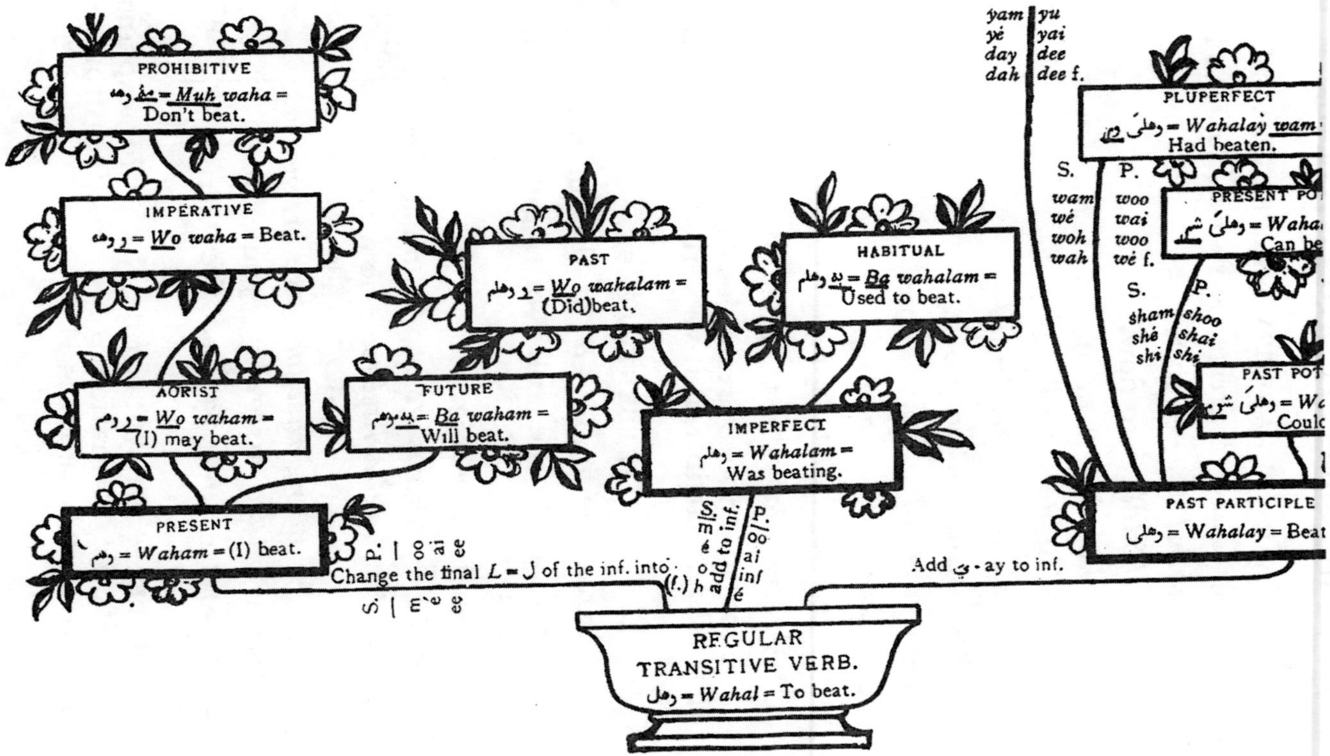
PROHIBITIVE
مه وهه = Muh waha = Don't beat.
IMPERATIVE
و وهه = Wo waha = Beat.
AORIST
و وهم = Wo waham = (I) may beat.
FUTURE
به وهم = Ba waham = Will beat.
PRESENT
وهم = Waham = (I) beat.
PAST
و وهلم = Wo wahalam = (Did)beat.
HABITUAL
به وهلم = Ba wahalam = Used to beat.
IMPERFECT
وهلم = Wahalam = Was beating.
PLUPERFECT
وهلیٔ وم = Wahalay wam
Had beaten.
PRESENT PO
وهلیٔ شم = Waha
Can be
PAST PO
وهلیٔ شوم = Wa
Coul
PAST PARTICIPLE
وهلی = Wahalay = Beat
yam yé day dah
yu yai dee dee f.
S. wam wé woh wah
P. woo wai woo wé f.
S. sham shé shi
P. shoo shai shi
Change the final L = ل of the inf. into
S. m é h (f.) add to inf.
P. oo ai inf é
S. m é ee
P. oo ai ee
Add ي - ay to inf.
REGULAR TRANSITIVE VERB.
وهل = Wahal = To beat.

REGULAR INTRANSITIVE VERBS CLASS II.

رسيدل *rasédal* to arrive ڎشيدل *sasédal* = to leak.
اوسيدل *osédal* to live.
بهيدل *bahédal* to flow.
زغليدل *zghalédal* to run.
تښتيدل *takhtédal* to flee.
زليدل *zalédal* to shine.
خوزيدل *khwazédal* to move.
رپيدل *rafédal* to tremble.
کړيدل *karédal* to pine.
غوړيدل *ghwarédal* to spread.
غوريدل *ghurédal* to thunder.

From the above examples it is quite clear that all regular intransitive verbs end in يدل = *édal*.

PRESENT TENSE.

Change the final د = *d* of the infinitive into ږ = *g* and apply the rules of regular transitive verb as :—

زۀ رسيږم	*zuh raségam*	I arrive.	Sing.
تۀ رسيږي	*tuh raségé*	thou arrivest.	
هغه رسيږي	*hagha raségee*	he arrives.	
,,	,, ,,	she ,,	
مونږ رسيږو	*mūng raségoo*	we arrive.	Plur.
تاسو رسيږئ	*tāso raségai*	you arrive.	
هغوی رسيږی	*haghūi raségee*	they arrive.	
,,	,, ,,	,, ,, (f.)	

NOTE :—See syntax rule No. 3 for explanation of the formation of transitive from in transitive verbs of class II.

DIAGRAM OF THE INTRANSITIVE VERB.

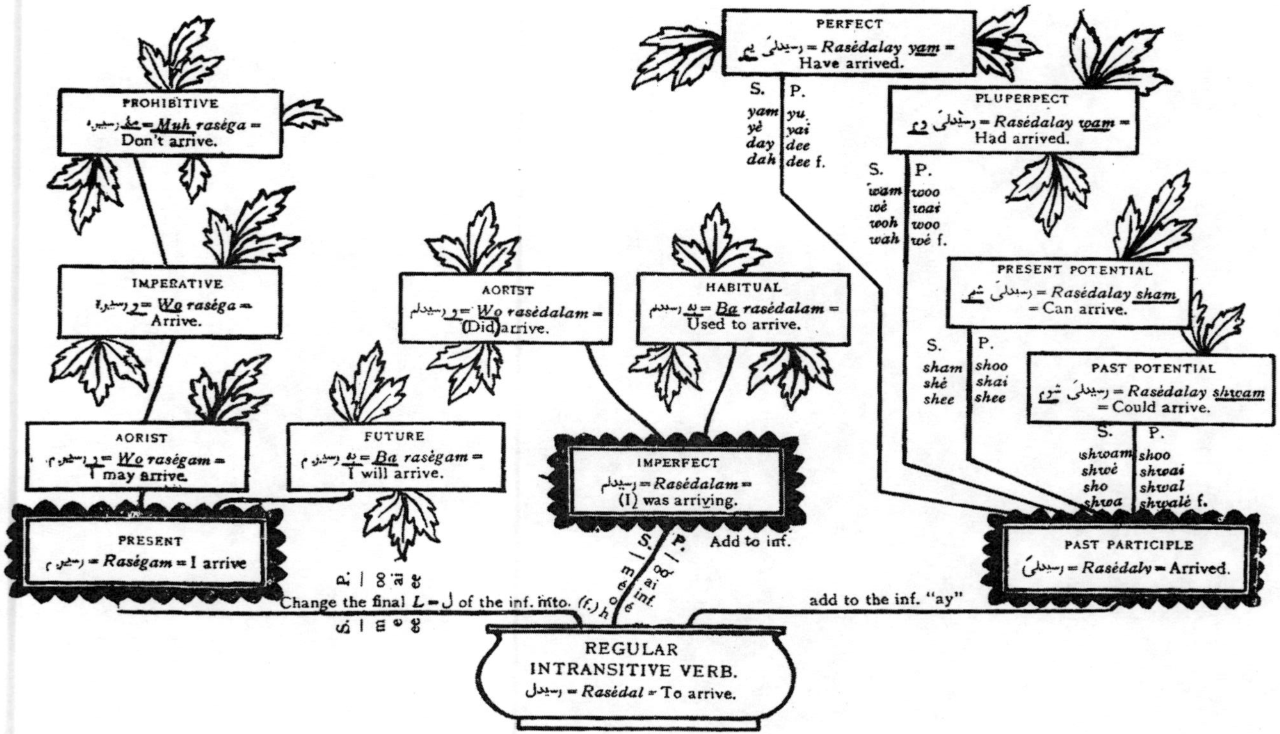

Diagram showing all the tenses of regular transitive verb. It is quite clear that و = *wo* and به = *ba* are added twice, once to the present to form aorist and future. Then to the imperfect to form past and habitual. All one needs to now are the Present, Imperfect, and Past participle. From these three principal parts of the verb all the other tenses are formed.

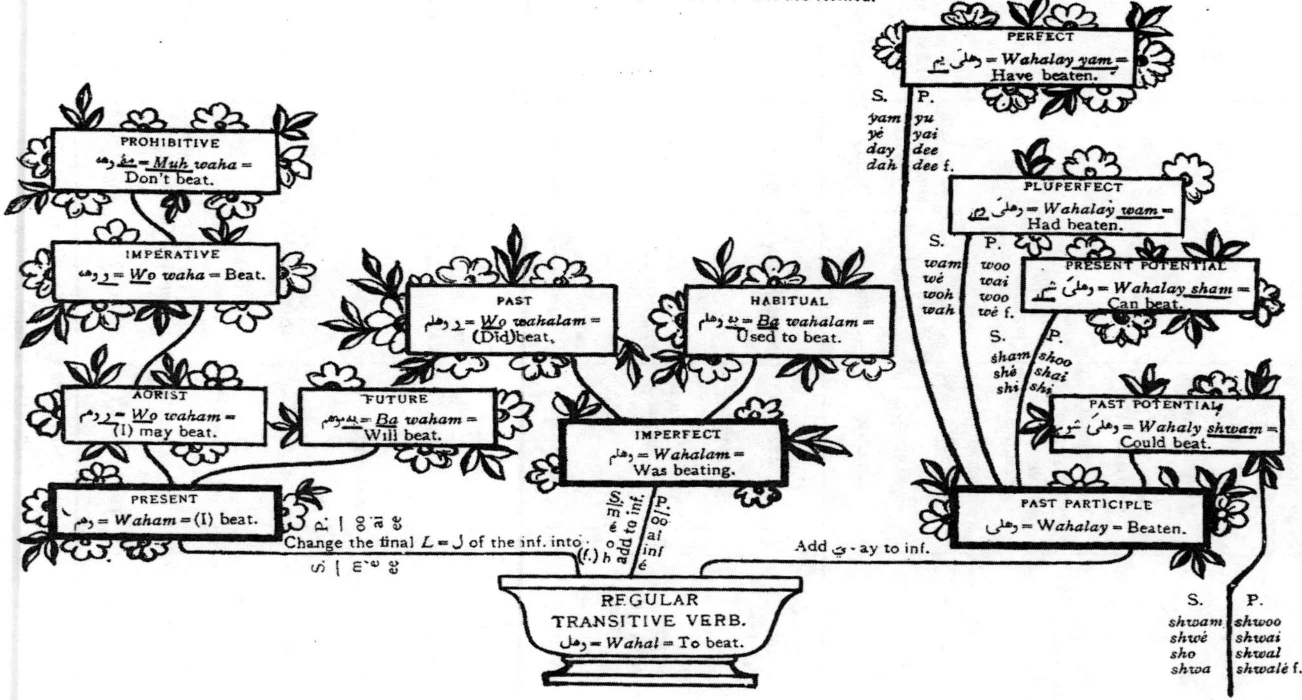

Irregular Transitive Verbs Class III.

Infinitive.	Imperative.	Prohibitive.	Past participle.		Past.
راوړل *Rāwral* to bring (in animate.)	راوړه *Rāwra* bring.	مه راوړه *muh rāwra* don't bring.	راوړلی *rāwralay* یا or راوړی *rāworay*	brought.	راوړلم *Rāwralam* یا or راوړم *Rawram* brought.
راوستل *Rāwastal* to lead. animate.	راوله *Rāwala* lead.	مه راوله *muh rāwala* don't lead.	راوستلی *rāwastalay* یا or راوستی *rāwastay*	Led.	راوستلم *Rāwastalam* یا or راوستم *Rāwastam* Led.
وړل *Vral* to take away. in animate.	یوسه *Yausa* take away.	مه وړه *muh vra* don't take away.	وړی *woray* یا or وړلی *wralay*	taken away	یوړلم *Yauralam* یا یوړم *Yauram* took away.
بیول *Biwal* to lead away. animate.	بوزه *Bōza* lead away.	مه بیایا *muh biyāya* don't lead away	بیولی *biwalay*	led away	بوتلم *Bōtlam* led away.
کیښودل *kèkhōdal* to place or put.	کېږده *Kégda* place.	مه ږده *muh gda* don't place.	کیښودلی *kèkhodalay* یا or ایښی *ikhāy*	placed	کیښودلم *kèkhōdalam* placed.
کول *kawal* to do.	کړه *Kra* do.	مه کوه *muh kawa* don't do.	کړی *kāray*	done	کړلم *kralam* یا or کړم *kram* did.
1. Imperfect راوړلم *rāwralam* was bringing. 2. Habitual به راوړلم *ba rāwralam* used to bring.	1. Aorist راوړم *rāwram* may bring.	1. Present :— راوړم *rāwram* I bring. 2. Future :— به راوړم *ba rāwram* will bring.	1. Perfect :— راوړلی یم *rāwralay yam* have brought. 2. Pluperfect. راوړلی وم *rāwralay wam* had brought. 3. Present poten راوړلی شم *rawralay sham* can bring. 4. Past poten. راوړلی یا راوړی شوم *rāwralay* or *rāworay shwam* = could bring.		

Irregular Intransitive Verbs Class IV.

Infinitive.	Imperative.	Prohibitive.	Past Participle.	Past.
تلل *tlal* to go.	لاړشه *lārsha* go.	مه ځه *muh za* don't go.	تلَي *talay* gone.	لاړم *lārm* I went.
راتلل *rātlal* to come.	راشه *rāsha* come.	مه راځه *muh rāza* don't come.	راغلَي *rāghalay* come.	راغلم *rāghlam* I came.
کیناستل *kénāstal* to sit.	کینه *kéna* sit.	مه کینه *muh kéna* don't sit.	کیناستلَي *kénāsta-lay* sat.	کیناستلم *kénāsta-lam* I sat.
څملاستل *samlāstal* to lie down.	څمله *samla* lie down.	مه څمله *muh samla* don't lie down.	څملاستلَي *samlāst-alay* laid down	څملاستلم *samlāsta-lam* I lay down.
کیدل یا *kédal* or شول *shwal* to become.	شه *sha* be or become.	مه کیږه *muh kéga* dont be or don't become.	شوی *shaway* been or become.	شوم *shwam* I became.
1. Imperfect. تلم یا تللم *tlam* or *talalam* was going. 2. Habitual. به تللم *ba tlalam* یا or به تلم *ba talam* used to go.	1. Aorist. لاړشم *lārsham* may go.	1. Present, ځم *zam* I go. 2. Future. به ځم *ba zam* will go.	1. Perfect. تلَی یم *talay yam* have gone. 2. Pluperfect. تلَی وم *talay wam* had gone. 3. Present Potential. تلَی شم *tlay sham* can go. 4. Past Potential تلَی شوم *tlay shwam* could go.	

Note:—In the verbs "to come, become and do" يَ = *ay*, should be added to the infinitive to form their potential mood and their irregular past participles should not be used as:—

راتلَی = *rātlay* کیدلی = *kédalay* کولَی = *kawalay* شم = *sham* and شوم = *shwam* and (not) (راغلَی = *rāghalay*, شوی = *shaway* or کړی = *karay*, شم = *sham* and شوم = *shwam*.)

Compound Verbs Class V & VI.

The Compound verbs are formed by adding adjectives and nouns to کول = *Kawal* and کیدل = *Kédal.*

	Transitive.			In Transitive.	
ورکول	*war kawal*	to give	ورکیدل	*war kédal*	to be given,
مړکول	*mar kawal*	to kill or put out.	مړکیدل	*mar kédal*	to die or to be put out.
جوړکول	*jōr kawal*	to make, build.	جوړکیدل	*jōr kédal*	to be made, to be built.
پوه کول	*pōh kawal*	to inform instruct.	پوهٔکیدل	*poh kédal*	to under-stand, to be instructed
لوکول	*law kawal*	to harvest.	لوکیدل	*law kédal*	to be harvested
اوبهٔکول	*obuh kawal*	to irrigate.	اوبهٔ کیدل	*obuh kédal*	to be irregated
خراپکول	*kharāp kawal*	to spoil.	خراپ کیدل	*kharāp kédal*	to be spoilt.
لرې کول	*laré kawal*	to open	لرې کیدل	*laré kédal*	to be opened.
پورې کول	*pōré kawal*	to shut.	پورې کیدل	*pōré kédal*	to be shut.
تپوس کول	*tapōs kawal*	to ask.	تپوس کیدل	*tapōs kédal*	to be asked.
پښتنه کول	*pukhtana kawal*	to ask	پښتنه کیدل	*pukh-tana kédal*	to be asked.

برباد کول	*barbād kawal*	to destroy.	برباد کيدل	*barbād kédal*	to be destroyed
کنډر کول	*kandar kawal*	to burgle.	کنډر کيدل	*kandar kédal*	to be burgled
ژوبل کول	*jhōbal kawal*	to wound	ژوبل کيدل	*jhōbal kédal*	to be wounded
خوږ کول	*khūg kawal*	to hurt.	خوږ کيدل	*khūg kédal*	to be hurt.
بل کول	*bal kawal*	to light.	بل کيدل	*bal kédal*	to be lit.
پري کول	*pré kawal*	to cut.	پرى کيدل	*pré kédal*	to be cut.
مات کول	*māt kawal*	to break.	مات کيدل	*māt kédal*	to be broken.

NOTE:—See syntax Rule No. 5. for full explanation of the formation of derivative verbs from Class V & VI.

CLASS VII.

Verbs which are irregular in the formation of Present and tenses derived from it.

Infinitive			Present.		
غوښتل	*ghukhtal*	to want.	غوارم	*ghwāram*	I want.
راغوښتل	*rāghukh-tal*	to send for.	راغوارم	*rāghwā-ram*	I send for
پريوتل	*préwatal*	to fall.	پريوځم	*préwō-zam*	I fall.
پوريوتل	*pōréwatal*	to cross.	پوريوځم	*pōréwo-zam*	I cross.

پرېښودل	*prékhōdal*	to leave, let off.	پرېږدم	*prégdam*	I leave.
پېژندل	*péjhandal*	to recognize.	پېژنم	*péjhanam*	I recognize.
مؤندل	*mūndal*	to get, obtain, receive, find.	مؤمم	*mūmam*	I get, obtain, receive, find.
ويشتل	*wishtal*	to shoot.	ولم	*wōlam*	I shoot.
وژل	*wajhal*	to kill.	وژنم	*wajhnam*	I kill.
لوستل	*lwastal*	to read.	لولم	*lwalam*	I read.
ليدل	*lidal*	to see.	وينم	*wīnam*	I see.
كتل	*katal*	to look.	گورم	*gōram*	I look.
اوريدل	*aurédal*	to hear.	اورم	*auram*	I hear.
اخستل	*akhistal*	to take.	اخلم	*akhlam*	I take.
اغوستل	*aghustal*	to wear, to put on, to dress.	اغوندم	*aghundam*	I put on. etc.
ختل	*khatal*	to climb.	خيژم	*khějham*	I climb.
الوتل	*alwatal*	to fly.	الؤځم	*alūzam*	I fly.
كنودل	*kanōdal*	to dig.	كنم	*kanam*	I dig.
اوريدل	*aurédal*	to hear.	اورم	*auram*	I hear.
ويل	*wayal*	to say, speak, tell.	وايم	*wāyam*	I say, speak, tell.
وتل	*watal*	to go out.	وځم	*wozam*	I go out.
راوتل	*rāwatal*	to come out.	راوځم	*rawozam*	I come out.
ويستل	*wistal*	to take out.	وباسم	*wobāsam*	I take out.
ننوتل	*nanawatal*	to go in.	ننوځم	*nanawozam*	I go in.

ننویستل	*nanawis-tal*	to take in.	ننباسم *nanabā-sam*	I take in.
خندل	*khandal*	to laugh.	خاندم *khāndam*	I laugh.
ژړل	*jharal*	to cry, weep.	ژاړم *jhāram*	I cry, I weep.
نښتل	*nakhatal*	to be caught.	نښلم *nakha-lam*	I am caught.
چاودل	*chāwdal*	to split, burst.	چوم *chwam*	I am burst.
لنبل	*lānbal*	to bathe.	لانبم *lānbam*	I bathe.
نیول	*niwal*	to catch, seize, arrest, hold.	نیسم *nīsam*	I catch etc :—
زنګل	*zangal*	to swing.	زانګم *zāngam*	I swing.
پاڅیدل	*pāsédal*	to get up.	پاڅم *pāsam* or *pāségam*	I get up.
راښکل	*rākhkal*	to pull.	راکاږم *rākāgam*	I pull.
نغښتل	*nghakh-tal*	to wrap-up.	نغاړم *nghāram*	I wrap-up.
پرانتل	*prānatal*	to untie.	پرانځم *prāna-zam*	I untie.

Section 10.

THE SYNTAX RULES.

1. Verbs commencing with را = *rā* در = *dar* ور = *war* پا = *pā* پري = *pré* پوری = *pōré* کې = *ké* نن = *nan* بې = *bé* تې = *té* do not take "و = *wo*" in their past, aorist and imperative:—

راوتل *rāwtal* to come out towards (me or us)

دروتل	*dar wtal*	to come out towards (thee or you)
وروتل	*war watal*	to come out towards (him or them, her, it)
پاڅيدل	*pāsédal*	to get up.
تيرباسل	*térbāsal*	to mislead.
پريوتل	*préwatal*	to fall.
پوريوتل	*poréwatal*	to cross.
کيښودل	*kékhōdal*	to put, place.
ننوتل	*nanawatal*	to go in, enter
بيلل	*bélal*	to lose.
راښکل	*rākhkal*	to pull.

EXAMPLE.

I got up زۀ پاڅيدم = *zuh pāsédam* (Not *wo pāsédam*) past).

May I get up پاڅم = *pāsam* (aorist)

Get up پاڅه = *pāsa* (The imperative)

EXCEPTIONS.

Which take *wo* after the را = *rā* در = *dar* and ور = *war* :—

راغوښتل	*rāghukhtal*	to send for.
رابلل	*rābalal*	to call for, recall.
رازغليدل	*rāzghalédal*	to run towards me or us.
راتښتيدل	*rā takhtédal*	to flee towards me or us.
راويستل	*rā wistal*	to bring out, towards me or us.

راوتل	*rā watal*	to come out towards me or us.
راگرزېدل	*rā garzédal*	to return.
رانغښتل	*rā nghakhtal*	to wrap up.
را گرزول	*rā garzawal*	to bring back, to make to return.
راشړل	*rā sharal*	to drive back towards me or us.

EXAMPLES.

ما هغه را و غوښتلو = *Mā hagha rā wo ghukhtalo* = I sent for him (past).

زهٔ يې را و غواړم = *Zuh yé rā wo ghwāram* = May I send for him? (aorist)

را و يې غواړه = *Rā wo yé ghwāra* = Send for him! (imperative).

NOTE :—Verbs which take را = *rā*, in the 1st person, take در = *dar*, and ور = *war* in the 2nd and 3rd person singular and plural as well as :—

هغه را و زغليدلو	*hagha rā wo zghalédalo*	he ran towards me or us.
هغه در و زغليدلو	*hagha dar wo zghalédalo*	he ran towards thee or you.
هغه ور و زغليدلو	*hagha war wo zghalédalo*	he ran towards him or them, her, it.

2 The subject of the following verbs although they are intransitive, is put in the Agentive case and the verb always goes into the 3rd person masculine plural in past tenses :—

دنګل	*dangal*	to jump.
غپل	*ghapal*	to bark.
خندل	*khandal*	to laugh.
ژړل	*jharal*	to weep.
زنګل	*zangal*	to swing.
تو کل	*tūkal*	to spit.
ټوخل	*tōkhal*	to cough.
لنبل	*lanbal*	to bathe.
جار باسل	*jārbāsal*	to vomit.

Examples as :—

ما و دنګل	*mā wō dangal*	I jumped.
سړي و دنګل	*sari wō dangal*	The man jumped.
جنۍ و دنګل	*jinai wō dangal*	The girl jumped.
سړو دنګلي دي	*saro dangali di*	The men have jumped.
ښځې دنګلې دي	*khazé dangali di*	The woman has jumped.
ما دنګلي وو	*mā dangali woo*	I had jumped.

In the absence of an object the following verbs also follow the above rules

ليکل	*likal*	to write.
لوستل	*lwastal*	to read.
ويل	*wayal*	to say, speak. tell.
کتل	*katal*	to look.
ليدل	*lidal*	to see.

غوښتل	*ghukhtal*	to wish, want.
اوريدل	*aurédal*	to hear.

As :—

ما وا وريدل	*Mā wā wrédal*	I heard.
تا وا وريدل	*Tā wā wrédal*	Thou heard
هلک وا وريدل	*Halak wā wrédal*	The boy heard.
جنۍ وا وريدل	*Jinai wā wrédal*	The girl heard.
سړو وا وريدل	*Saro wā wrédal*	The men heard
ښځو وا وريدل	*Khazo wā wrédal*	The women heard.
ما اوريدلي دي	*Mā aurédali di*	I have heard.
ما اوريدلي وو	*Mā aurédali woo*	I had heard.
جنۍ اوريدلي وو	*Jinai aurédali woo*	The girl had heard.
هلک اوريدلي وو	*Halak aurédali woo*	The boy had heard.
ما و ليکل چه	*Mā wo likal chi...*	I wrote that...
ما په اخبار کښې ولوستل	*Mā puh akhbār ké wo lwastal*	I read in the paper.
ما په اخبار کښې لوستلي دي	*Mā puh akhbār ké lwastali di*	I have read in the paper.

3. To form transitive from class II, Regular intransitive verbs, change يدل = *édal* of the infinitives into ول = *awal* as :—

رسيدل *rasédal*	to arrive	رسول *rasawal*	to make to arrive
اوسيدل *osédal*	to live	اوسول *osawal*	to make to live

پاڅیدل *pāsédal* to get up پاڅول *pāsawal* to make to get up.

NOTE :—In conversation some times the present tense of Class II is formed irregularly.

رسیدل	*rasédal*	to arrive	رسم	*rasam*	I arrive
اوسیدل	*osédal*	to live	اوسم	*ōsam*	I live
زغلیدل	*zghalédal*	to run	زغلم	*zghalam*	I run
تښتیدل	*takhtédal*	to flee	تښتم	*takhtam*	I flee
خوزیدل	*khwazédal*	to move	خوزم	*khwazam*	I move
رپیدل	*rapédal*	to tremble	رپم	*rapam*	I tremble
څڅیدل	*sasédal*	to leak	څڅم	*sāsam*	I leak.

4. Compound verbs formed from adjectives never take و = *wo*, in their past, aorist and imperative and those formed from nouns always do as :—

ما میز صاف کړلو *mā méz sāf kralo* I cleaned the table.

ستا بوټونه صاف کړم *stā būtūna sāf kram ?* May I clean your boots ?

لوکوټی یې صاف کړه *lūkūti yé sāf kra* Please clean them.

ما کار و کړلو *mā kār wo kralo* I worked.

زۀ کار وکړم *zuh kār wo kram* May I work ?

خپل کار و کړه *khpal kār wo kra* Do your work.

5. Compound verbs formed from some adjectives are Derivative Verbs which are formed by leaving out the first letter ک = *k* of کول = *kawal* and کیدل = *kédal* and add *zabar* over

the last letter of the adjective only in case of transitive verb, as :—

from صاف کول *sāf kawal* صافول *sāfawal* to clean.
from صاف کیدل *sāf kédal* صافیدل *sāfédal* to be cleaned.

from پوه کول *pōh kawal* پوهول *pōhawal* to inform
from پوه کیدل *pōh kédal* پوهیدل *pōhédal* to understand.

EXAMPLES.

زهٔ صافوم	*zuh sāfawam*	I clean.
زهٔ به صافوم	*zuh be sāfawam*	I will clean.
مهٔ صافوه	*muh sāfawa*	don't clean.
ما صافولو	*mā safawalo*	I was cleaning.
زهٔ صافولی شم	*zuh sāfawalay sham*	I can clean.

NOTE :—In the Past, Aorist, Imperative and Past Participle of Derivative Verbs however کول = *kawal*, and کیدل = *kédal*, are conjugated in full.

EXAMPLES.

ما میز صاف کړلو	*mā méz sāf kralo*	I cleaned the table.
صاف کړم	*sāf kram ?*	my I clean ?
هو صاف کړه	*ho sāf kra*	yes, clean.
میز تیار شو	*méz tayār sho*	the table was (became) ready.
تیار شم	*tayār sham ?*	may I became ? ready ?

هو تیار شه *ho tayār sha* yes, be ready.

Not: ما میز و صافولو *mā mēz wo sāfawalo.*

وصافوم = *wo sāfawam* or وصافوه = *wo sāfwa*

The list of adjectives from which the derivative Verbs are formed.

Adjective.		Verbs.		
خراپ	*kharāp*	خراپول	*kharapawal*	to spoil.
جوړ	*jor*	جوړول	*jorawal*	to make, build.
پوه	*poh*	پوهول	*pohawal*	to inform or instruct.
موړ	*mōr*	موړول یا	*mōrawal* or	
		مړول	*marawal*	to feed.
لوند	*lūnd*	لوندول	*lūndawal*	to make wet.
کوږ	*kōg*	کوږول یا	*kōgawal* or	to make crooked.
		کږول	*kagawal*	
دروند	*drūnd*	دروندول	*drundawal*	
		یا درنول	or *dranawal*	to make heavy.
تود	*tōd*	تودول	*tōudawal*	to make hot.
پوښ	*pōkh*	پښول یا	*pakhawal* or	
		پوښول	*pokhawal*	to cook.
تریو	*triw*	تریوول	*triwawal*	to make sour
خوږ	*khōg*	خوږول یا	*khōgawal* or	
		خوږول	*khwagawal*	to make sweet.
تریښ	*trikh*	تریښول یا	*trikhawal* or	
		ترښول	*tarkhawal*	to make bitter.

Adjective.		Verbs.		
خوږ *khūg*	خوږول	*khūgawal*	to hurt.
وروست *vrōst*	وروستول يا	*vrostawal* or	
	ورستول	*vrastawal*	to make rotton.
شين *shin*	شينول	*shinawal*	to make green
ړوند *rūnd*	ړوندول يا	*rūndawal* or	
	ړندول	*randawal*	to make blind.
سپين *spīn*	سپينول	*spinawal*	to make white.
زيړ *ziar*	زيړول	*ziarawal*	to make yellow.
بند *band*	بندول	*bandawal*	to close.
لوی *loi*	لويول	*loyawal*	nurse up or make bigger.

PRESENT CONTINUOUS.

6. When the action is continuous use simple present in the first sentence and simple future in the second, the 1st: sentence commences with كه = *kuh* if, and the 2nd: with نو = *no* then.

EXAMPLE.

كه هغه راځی نوزه به ځم = *kuh hagha rāzee, no zuh ba zam*

If he keeps on coming, I shall keep on going.

PAST CONTINUOUS.

7. Use imperfect in the first sentence and Habitual in the 2nd as:—

کۀ هغه راتلو، نوزۀ به تلم *kuh hagha-rātlo, nō zuh ba tlam*
If he had kept on coming I would have kept on going.

PRESENT CONDITIONAL.

8 Use aorist in the first sentence and aorist preceded by بۀ = *ba* in the 2nd as:—

کۀ هغه راشي، نوزۀ به لاړشم *kuh hagha rāshee, no zuh ba lārsham* If he comes I will go.

NOTE:—Some times in the present conditional idiomatically, the Past tense is used instead of the aorist, in the first clause when the condition is assumed to be realised, as :—

کۀ تا دا کار وکړلو نو انعام به درکړم *kuh tā dā kār wokralo, no inām ba darkram*
If you do this work I will reward you.

PAST CONDITIONAL.

9. Use the word وی = *way* unchangeably after the uninflected Past Participle in the first sentence and pluperfect preceded by بۀ = *ba*, in the 2nd: as:—

کۀ هغه راغلی وی نوزۀ به تلی وم *kuh hagha rāghalay way, nō zub ba talāy wam*
If he had come, I would have gone.

PAST POTENTIAL CONDITIONAL.

10. Use the word شوی = *shway*, unchangeably after the original uninflected Past participle

in the first half and Pluperfect tense preceded by به = *ba*, in the 2nd as :—

کهٔ زهٔ راتلیَ شویَ نوزه به را غلیَ وم	*kuh zuh rātlay shway, no zuh ba rāghalay wam*	If I could have come, I would have
کهٔ مِ وهلیَ شویَ نو بهِ م وهلیَ وهٔ	*kuh mé wahalay, shway, no ba mé wahalay woh*	If I could have beaten him, I would have done so.

PASSIVE VOICE.

11. In Pushtu the Passive Voice is only used in those cases wnen the subject of the verb is not mentioned at all.

Formation :—

Conjugate the required tense of کېدل = *kėdal*, after the uninflected Past Participle of an other Verb as :—

ډوډئ خوړلی کېږي	*dodai khwaralay kėgi*	The bread is being eaten.
ډوډئ به خوړلیَ کېږي	*dodai ba khwaralay kėgi*	The bread will be eaten.
ډوډئ خوړلیَ شویَ ده	*dodai khwa-ralay shawé dah*	The bread has been eaten.

NOTE :—To form Passive Past and Aorist add یَ = *ay* to the Past Tense 3rd. Person masculine Plural with کیدل = *kédal* conjugated after it *e. g.*

هغه و وهلی شو	*hagha wo wahalay sho*	He was beaten.
کهٔ هغه و وهلیَ شيِ	*kuh hagha wo wāhalay shī*	If he is beaten.
کتاب یوړلیَ شو	*kitāb yauralay sho*	The book was taken away.
کهٔ کتاب یوړلیَ شيِ	*kuh kitāb yauralay shī*	If the book is taken away.
آس بوتللیَ یا بوتليَ شو	*āss bōtlalay* or *bōtlay sho*	The horse was taken away.
کهٔ آس بو تللیَ یا بوتلیَ شيِ	*kuh āss bōtlalay* or *botlay shi*	If the horse is taken away.
کار وکړیَ شو (یا وکړلیَ شو)	*kār wo kray sho* or *kār wo kralay shō*	The work was done.
کهٔ کار وکړیَ شيِ یا وکړلیَ شيِ	*kuh kār wo kray shi* or *wo kralay shi*	If the work is done.
میز صاف کړیَ شو یا کړلیَ شو	*méz sāf kray sho* or *kralay sho*	The table was cleaned.
کهٔ میز صاف کړیَ یا کړلیَ شيِ	*kuh méz sāf kray* or *kralay shi*	If the table is cleaned.

NOTE :—کړیَ = *kray*, is a short form of کړلیَ *kralay*.

12. The Infinitive of Purpose is always inflected and it is followed by the Post Position دَ دَ پاره = *da dapāra* as :—

زهٔ دَ رپوټ کولو دَ پاره را غلی یم	*zuh da rapōt kawalo dapāra rāghalay yam*	I have come to make a report.

13. In the Negative Past and Aorist, the نهٔ—*nuh*, is placed after the following Particles:—
را *rā* در *dar* ور *war* پا *pā* پرې *pré* پورې *pōré*
و *wo* وا *wā* لا *lā* کې *ké* بې *bé* ننه *nan*
پرا *prā*, as :—

هغه را غلو	*hagha rāghlo*	He came.
هغه را نهٔ غلو	*hagha rā nuhghlo*	He did not come.
زهٔ لاړم	*zuh lāram*	I went.
زهٔ لا نهٔ ړم	*zuh lā nuh ram*	I did not go.
تهٔ پا څیدلی	*tuh pāsédalé*	You got up.
تهٔ پا نهٔ څیدلی	*tuh pā nuhsédalé*	You did not get up.
ما و ویل	*mā wo wayal*	I said, spoke or told
ما و نهٔ ویل	*mā wo nuh wayal*	I did not say etc.
مونږ واخستلو	*mūng wā khistalo*	We took it.
مونږ وا نهٔ خستلو	*mūng wā nuh khīstalo*	We did not take it.
تاسو کیښودلو	*tāso kékhōdalo*	You placed it.
تاسو کېنهٔ ښودلو	*tāso ké nuh khōdalo*	You did not place it.

هغوی ننو تل	*haghui nanawatal*	They entered.
هغوی ننهٔ وتل	*haghui nana nuh watal*	They did not enter.
چا پرا نتلو	*chā prānatlo*	Who opened it ?
چا پرا نهٔ نتلو	*chā prānuh natlo*	Who did not open it ?

14. In the case of all verbs commencing with ا = *ā*, (alif) the sound of و = *wo*, becomes وا *wā*, in their Past, Aorist and Imperative as :—

ما یو کتاب واخستلو	*mā yau kitāb wākhistalo*	I took a book.

15. When an infinitive is used after an imperative, the last part of the sentence should be put into the aorist preceded by چه = *chi* as :—

ور ته و وایه چه لاړ شي	*warta wō wāya chi lārshee*	Tell him to go.

16. Use the word ځان = *zān*, self or خپل ځان *khpal zān* oneself when the person of the subject is concerned as :—

یو کتاب م دَ ځان سره وا خستلو	*yau kitāb mé da zān sara wākhistalo*	I took a book with me.
څهٔ او بهٔ دَ ځان سره واخله	*suh obuh da zān sara wākhla*	Take some water with you.

17. The words تن = *tana* or کس = *kasa* = individuals, are used before persons as :—

شل تنَ سړیِ راغلل	*shal tana sari rāghlal*	Twenty men came
څلور تنَ ښځی	*salōr tana khazé*	Four women.
پنځهٔ کسَ ښځی	*pinzuh kasa khazé*	Five women.
څو کسَ	*sō kasa*	How many persons ?

18. When a possessive pronoun refers to the nominative of the sentence it should always be translated by خپل = *khpal.* own :—

زهٔ خپل کور ته ځم	*zuh khpal kōr ta zam*	I go to my house.
ټول خپلو خپلو کورونو ته لاړل	*tōl khpalo khpalo korūnō ta lāral*	Each man went. to his own house, or they all went to their own houses.
زهٔ خپله کمره کښیں وم	*zuh khpala kamra ké wam*	I was in my room

19. The particle د = *dé.* is used before the aorist tense at the end of a sentence only in the 3rd person singular and plural to express command and permission, but to show negation, permission and continuation use Present Tense as :—

هغهٔ د لاړ شی	*hagha dé lārshee*	He should go.

د هغهٔ خور دِ هم لاړه شي	*da haghuh khōr dė hum lāra shee*	His sister should also go.
هغه دِ نهٔ راځي	*hagha dė nuh rāzee*	He should not come.
هغه د راځی یا راځي دِ	*hagha dė rāzee* or *rāzee dė*	He may come or he is allowed to come or let him come.
هغه دِ مدام راځي راځي	*hagha dė mudām rāzee*	He should always come.

NOTE (A)—لاړ = *lār* is used as an adjective declinable .

NOTE (B)—د = *dė* with لکه = *laka* after it is used after the subject of the verb in all persons to express the following idioms *e. g.*

تهٔ دلکه خوب کوی او زهٔ د لکه ستا بوټونه صافوم	*tuh dė laka khōb kawė aw zuh dė lakā stā būtūna sāfawam*	Is it reasonable that you should go to sleep and I should cleam your boots.

20. Use the word پکار = *pakār di* it is necessary, after the uninflected infinitive at the end of a sentence and the subject of the verb should be put into the dative case to express should, must or ought as :—

ماله تلل پکاردي	*mā la tlal pakār di*	lit To me going necessary is I must go.

تا له تلل پکاردي *tā la tlal pakār di* You should go.
مونږ له پښهٔ ښار (ښهر) *mūng la puh khār* We must live in
کښې اوسيدل پکاردي *ké osédal pakār di* The city.

21. Use the word پکار دي چه = *pakār di chi* at the beginning of a sentence followed by the aorist tense to express the same meaning as above as :—

پکاردی چه زهٔ پريډ ته لاړشم *pakār di chi zuh paraid ta lārsham* I must go on parade.

پکار دی چه تا سو وختی لاړشئ *pakār dī chi tāso wakhtī lārshai* You must go earlier.

22. To express should have or ought to have, use پکار وُو چه = *pakār woo chi* at the beginning of a sentence followed by وی = *way* after the uninflected past participle at the end of a sentence as :—

پکار وُو چه زهٔ تلَی وی *pakār woo chi zuh talay way* I ought to have gone.

پکار وُو چه هغه راغلَی وی *pakār woo chi hagha rāghalay way* He should have come.

23. وي = *wi* the aorist tense of the verb "to be", is only used in the 3rd person singular and plural to express doubt, continuation, present conditional in the verb "to be" and general statement as :—

ګُند هغه هلته وي	*gundė haga haltā wi*	Perhaps he is there.
هغه مدام په ښهر کښې وي	*haga mudām puh khahar kė wi*	He is always in the city.
که هغه په مردان کښې وي	*kuh hagha puh mardān kė wi*	If he is in Mardan.
نو زه به ورسره خبري وکړم	*no zuh ba warsara khabarė wo karm*	I will speak to him.
په دې وطن کښې هر رنګ ښکار وي	*pa dė watan kė har rang khkār wi*	There are all kinds of shooting in this country.

24. Aorist preceded by به = *ba* is called strong future, which stands for certainty and fixed time as :—

هغه به صبا راشي	*hagha ba sabā rāshee*	He will (certainly) come tomorrow.
هغه به په کور کښې وي	*hagha ba puh kōr kė wi*	He will (certainly) be in the house.

25. The Imperative formed from the Present Tense denotes continuation, or habit as :—

هره ورځ زما کور ته راځه	*hara wraz zamā kōr ta rāza*	Come to my house every day.
هره ورځ مدرسې ته ځه	*hara wraz madrasė ta za*	Go to the school every day.

26. The Plural of Onomatopœic Nouns is formed by adding ـَـهار—*ahār,* which takes the verb to be into 3rd person masculine singular, as :—

ډز	*daz*	sound of a shot.	ډزهار	*dazahār*	sound of shots.
کړپ	*krap*	foot fall	کړپهار	*krapahār*	sound of footfalls.
شرنګ	*shrang*	chink of money.	شړنګهار	*shranga-hār*	chink of rupees.
پُس	*pus*	sound of whisper	پُسهار	*pasahār*	whispering.
هینړ	*henr*	neigh of a horse.	هینړهار	*henrahār*	neighing of horses.

27. Use the word لګیا = *lagyā* = busy, as an adjective with the subject of the Verb, when the action is continuous as :—

زهٔ لګیا یم پښتو زده کوم	*zuh lagyā yam pukhtu zda kawam*	I am busy learning Pushtu.
هغه لګیا دی چِټی لیکی	*hagha lagyā day chitai likee*	He is busy writing letters.
مونږ لګیا یو غنم کړو	*mūng lagyā yū ghanam karoo*	We are busy sowing wheat.

28. The following words take the Genitive Case followed by the Verb to be (بدی = *badi* is the only one which takes the aorist of "to become".)

خوښ	*khwakh*	pleasant.
پکار	*pakār*	required.
بدي	*badi*	unpleasant.
پېرزو	*pérzo*	wish.

EXAMPLES.

دا کتاب ځما خوښ دی	*dā kitāb zamā khwakh day*	I like this book.
ځما دری روپۍ پکار دي	*zamā dré rupai pakār dee*	I requirė three rupees.
دَ هغهٔ وروز ځما بدي شي	*da haghuh vror zamā badi shee*	I hate his brother.
دا انعام ځما پهٔ تا پېروز دی	*dā ināam zamā puh tā pérzo day*	I wish you to have this reward.

29. The word معلوم = *mālūm* = known, takes dative case followed by the Verb to be as:—

دا ما ته معلوم دي	*dā mā ta mālūm day*	I know this.

30. The phrases given below are followed by the aorist tense :—

راځه چه	*rāza chi*	Let us.
پرېږده چه	*prégda chi*	Let him, them, her, it.

EXAMPLES.

راځه چه دغه کلي ته لاړشو	*rāza chi dagha kali ta lārshoo*	Let us go to that village.
پرېږده چه لاړشي	*prégda chi lārshee*	Let him go.

31. The verbs "to sell" and "sell for" always take the preposition پهٔ باند = *puh bāndé* on as :—

ما خپل آس په هغهٔ پهٔ باند پهٔ لس روپئ خرڅ کړلو	*mā khpal ass puh haghuh bāndé puh las rūpai khars kralo*	I sold my horse to him for 10 rupees.

32. The verb "to understand" takes پهٔ = *puh* as :—

زهٔ پهٔ پښتو پوهيږم	*zuh puh pukhtu pōhégam*	I understand Pushtu.

33. پس = *pas* = after (in time) does not inflect any nouns of time as :—

درى مياشتى پس	*dré miāshté pas*	After three months.
څلور کال پس	*salōr kāla pas*	After four years.

34. پسى = *pasé* after (position or business) inflects its nouns or pronouns e. g.

ما پسى دفتر ته راشه	*mā pasé daftar ta rāsha*	Come after me to the office.
زهٔ نوکري پسي راغلى يم	*zuh naukarai pasé rāghalay yam*	I have come after a job.

35. The following Verbs take Ablative Case (لهٔ - نه = *luh - na*) from.

تپوس کول يا پښتنه کول	*tapōs kawal* or *pukhtana kawal*	To ask.

ويريدل	*veyarėdal*	to fear.
پوريوتل	*pōrėwatal*	to cross.
هير كيدل	*hėr kėdal*	to be forgotten.

EXAMPLES.

لهٔ هغهٔ ند تپوس وكړه	*luh haghuh na tapōs wokra*	Ask him.
لهٔ سيند نه پوريوتلم	*luh sind na pōré-watalam*	I crossed the river.
را نه كتاب هير شو	*rā na kitāb hėr shō*	I forgot the book.

36. When the action is unintentional an Intransitive Verb with the Ablative case should be used as :—

گلاس را نه مات شو	*galās rā na māt shō*	I broke the glass (by accident).

37. To do something by means of any thing, the indirect object is always governed by پهٔ - باند = *puh - bāndė* on as :—

زهٔ پهٔ قلم باندِ ليكم	*zuh puh qalam bāndė likam*	I write with a pen.
زهٔ يى پهٔ لرگىِ و وهلم	*zuh yé puh largi wo wahalam*	He beat me with a stick.

38. For the Pluperfect Tense after "when" the past tense should be used and for Perfect, the Aorist as :—

كله چه ما خپل كار و كړلو يا وكړ	*kala chi mā khpal kār wō kralo* or *wo kar*	When I had done my work

کله چه زهٔ ډوډيئ و خورم	*kala chi zuh dodai wo khuram*	When I have eaten my food.

39. "Until" at the beginning of an English sentence is always translated by ترڅو پورې چه = *tar sō pōré chi.* and followed by the Negative Aorist tense as :—

ترڅو پورې چه خما دفتر له رانهٔ شي	*tar sō poré chi zamā daftar la rā nuh shé*	Until you come to my office.

40. "Since" (in the sense of time) at the beginning of an English sentence, is translated by کله راسې چه = *kala rāsé chi,* as :—

کله راسې چه هغه خما نوکر دی	*kala rāsé chi hagha zamā naukar day*	Since he has been in my service.

41. To express "See if" the negative tense with خو *kho,* before it, should be used as :—

ګوره چه خما کتاب پهٔ ميز باندې خو نشته	*gora chi zamā kitāb puh méz bāndé kho nishta*	See if my book is on the table.

42. To express Present Optative, change the last م = *m*, of the past tense 1st. person singular into ی = *ay*, for all persons.

To express Past Optative, use the word *way*, unchanged after the uninflected past participle and to form Past Potential Optative, use the word شوی = *shway.* unchanged after the original uninflected past participle. All these Optative expressions commence with :—

ارمان دی چه	*armān day chi*	I wish that (Lit : Iregret.)

EXAMPLE.

ارمان دی چه زهٔ لاړی	*armān day chi zuh lāray*	I wish I could go.
ارمان دی چه زهٔ تلی وی	*armān day chi zuh talay way*	I wish I had gone.
ارمان دی چه زهٔ تلی شوی	*armān day chi zuh tlay shway*	I wish I could have gone.

43. To express compulsion, کام نا کام = *kām nā kām* or خوا مخواه = *khwā makhwāh* = some-how or other, should be used as :—

زهٔ خوا مخواه لاړم	*zuh khwā makhwāh lāram*	I had to go.
ما کام نا کام نوم کټ کړو	*mā kām nā kām nūm kat kro*	I had to resign.
زهٔ به خوا مخواه ځم	*zuh ba khwā makhwāh zam*	I will have to go.

44. Adverbial phrases of time and place are sometimes put before the subject of the verb as :—

پهٔ شپږ بجې زهٔ به د فتر ته لاړ شم	*puh shpag bajé zuh ba daftar ta lārsham*	I will go to the office at 6.

45. شته = *shta* Is there or are there ? It is also used for a question and an answer to a question in the verb to have, but in case of using any interrogative, Adjective and Adverb in the sentence, شته = *shta* can not be used as :—

تا سخه كتاب شته	*tā sakha kitāb shta*	Have you a book ?
هو ما سخه كتاب شته	*ho mā sakha kitāb shta*	Yes, I have a book.
خو ما سخه قلم نشته	*kho mā sakha qalam nishta*	But I have not a pen.
تا سخه څومره كتابونه دي	*tā sakha sōmra kitabūna di*	How many books have you ?
تا سخه كوم كتاب دي	*tā sakha kum kitāb day*	What book have you ?
تا سخه ډير دولت دي	*tā sakha dér daulat day ?*	Have you much wealth ?

46. The post position سخه = *sakha* = In the possession of, can be used when the object possessed, is light and moveable and can be carried about.

In the case of parts of the body, relations and heavy property the possessive case should be used as:—

ما سخه يو قلم دى	*mā sakha yau qalam day*	I have a pen.
ملک سخه يوه اسپه ده	*malak sakha yawa aspa dah*	The headman owns a mare.

ځما يوه سترګه ده	*zamā yawa starga dah*	I have one eye.
ستا وروَر شته	*stā vrōr shta?*	Have you a brother?
ستا کور شته	*stā kōr shta*	Have you a house?

47. The use of two similar numerals together denotes "each" as :—

يو يو ته دوه دوه انې ورکړه	*yau yau ta dwa dwa ané warkra*	Give them two annas each.

48. The Past Conditional of the verb to be is formed by using the word وَی = *way* (indeclineable) at the end of a sentence as :—

کهٔ زهٔ هلته وَی	*kuh zuh halta way*	If I had been there.
کهٔ تهٔ هلته وَی	*kuh tụh halta way*	If you had been there.
کهٔ خان هلته وَی	*kuh khān halta way*	If the khan had been there.

49. In the Negative Tenses formed from the Past Participle, the Past Participle in conversation is sometimes put last as :—

هغه نهٔ دَی راغلی	*hagha nuh day rāghalay*	He has not come.
خان نهٔ وهٔ راغلَی	*khān nuh woh rạghalay*	The Khan had not come.
زهٔ نهٔ شم راتلَی	*zuh nuḥ sham rātlay*	I cannot come.

ښځه پهٔ لار نهٔ شوه تلی *khaza puh lāra nuh shwa tlay* The woman could not go on the road.

50. In Yusafzai Pushtu the last لو = *lo*, of the 3rd. person Masculine singular of the past tense is left out as :—

کینا ستلو *kénāstalo* or کیناست *kénāst* He sat.

څملا ستلو *samlāstalo* or څملاست *samlāst* He lay down.

51. The following nouns take the verb in the 3rd. person masculine singular :—

مال	*māl*	Cattle.
یرغمل	*yarghamal*	Hostage or Hostages.
فوځ	*fauz*	Troops, Army.
ملاتړ	*mlā tar*	Followers, Fighting men.
دښمن	*dukhman*	Enemy (in War.)

52. The following words take the verb in the 3rd ; person Masculine Plural :—

دروغ	*darōgh*	Lie.
رښتیا	*rikhtiā*	Truth.
کنزل	*kanzal*	Abuse,
څهٔ	*suh*	What, anything.
هیڅ	*hiss*	Nothing (takes negative tense.)

53. To forget = هیر کول = *hér kawal*, is only used transitively if the act of forgetting is delibrate ; ordinarily = هیر کیدل = *hér kédal*. with the ablative case is used e. g.

مامهٔ هیروه = *mā muh hérawa* = Don't forget-me

پۀ دفتر کښې کتاب رانه هېر شو	*puh daftar ké kitāb rā na hér sho*	I forgot the book in the office.

Lit:—In the office the book from me was forgotten.

54. (A) Terms of politeness used in addressing the following are :—

Old man	کاکا جي يا کاکا	*kākā ji* or *kākā*	Uncle.
Blind man	حافظ	*hāfiza*	The man who knows the Quran by heart.
Stranger	ځوان	*zowāna*	Young man.
Known person	هلک	*halaka*	Boy.
Father	بابا	*bābā*	Father.
Mother	ادي	*adé*	Mother.
Brother	لالا	*lālā*	Brother.
Sister (older)	بی بی	*bébé*	Sister.
Uncle	چاچا	*chāchā*	Uncle.
Grand-mother	نانا	*nā nā*	Grand-mother.
Maternal uncle	ماما	*māmā*	Maternal uncle.
Wife or husband	وي	*way*	Oh !
Urdu knowing person	مرزا صاحب	*mirzā sāhib*	Urdu writer.
English knowing person	بابو صاحب	*bābū sāhib*	Clerk.
A sweeper	جمعدار	*jamādār*	Jemadar.
Mali	چودري	*chōwdhri*	Manager.

(B) The following are the terms of calling and driving away different kinds of animals etc :—

	Calling.	Driving away.
Dog	تو تو تو *to to to*	کوری شه یا چخی شه *kurésha* or *chakhaysha*
Cat	پیش پیش پیش *peesh peesh peesh*	پشی شه *pashéysha.*
Cow or Bullock	شو شو شو *sho sho sho*	هاوشه *hawsha*
Buffalo	تی تی تی *té té té*	هي شه *hai sha*
Hawk	بیا بیا بیا *biā biā biā*	سُو سُو سُو *sū sū sū* or هان هان هان *hān hān hān*
Goat	بچی بچی بچی *baché baché baché*	کچی شه *kaché sha*
Sheep	درری درری درری *darray darray darray*	درری شه *darray sha*
Horse or Donkey	کوُر کوُر کوُر *koor koor koor*	تپو شه *tpo sha*
Hen or Cock	پاپ پاپ پاپ *pāp pāp pāp*	کړی شه *karé sha*
Camel	پش پش پش *pash pash pash*	اوشا *oosha*
Crow	آ آ آ *ā ā ā*	دو شه *dōsha*

(C) Driving a person out ورک شه = *vraksha* = Confound you, go and lose yourself.

(D) When speaking of any defective person use the word معذور = *mazūr* = the one who has objection.

هغه په يوه ستركه معذور دى	*hagha puh yawa starga māzūr day*	He has only one Eye.
هغه په لاس معذور دى	*hagha puh lās māzūr day*	He has only one hand.
هغه په خپه معذور دى	*hagha puh khpa māzūr day*	He has only one foot or leg.

55. When two similar post positions are used together, their meaning is intensified as :—

ورستو ورستو راځه	*vrosto vrosto rāza*	Come far behind.
لاندې لاندې	*lāndé lāndé*	Right underneath, the lower most ones.
پورته پورته	*pōrta pōrta*	Upper most ones.
مخکښې مخکښې ځه	*makhké makhké zah*	Go right ahead.

56. The following words have an additional meaning derived from the characteristic of the language and the people as :—

پښتو	*pukhtu*	Pashto or modesty.
پښتون	*pukhtūn*	Pathan or modest, self respecting, firm.

EXAMPLES.

پۀ هغۀ کښې هيڅ پښتو نشته	*puh haghuh ké hiss pukhtō nishta*	He has no modesty (shame) in him.
کرنيل صاحب يو پښتون سړی دی	*karnél sāhib yau pukhtūn saray day*	The colonel is a modest yet firm person.

57. The following words are used as regular adjectives with the verb to be :—

ناست	*nāst*	Sitting.
ولاړ	*walār*	Standing.
ملاست	*mlāst*	Lying.
اودۀ	*ūduh*	Sleeping.

EXAMPLE

هغه پۀ کرسئ نا ست دی	*hagha puh kursai nāst day*	Lit: he is seated on the chair = he is sitting on the chair.
جنئ پۀ کر سئ ناسته ده	*jinaī puh kursai nāsta dah*	The girl is sitting (seated) on the chair.

58. خندل=*khandal*, to laugh takes پوری=*pōré* as :—

هغۀ ما پوری و خندل	*haghuh mā poré wo khandal*	He laughed at me
ما هغۀ پوری و خندل	*mā haghuh pōré wo khandal*	I laughed at him.

59. The future perfect and past dubious are formed by conjugating the future tense of the verb to be after the past participle of another verb as :—

هغه به راغلیَ وي	*hagka ba rāghalay wee*	He must, will, or may have come.

NOTE :— به = *ba* the sign of the future can be put anywhere after the subject of the verb, so long as it is before the verb as :—

زهٔ به پهٔ پنځهٔ بجې دَ کرنیل صاحب سره ښکار دَ پاره ځم	*zuh ba puh pinzuh bajé da karnail sāhib sara khkār da pāra zam*	I will go for shooting with the colonel at 5 o'clook.

60. To express "to be about to" either change the final ل = *l* of the infinitive into ونکیَ = *ūnkay* or use the preposition پهٔ-کې = *puh-ké* with the verbal nouns as :—

هغه راتلونکیَ دیَ	*hagha rātlūnkay day*	He is about to come.
هغه پهٔ راتلوکښې دی	*hagha puh rātlo ké day*	He is about to come.

61. To express "to be about to be" conjugate the verb راتلل = *rātlal* = to come or کیدل = *kédal* = become after the verbal nouns governed by پهٔ-باند = *puh-bāndé* as :—

کوهیَ پهٔ ډکیدلو راغيَ	*kuhy puh dakédalo rāghay*	the well is about to become full
کوهي په ډکیدلو شو	,, ,, ,, *sho*	
کوهیَ په ډکیدلو دی	,, ,, ,, *day*	

62. To express "either......or," use یا = *yā* at the beginning of both sentences and to express "neither nor," use نهٔ = *nuh* at the begining of both sentences as :—

یا دا واخله یا هغه واخله	*yā dā wākhla yā hagha wākhla*	take either this or that.
زهٔ نهٔ دا اخلم نهٔ هغه اخلم	*zuh nuh dā akhlam nuh hagha akhlam*	I will take neither this nor that.

63. یادکول = *yād kawal* to remind and ویل = *wayal* to say, speak or tell, take the dative case ته = *ta* = to.

ما ته یاد کړه	*mā ta yād kra*	Remind me.
ورته و وایه	*war ta wo wāya*	Tell him.

64. In some districts the imperfect tense 3rd. person masculine singular and plural of the Class II, III, IV and VII verbs, is formed by changing the final ل = *l*, of the infinitive into هٔ = *uh*, as :—

هغه رسیدهٔ	*hagha raséduh*	He was arriving.
هغوی رسیدهٔ	*haghui raséduh*	They were arriving.
ما هغه راوستهٔ	*mā hagha rāwastuh*	I was bringing him.
ما هغوی راوستهٔ	*mā haghui rāwastuh*	I was bringing them.
هغه مړ کیدهٔ	*hagha mar kéduh*	He was dying.

هغوی مړۀ کیدۀ	*haghui mruh kéduh*	they were dying.
ما کتاب لوستۀ	*mā kitāb lwastuh*	I was reading a book.
ما کتابونه لوستۀ	*mā kitābūna lwastuh*	I was reading books.

In Class I. Verbs the above rule applies only to 3rd. person masculine singular as :—

ما هغه و وهۀ	*mā hagha wo wahuh*	I beat him, struck him.
ما هغوی و وهل	*mā hughui wo wahal*	I beat them, struck them.

Some times the imperfect tense 3rd person masculine singular is formed irregularly :—

هغه تۀ	*hagha tuh*	He was going.
هغه راتۀ	*hagha rātuh*	He was coming.

65. Sometimes in forming the potential mood the final ل = *l*, of the past participle is dropped.

زۀ رسیدی شم	*zuh raséday sham*	I can arrive.
زۀ او سیدی شم	*zuh oséday sham*	I can live.
زۀ رسیدی نۀ شم	*zuh raséday nuh sham*	I cannot arrive.
زۀ کینا ستی شوم	*zuh kénāstay shwam*	I could sit.
زۀ راوړی شم	*zuh rāwray sham*	I can bring.
ما راوړی شو	*mā rawray sho*	I could bring.

66. The past tense of the following verbs is sometimes formed thus :—

راتلل = *rātlal* = to come,

	Singular.			Plural.	
راغم	*rāgham*	(I) came	راغؤ	*rāghū*	(we) came.
راغې	*rāghé*	(thou) came	راغئ	*raghai*	(you) came.
راغی	*rāghay* or *rāgho*	(he) came	راغۀ	*rāghuh*	(they) came.
راغه	*rāgha*	(She) came (F)	راغی	*rāghé*	(they) came. (F. P.)

کول = *kawal* = to do.

(زۀ یی مړ) کړم	(*zuh yé mar*) *kram*	(He killed) me.
(ته یئ مړ) کړی	(*tuh yé mar*) *kré*	(he killed) thee.
(هغه یی مړ) کړو	(*hagha yé mar*) *kro*	(He killed) him.
(هغه یی مړه) کړه	(*hagha yé mra*) *kra*	(He killed) her (F. S.)
(مونږ یي مړۀ) کړؤ	(*mūng yé mruh*) *kroo*	(He killed) us.
(تاسو ئی مړۀ) کړئ	*tāsō yé mruh*) *krai*	(He killed) you.
(هغوی یی مړۀ) کړۀ	(*haghui yé mruh* *kruh*	(He killed) them.
(هغوی یی مړی) کړی	(*haghui yé mré*) *kré*	(He killed) them (F. P.)

کیدل = *kédal* = to become.

شولم *shwalam*	(I) became.	شولو *shwaloo*	(we) become.
شولی *shwalé*	(thou) become.	شولئ *shwalai*	(you) became.
شولویاشهٔ *shwalo* or *shuh*	(he) become.	شوهٔ *shwuh*	(they) became.
شوله *shwalah*	(she) became.	شوي *shwé*	(they) became. (F. P.)

ویل *wayal*	to say, speak, tell.
ما ووِ *mā wo wé*	I said, spoke, or told.
ما وِ *mā wé*	I was saying. (Imperf. tense.)

67. To express "unless or until" use the negative aorist tense of the required verb as :—

کهٔ تهٔ پخپله رانهٔ شی *kuh tuh pakh-pala rā nuh shé*	Unles you come yourself.
ترڅو پورې‌چه زهٔ را نهٔشم *tar so pōré chi zuh rā nuh sham*	Until I come myself.

68. داړه = *dāra* raid or raiding party and جُرم = *jurm* fine (on the village or tribe) both take the verb to fall = پریوتل = *préwatal.*

خما پهٔ کلي باندې داړه پریوتله *zamā puh kali bāndé dāra préwatala*	My village was raided.
خما پهٔ کلي باندې جُرم پریوتلو *zamā puh kali bāndé jurm préwatalo*	My village was fined.

69. افسوس = *afsōs*, sorrow. must always be used with کول = *kawal* = to do, as :—

زهٔ افسوس کوم = *zuh afsōs kawam*, I am sorry.

70. Nouns ending in consonants governed by ablative case sometimes take ـَ *zabar* over the last consonant letter of the noun instead of نه = *na*, the second Part of the Post position as :—

لهٔ کور نه *luh kōr na* or له کورَ *luh kōra*
From the house.

لهٔ مسکوټ نه *luh miskōt na* or لهٔ مسکوټَ *luh miskota*
From the Mess.

71. بل = *bal*, next or other (stands for number) Its Plural is نور = *nōr*, = more or others (Stands for both number and quantity) as :—

بل سړی راغی	*bal saray rāghay*	Another man came.
نوری اوبهٔ نشته	*noré obuh nishta*	There is no more water.

72. څو = *so*, how many (stands for number.) څومره = *somrā*, how many or how much (Stands both for number and quantity) e. g.

څو هلکان دی	*so halakān di*	How many boys are there.
پهٔ گلاس کښی څومره اوبهٔ دي	*puh gélās ké sōmra obuh di*	How much water is there in the glass.

73. When an adjective is used to qualify two or more nouns of different Genders the verb agrees with last one as :—

يو سړی او دوه ښځې ناستې وې	*yau saray aw dwa khazé nāsté wé*	One man and two women were sitting.

74. When two or three or more than three nouns of different genders are used in the sentence, the verb agrees with the last one and if two nouns of different genders in the singular number are used, the verb goes into the 3rd person masculine plural. In the case of the verb "to be" however agreement is with the last noun as :—

هلته دوه سړي او درې هلكان او درې ښځې وې	*halta dwa sarī aw dré halakān aw dré khazé wé*	There were two men and three boys and three women three.
په كور كښې څلور ښځې او دوه سړي وُو	*puh kōr ké salōr khazé aw dwa sari woo*	There were four women and two men there in the house.
يو هلك او يوه جنۍ ولاړ وُو	*yau halak aw yawa jinai walār woo*	One boy and one girl were standing
هلته يو هلك او يوه جنۍ دَه	*halta yau halak aw yawa jinai dah*	There are one boy and one girl there.
خما په خيال كښې يوه جنۍ او يو هلك وُه	*zamā puh kheyāl ké yawa jinai aw yau halāk woh*	I thing there were one girl and one boy there.

75. خپل = *khpal* Own—comes under the rules of regular adjectives ending in consonants and is used as a reflexive pronoun as :—

زهٔ خپل کورته ځم	*zuh khpal hōr ta zam*	I go to my house.
ځما خپل کورونه دي	*zamā khpal kōrūna di*	They are my own houses.
ځما خپله لوُر دَه	*zamā khpala lūr dah*	She is my own daughter.
ځما خپلې لوُنړه دي	*zamā khpalé lūnra di*	They are my own daughters.
دَ خپلې اسپې زين راوړه	*da khpalé aspé zin rāwra*	Bring the saddle of your mare.
خپلو اسپوته واښهٔ واچوه	*khpalo aspo ta wākhuh wāchawa*	Give grass to your mares.
موُنږ خپلو کورونو ته ځوُ	*mūng khpalo kōrūno ta zoo*	We are going to our houses.

NOTE :—When the particle په = *pa* is prefixed to خپل = *kapal*, the ه = *h* of the particle په = *pa* is placed after the same word :—

پخپله = *pakhpala* = Myself, yourself, himself, herself, itself, etc.

زهٔ پخپله ځم	*zūh pakhpala zam*	I go or will go myself.
هغه به پخپله راشي	*hagha ba pakhpala rāshi*	He will come himself.

76. The Causative verbs are formed by using the preposition پهٔ-باندې = *puh-bāndé* with a transitive verb as :—

ما پهٔ منشی باندې چهٹی ولیکله	*mā puh munshi bāndé chitai wo likalah*	I made the munshi write a letter.

77. The interrogative is often used to indicate strong negative as :—

ما سخه روپئ چرته دي	*mā sakha rupai charta di?*	I have no money at all.

78. The past participle of any verb can be used as an adjective as :—

تښتیدلی آس	*takhtédalay āss*	Run away horse.
وهلی شوی سړي	*wahalay shaway saray*	The beaten man.

79. Prefix دَ = *da* = of, (the genitive) to a noun to use it as an adjective as :—

د میوی دوکان	*da mewé dūkān*	The fruit shop.
دَ کور خاوند	*da kōr khāwand*	The owner of the house.

80. لوکوټی = *lūkūti* or لږ = *lag* = little, is used at the beginning of a sentence to express "Please" as :—

لوکوټي زر راشه	*lūkūti zar rāsha*	Please come quickly.

لږکوټيِ اوبهٔ راوړه	*lūkūti obuh rāwra*	Please bring some water.
لږى اوبهٔ راکړه	*lagé obuh rākra*	Please give me some water.

81. غوندې = *ghundé* Like, added to adjectives signifies "Somewhat" :—

وړوکی غوندي	*warūkay ghundé*	somewhat small or smallish.
سپين غوندي	*spin ghundé*	somewhat white or whitish.

82. The plural is used for the 2nd and 3rd person singular for politeness, but if the name of the person is mentioned then the Verb remains singular as :—

تاسو كله راغليِ يئ	*tāso kala rāghali yai*	instead of.
تهٔ كله راغلى يې	*tuh kala rāghalay yé*	When have you come ?
هغوئِ كله راغليِ دي	*haghūi kala rāghali dī*	Instead of.
هغهٔ كله راغلى دى	*hagha kala rāghalay day*	(lit) when has he come, when did he come ?
افضل خان كله تلى دى	*afzal khān kala talay day*	when did Afzal Khan go ?

83. پهٔ مخه راتلل = *puh makha rātlal* to meet. When using this in a sentence, the subject of the English verb is always left out as :

هغه پهٔ مښه راغلو	*hagha puh makha rāghlo*	I met him.
هغه پهٔ مښه درَغلو	*hagha puh makha daraghlo*	Thou met him.
هغه پهٔ مښه ورَغلو	*hagha puh makha waraghlo*	He met him.

84. To express strong negation in question form repeat, the tense in affirmative after the negative tense with خو = *kho* before it as :—

زهٔ ستا نوکر خو نهٔیم چهٔ نوکریم	***zuh stā naukar kho nuh yam chi naukar yam***	I am not your servant am I ?

85. The expression "Will you" the sign of a question or force after an imperative in English is always translated by کهٔ نهٔ = ***ka na*** = if not, or not as :—

دا واخله کهٔ نهٔ *dā wākhla ka na* take this will you ?

but when used with هو = *ho*, it means "Of course" as :—

هو کهٔ نهٔ *ho ka na* of course, certainly.

86. For blessing and cursing use دې = *dé* before the imperative for 2nd person singular as :—

خدای دې لاټ کړه	*khudāi dé lāt kra*	May God make you a lord.
خدای د خوار کړه	*khudāi dé khwār kra*	May God make you poor.

NOTE:—For the rest of the persons use the following particles.

مِ = *mé*	Singular.	مو = *mo*	Plural.
دِ = *dé*		مو = *mo*	
يې = *yé*		يې = *yé*	

before the aorist tense 3rd, person with دِ = *dé* before it as:—

خدای مِ دِ خان کړي	***khudāi mé dé khān kri***	May God make me a Khan.
خدای مو دِ خوار کړي	***khudāi mō dé khwār kri***	May God make you poor.
خدای دِ يې خوار کړي	***khudāi dé yé khwār kri***	May God make him (them) poor.

NOTE:—The above particles are idiomatically used after:—

را = ***rā*** در = ***dar*** ور = ***war*** پا = ***pā*** پرې = ***pré***
پورې = ***pōré*** کې = ***ké*** وُ = ***wo*** وا = ***wā*** نن = ***nan***
بې = ***bé***, e. g.

را يې نهٔ کړ	***rā yé nuh kar***	He did not give it to me.
پا يې نهٔ ښولو	***pa yé nūh sawalo***	He did not make him get up.
وُ مِ نهٔ ويل	***wo mé nuh wayal***	I did not say.

کیم نهٔ ږو دلو *ké mé nuh khōdalo* I did not place it.

رایې نهٔ وړو *rā yé nuh vro* He did not bring it.

87. An inanimate object can never be used in the Agentive case. The verb is changed into intransitive governed by the Ablative case as :—

ستا چټۍ مې ولوستله او ور نه پوه شوم چه تهٔ نوره نوکری نه کوی

stā chitai mé wo lwastalah aw war na poh shwam chi tuh nōra naukari nuh kawé

I read your letter which made me think that you were not going to serve any more.

لهٔ دی سیند نه خمونږ ټوله زمکه اوبهٔ کیږي

luh dé sind na zamūng tōla zmaka obuh kégi

This river irrigates all our land.

خمونږ پټو له پهٔ وله کښې اوبهٔ راځی یا له ولې نه اوبهٔ راځی

zamūng patō la puh wala ké obuh rāzee or *luh walé na obuh rāzee* The irrigation channel brings water to our fields.

88. The first letter of a noun is changed into م = *m* and then it is repeated for emphasis and etc. but when the noun begins with م = *m* it should be repeated without any alteration as :—

تا سخه کتاب متاب شته *tā sakha kitab mitāb shta* Have you any book etc ?

پهٔ کمره کښې څه میز میز شته *puh kamra ké suh méz méz shta* Is there any table etc. in the room ?

NOTE :—The following are the exceptions :—

غبږ غوبږ	*ghag ghūg*	Human voice (in answer)
هان هون	*hān hūn*	,, ,, ,,
ټس ټوس یا	*tas tūs* or	
ډز ډوز	*daz dūz*	Sniping.
غلا غلتیا	*ghlā ghultia*	Theft etc.
کاڼړي بوټي	*kānri būti*	Stones etc.
کډوډ کور	*karū kōr*	Rendered homeless.
چنګ رباب	*chang rabāp*	Squandered.
خل پل	*khal pal*	Leaves and twigs.
غال بول	*ghāl būl*	Harum scarum.
ټیل ما ټیل	*tail mātail*	Pushing each other.
درب دروب	*drab drūb*	Fisticuffs.
ګړ ګوړ	*gār gūr*	Thunder and lightning.

89. The use of خو = *kho* = but

دغه کتاب خو راکړه	*dāgha kitāb kho rākra*	Just hand me that book please.
زه خو دا کار نه کوم	*zuh khō dā kār nuh kawam*	I shall not do this really.
دا سړی خو زما نوکر وه	*dā saray khō zamā naukar woh*	I believe this man was my servant.
هغه خو به پاس شي	*hagha khō ba pāss shi*	He will certainly pass.
آخر ګوره خوچه دې به څه نتیجه وي	*ākher gora kho chi da dé ba suh natija wee*	Any way do at least wait and see what the result of it will be.

تهٔ نا جوړ خو نهٔ یې	*tuh nā jōr kho nuh yé*	I hope you are not ill. (you look as if you are.)
جوړ خو یې که نه	*jōr kho yé ka na*	I hope you are well. (you look as if you are not.)
کم عقل خو دی خو غل نهٔ دی	*kam aqal khō day kho ghal nuh day*	Admitted that he is a fool but he is not a thief.
دا خو رښتیا خبره دَه	*dā kho rikhtiā khabara dah*	This indeed is true.
زهٔ خو نهٔ ځم	*zuh khō nuh zam*	I (as you know) am not going.

پښتو خو پښتو دَه چه زهٔ پهٔ انګریزي هم نهٔ پو هیږم

pukhtō kho pukhtō dah chi zuh puh angrézai hum nuh pōhégam

or

پښتو خو پریږده چه زهٔ پهٔ انګریزي هم نهٔ پو هیږم

pukhtō kho prégda chi zuh puh angrézai hum nuh pōhégam

Let alone (or to say nothing of) Pushtu I do not even understand English.

ښه دا کار خو وشو	*kha dā kār khō wo shō*	Well that is done.
یو خو هغهٔ غریب دی بل بد خوئ دی	*yau khō hagha gharib day, bal bad khūi day*	For one thing (or first) he is poor, and for another (or secondly) bad tempered,

90. When a noun is repeated, it denotes entirety plurality and variety as :—

ما هغه کټ پهٔ کټ ولټولو	*mā hagha kat puh kat wo latawalo*	I searched for him in each and every bed.
رښتيا رښتيا وايه	*rikhtiā rīkhtiā wāya*	Speak the truth and nothing but the truth (i. e. the whole truth.)
مؤ نږ پهٔ سرک سرک راغلؤ	*mūng puh sarāk sarāk rāghlū*	We came by the road the whole way.
اوس هغه در پهٔ در ګرځي	*us hagha dar puh dar garzee*	Now he wanders about begging from door to door

91. When a personal or pronominal adjective is repeated, it denotes plurality, variety and distribution.

تا څهٔ څهٔ وليدل *tā suh suh wo lidal*

What various things did you see ?

پهٔ هغه وخت هلته څوک څوک موجود وؤ *puh hagha wakht halta sōk sōk maujūd woo.*

What people were individually present there at that time ?

کوم کوم چه وګټي نو انعام به ومؤمي *kum kum chi wo gati no inām ba wo mūmee*

Every one of those who wins will get a reward.

ځيني ځيني سړي هلته پاتي دي *ziné ziné saray halta paté day*

There were only a few people left there.

بعضي بعضي په کښې ډیر منُصف وُه — *bazé bazé pa ké dér munsif woh*

Some of them (considered individually) were very just.

هر سړی خپل خپل کور ته لاړ — *har saray khpal khpal kōr ta lār*

Everyone of them went to his own house.

ټول خپلو خپلو کورونو ته لاړل — *tōl khpalō khpalō kōrūno ta lāral*

All went to their respective houses.

ما هغه هغه یا داسی داسی خیزونه ولیدل چه ورته حیران پاتی شوم — *mā hagha hagha* or *dāsé dāsé sizūna wo lidal chi war ta hairan pāté shwam*

I was astonished to see such things.

څۀ څۀ یا څۀ نا څۀ — *suh suh* or *suh nā suh*

Somewhat or to some extent.

هغه څۀ نا څۀ انګریزی ویلَی شي	*hagha suh nā suh angrezi wayalay shee*	He can speak English a little (to some extent.)
اوس هغه څۀ نا څۀ جوړ دَی	*os hagha suh nā suh jōr day*	He is somewhat better now.

92. خوک = *sōk* = who, څۀ = *suh* = what, repeated in negative sentences have the additional idiomatic meaning of all or whole. as :—

هلته خوک خوک نۀ وُه ؟	*halta sōk sōk nuh woh*	Who was not present there ? (name them individually) ? or every body was there.

ما څۀ څۀ ونۀ ليدل ؟	*mā suh suh wo nuh lidal*	I saw everything (lit : what was it that I did not see?)

93. When an adjective is repeated it denotes plurality, entirety, and variety or distribution.

پۀ هر طرف اوچت اوچت کورونه وو	*puh har taraf ūchat ūchat korūna woo*	There were tall houses on every side.
لۀ سړک نه پورې غاړه لوی لوی پټی وو	*luh sarak na poré ghāra lōi lōi pati woo*	Beyond the road there were many large fields.
لۀ چاونړۍ نه باهر شنۀ شنۀ فصلونه دي	*luh chāwnrai na bāhar shnuh shnuh faslūna di*	Outside the cantonment there are many green crops.

دَ هغوی لنډی لنډی ږیری وي *da haghūi landé landé giré wi*

They have (generally) short beards.

ورته تازه تازه پئی ورکوه *war ta tāza tāza pai war kawa*

Give him (or them) very fresh milk or give him milk while it is still fresh.

یخه یخه هوا الوزي *yakha yakha hawā alūzee*

A nice cool breeze is blowing (continued and agreeable intensity).

ورته پنځۀ پنځۀ انې ورکړه *war ta pinzuh pinzuh ané war kra*

Give them five annas each.

صاحب سخه ښې ښې جامې دي *sāhib sakha khė khė jāmė di*

The sahib has many good clothes.

ورسخه خرڅ دَ پاره لس لس روپئ دی *war sakha khars da pāra las las rupai di*

Each of them has ten rupees to spend.

تا سو تولو ته به پاؤ باندِ څلور څلور روپئ ملاؤ شي *tāso tōlo ta ba pāw bāndė salōr salōr rūpai milāw shi*

Everyone of you will get Rs. 4/4/-.

94. When an imperfect tense or a verbal noun is repeated it denotes continuity.

تلم تلم کابل ته ورسیدم *tlam tlam kābal ta wo rasėdam*

I went on till I reached Kabul.

هغه پهٔ لوستو لوستو کښې لیونَی شو *hagha puh lwasto lwasto kė lėwanay sho*

By continually reading he went mad.

پهٔ ناستې ناستې ستړیَ شوم *puh nāstė nāstė staray shwam.*

I became tired of continued idleness.

پهٔ ملاستې ملاستې یې روټې وخوړله *puh mlāstė mlāstė yė rōtai wo khwarala*

He ate his food lying down all the time.

پهٔ لیدو لیدو مې زړهٔ باغ باغ کیږي *puh līdo lido mė zruh bāgh bāgh kėgee*

By continuously looking I am delighted.

جوړ پهٔ جوړ *jōr puh jōr* — Like servant like master (or wife and husband both are of the same nature)

96. To form a question in the absence of any interrogative word use کهٔ نه = *kuh na* = or not, at the end of a sentence. Also, as in other languages a rising intonation at the end of a remark implies a question.

خان اوس پهٔ هسپتال کښې دې کهٔ نه ؟ *Khān oss puh haspatāl ké day kuh na*

Is the Khan in the hospital now?

97. کهٔ نه = *kuh na* = or not, is some times put at the end of a sentence to make it interrogative and invites an answer accordingly as the rest of the sentence is couched e. g. if the rest of the sentence is put affirmatively the answer is expected to be in the affirmative, but if it is worded negatively, the answer is expected to be in the negative as :—

تهٔ خو به صبا ځې کهٔ نه *tuh kho ba sabā zé kuh na*

I believe you will go tomorrow, wont you?

بیا خو به داسې کارنهٔ کوې کهٔ نه *biā kho ba dāsé kār nuh kawé ka na*

Well, I hope you will not do so in future, will you?

98. The names of places ending in ي = *i* are considered masculine plural, therefore when governed by any preposition they should be put into the oblique plural as :—

لهٔ پبونه دی خوا	*luh pabō na dé khwā*	This side of Pabbi.
صبا زهٔ مټنوته ځم	*sabā zuh matano ta zam*	I am going to Mattani tomorrow.

99. To show dislike or anger add ی = *ay*, گی = *gay*, to proper nouns and titles ending in consonants or vowels respectively.

احمد	*ahmad*	احمدی	*ahmaday*
مُلا	*mulā*	ملا گی	*mulāgay*

100. To animate or inanimate articles add گی = *gay*, to express smallness or poor quality as :—

ټټو	*tattū*	Pony	ټټو گی	*tatūgay*	Small pony.
تم تم	*tam tam*	Tonga	تم تم گی	*tam tamgay*	Ordinary kind of tonga.

101. Generic Plural Animals etc. when seen in numbers from a distance are sometimes referred to as feminine plural and sometimes as masculine plural regardless of their actual sex.

e. g. Feminine Plural.

میښی	*Mékhé*	Buffaloes.
ګډی	*gadé*	Sheep.
کونتری	*kōntaré*	Pigeons.

Masculine Pural.

میلؤ ګان	*mėlūgān*	Bears.
اوښان	*ukhān*	Camels.
ډنګر	*dangar*	Cattle.
ها تیاں	*hāthiān*	Elephants.
قار غان	*qārghān*	Crows.
ټپۇ ښان	*tapūsān*	Kites.
طو طیان	*tōtyān*	Parrots.
امزري	*amzari*	Tigers.
بیزو ګان	*bizōgān*	Monkeys.

102. لرل = *laral* to have. is rarely used except in the present and imperative.

زۀ یو کتاب لرم	*zuh yau kitāb laram*	I have a book.
ټول رسد تیار لره	*tōl rasad tayār lara*	Have all supplies ready.

103. ماره = *māra*, give me, the imperative, has no infinitive, it only derived from Persian Dative case مارا *mā rā* = to me as :—

دا کتاب مارا	*dā kītāb māra*	Give me that book.

104. مینهٔ کیدل = *mina kėdal* to have a desire for, takes Dative case and is followed by the genitive case :—

خما تلو ته مینه کیږي	*zamā tlo ta mina kėgee*	I have a desire to go.

105. The following nouns are masculine in the singular and feminine in the plural :—

مرز	*maraz*	Quail	مرزی	*marazé*	F. P.
کنډر	*kandar*	ruined house	کنډری	*kandaré*	F. P.
کوتک	*kōtak*	big stick	کوتکی	*kōtaké*	F. P.
ډز	*daz*	Gun shot (report)	ډزی	*dazé*	F. P.

106. Some nouns are feminine in the singular and masculine in the plural as :—

ګناه *gunāh* Sin ګناهونه *gunāhūna* Sins M. P.

107. خدمت کول = *khidmat kawal* = To serve (without payment) takes genitive case as :—

مونږ د سرکار خدمت کړی دی *mūng dā sarkār khidmat karay day*
We have served Government.

108. Use simple imperfect when the desire of a person i. e. subject of the verb is expressed as :—

کهٔ هغه راتلو نو را د شي *kuh hagha rātla no rā dé shee*
Let him come if he wishes to come.

109. In the imperative of a transitive verb the direct object must be expressed as :—

را یی کړه	*rā yé kra*	Give it to me.
وریی کړه	*war yé kra*	Give it to him.

وییٰ وهه *wo yé waha* Beat him.
کیم نوه *ké mé nawa* Make me sit.

110. When the intention of the subject in the conditional form is expressed, use the original uninflected past participle in the 1st sentence and the required tense in the 2nd; half as :—

کهٔ هغه راتلیٰ نو به راغلی وهٔ *kuh hagha rātlay nō ba rāghalay woh*
If he meant to come he would have come.

111. To express "nearly" or "about" use یو = *yau* = one. before the required numerals as :—

یو دوه سو *yaw dwa sawa* nearly two hundred.

112. List of common female animals and their male young.

غوا	*ghwā*	Cow	سخیٰ	*skhay*	calf.
میښه	*mékha*	Buffalo	کټیٰ	*katay*	Buffalo calf.
اسپه	*aspa*	mare	کوٗ چانړیٰ	*kūcha nray*	Colt.
ګډه	*gada*	Sheep	اوریٰ	*oray*	Lamb.
چیلۍ	*chélai*	She goat	بکریٰ	*bakray*	Kid.
اوښ	*ūkha*	Female camel	جونګیٰ	*jōngay*	young camel.
سپۍ	*spai*	Bitch	کوٗتری	*kūtré*	pup.

113. پۀ قهر کیدل = *puh qahar kėdal* to be enraged with. takes Dative case as :—

ما ته پۀ قهر شو	*mā ta puh qahar sho*	He got angry with me.

114. خپه کیدل = *khapa kėdal* to be angry with, takes لۀ-نه = *luh-na* as :—

هغه رانه خپه شو یا هغه لۀ ما نه خپه شو	*hagha rā na khapa sho* or *hagha luh mā na khapa sho*	He got angry with me.
لۀ ما نه مۀ خپه کیږه	*luh mā na muh khapa kėga*	Don't be angry with me.

115. بلا = *balā* = calamity, when used before plural nouns means innumerable and before singular number, denotes greatness, the biggest size and the best qualification of a person as :—

پۀ جماعت کښې بلا خلق دی	*puh jumāit kė balā khalq dee*	There are innumerable people in the mosque.
هغه بلا سړی دی	*hagha balā saray day*	He is an exceptionable person.

. 116. The Definite Habitual expressing a condition is formed by prefixing به = *ba* to the past definite as :—

چه ښهر ته به راغلو نو زۀ به یې ولیدم او بیا به لاړو *chi khahar ta ba rāghlo no zuh ba yé wo lidalam aw biā ba lāro*

Whenever he came to the city, he would come to see me and then go back.

117. The Potential Habitual in the form of conditional in the 2nd half is formed by pre fixing به = *ba*, to the past potential.

کهٔ سرکار ټول وطن ته دَ ټوپکو ساتلو اجازت ورکړی وی - نو څنګه به م ټول په قابو کېښ ساتلی شول	*kuh sarkār tōl watan ta dạ tōpakō sātalō ijā-zat warkaray way, nō sanga ba mé tōl puh qābū ké sātalay shwal.*

If the Government had allowed the whole country to keep rifles, how could I keep them all in hand.

118. هسی نه وی چه = *hasé nuh wi chi* = Lest. is followed by the *A*orist tense as :—

هسی نه وِي چه هغه راشيِ	*hasé nuh wi chi hagha rāshee*

Lest he should come.

NOTE :—Also the use of چرته = *charta,* in this connection.

چرته هغه را نه شيِ	*charta hagha rā nuh shee.*

I hope he will not come (i.e. I fear lest he should come.)

119. Politely speaking when referring to the son of gentleman call him صاحبزاده = *Sahibzāda*, or برخوردار = *Barkhurdār* and when referring to ones own son, call him غلام = *ghulām* = Slave. Similarly when talking about the house of a gentleman (other than your own) you will call it

دولت خانه = *daulat khāna* = (abode of wealth) and when talking of your own house, you will call it.

غریب خانه = *gharib khāna* = Humble cottage, as :—

ستا سو دَ برخوردار نوم څهٔ دی *stāso da burkhurdār nūm suh day*
What is the name of your son ?

داستاسو غلام به جواب دروړی *dāstaso ghulām ba jawāb dar wree*
This son of mine lit your slave will bring you the answer.

ستا سو دولت خانه چرته دَه *stāso daulat khāna charta dah*
Where is your house ?

ځما غریب خانه پهٔ ښهر کښې دَه *zamā gharib khāna puh khahar ké dah*
My house is in the city.

120. When visiting a patient, or referring to an unpleasant subject, say, first :—

نصیبِ دشمنان *nasibé dushmanān*

May it (disease) fall to the lot of your enemies.

When praising something or somebody belonging to another person say :—

ماشاء الله *mā shā allāh* As God wills.
چشمِ بد دُور *chéshmé bad dūr* Far be the evil eye.

نصیب دشمنان دا کله راسی ناجوړ شوی یی — *nasibé dushmanān dā kala rāsé nā jora shaway yé*

May your disease become the lot of your enemies. How long have you been ill ?

ماشاء الله ستا سو برخوردار پهٔ جماعت کښې اول لمبر دی — *mā sha allah stāso barkhurdār puh jamāat ké awal lambar day*

By God's will your son is first in the class.

چشم بد دور ستا سو موټر دَ چاونړۍ دَ موټرونو پلار دی — *cheshmé bad dūr stāṣō mōtar da chāunrai da mōtarūno plār day*

Far be the evil eye, your motor is the best in the cantt; (lit: is the father of motors in the Cantt.)

121. Strong Negation is sometimes expressed by using خاورې = *khāwré* = dust, with the subject of the verb as :—

هغه به په دی خاوری پوه شی څهٔ — *hagha ba pa dé khāwré poh shee suh*

How on earth can he understand this ?

122. Interrogatives are often used to express strong negation, surprise and impossibility as :—

زهٔ په دی کښې څهٔ کولی شم — *zuh pa dé ké suh kawalay sham*

What can I do in this matter! (or it is impossible for me to do anything in this matter).

زهٔ څنګه هلته لاړ شم — *zuh sangā halta lār sham*

How can I go there or I cannot go there or it is impossible for me to go there.

تۀ په دی څۀ پوهیږې *tuh pa dė suh pōhėgė*

How do you know of this ? (you know nothing of this).

هغه کله کابل ته تلی دی *hagha kala kabal ta talay day*

When has he been to Kabul ? (i e. he has never been to Kabul).

123. Many Arabic and Persian adverbs are commonly used :—

اتفاقاً	*ittefāqan*	by chance.
خصوصاً	*khusūsan*	especially.
تخمیناً	*takhminan*	nearly.
قریباً	*qariban*	nearly.
فوراً	*fauran*	at once.
جبراً	*jabran*	by force.
مثلاً	*masalan*	for instance.
عموماً	*umūman*	generally.
ارادتاً	*irādatan*	intentionally.

etc :—

124. Some idiomatic uses of چرته—*charta* where.

چرته زۀ او چرته تۀ *charta zuh aw charta tuh*

there is all the difference between you and me (lit : where am I and where are you.) ?

چرته هغه بادشاهی او چرته دا غریبی *charta hagha bādshāhi aw charta dā gharibi*

Once there was such a good time and now there is this poverty.

زهٔ چر ته او تهٔ چر ته — *zuh charta aw tuh charta*

We were far apart from each other or you found me merely by luck.

چر ته یې کېږده — *charta yé kégda*

Place it somewhere.

ګوره کهٔ چر ته څوک راشي — *gōra kuh charta sōk rāshee*

Wait and perchance someone may come.

ما چر ته ایښیَ دیَ — *mā charta ikhay day*

I have placed it somewhere.

پهم کوه چه چر ته نا جوړنه شې — *paham kawa chi charta nā jōra nuh shé*

Be careful lest you should fall ill.

چر ته ورک شویَ خو نه دیَ — *charta vrak shaway kho nuh day*

I hope he or it has not been lost by any chance.

125. Direct narration is always used in place of indirect narration as :—

هغهٔ و وِ چه زما نوُم جان دیَ — *haghuh wō wé chi zamā nāu Jān day*

He said his name was John.

هغهٔ و وِ چه زهٔ به لاړ شم — *haghuh wo wé chi zuh ba lār sham*

He said that he would go.

126. The required tense of کیدل = *kédal* with the ablative can be used to express Potential mood.

دا کارلهٔ تا نه کیږی	*dā kār luh tā na kégee*	You can do this.
دا کارلهٔ ما نه نهٔ کیږی	*da kār luh mā na nuh kégee*	I cannot do this.
داسی کار لهٔ ما نه نهٔ کیدو	*dāsé kār luh mā na nuh kédo*	I could not do such work.
لهٔ ما نه دانهٔ اوچتیږی	*luh mā na dā nuh ūchatégee*	I cannot lift this up.

127. The negative potential mood with the ablative case is also used to express impossibility and strong negation as :—

لهٔ ما نه نهٔ شی کیدی *luh mā na nuh shi kéday*

I am not going to do it or it is impossible for me to do it. (lit: from me it cannot become).

128. Pathans themselves are often puzzled to know which is the subject and which is the object in sentences with a transitive verb, where the subject and object both are singular in number and the subject remains uninflected in form in the agentive case.

To distinguish the subject لږی کیدل = *lagé kédal* to act, is conjugated after it as :—

احمد خان لږی شو محمد خان یی ووهلو *Ahmad Khan lagé sho, Muhamad Khan yé wo wahalo*

Ahmad Khan beat Muhamad Khan.

NOTE:—Normally the subject in the sentence is put first, but colloquially this is often disregarded.

129. The following nouns take ورکول = *war kawal* to give.

شکست ورکول *shikast war kawal* To defeat.
مدد ورکول *madad war kawal* To help.
قرض ورکول *qarz war kawal* To lend.
لاس ورکول *lās war kawal* To shake hands, help.
رنګ ورکول *rang war kawal* To colour, dye.
ګُذار ور کول *gūzār war kawal* To give a blow.
ربړ ور کول *rabar war kawal* To trouble.
سزا ور کول *sazā war kawal* To punish.

130. The following nouns take اخستل = *akhistal* = to take.

ساه اخستل *sāh akhistal* To breathe.
پناه اخستل *panāh akhistal* To take refuge.
لهٔـنه پور اخستل *luh-na pōr akhistal* To borrow.
لهٔـنهٔ خولهٔ اخستل *luh-na khuluh akhistal* To kiss.

131. The following nouns take لګول = *lagawal* = to add, to put, to apply etc, as :—

لاس لګول *lās lagawal* To fight, touch.
اور لګول *aur lagawal* To set fire to.
قُلپ لګول *qulp lagawal* To lock.

ډيل لګول	*dīl lagawal*	To delay.
زور لګول	*zōr lagawal*	To exert strength.
پته لګول	*pata lagawal*	To trace.
ګلونه لګول	*gulūna lagawal*	To arrange flowers (in vases)
ميز لګول	*méz lagawal*	To arrange table.
روپۍ لګول	*rupai lagawal*	To spend money.
ډيره لګول	*déra lagawal*	To pitch a tent, or encamp.
دوکان لګول	*dūkān lagawal*	To open shop.

132. The following nouns take لګيدل = *lagédal* = to be applied.

پۀ-باندې اور لګيدل	*puh-bāndé aur lagédal*	To catch fire.
پۀ-باندې لوږه لګيدل	*puh-bāndé luaga lagédal*	To feel hungry.
پۀ-باندې تنده لګيدل	*puh-bāndé tanda lagédal*	To feel thirsty.
پۀ-باندې بد لګيدل	*puh-bāndé bad lagédal*	To take ill.
پۀ-باندې باد لګيدل	*puh-bāndé bād lagédal*	To blow (wind.)
پۀ-باندې ښۀ لګيدل	*puh-bāndé khuh lagédal*	To like the sight of.

133. The following nouns take راتلل = *rātlal* to come.

(تۀ) غُصه راتلل	*(ta) ghusa rātlal*	To feel angry.

پۀ-بانډې رحم راتلل	(puh-bāndé) raham rātlal	To feel compassion.
(تۀ) ژبه راتلل	(ta) jhuba rātlal	To know (the language).
(پۀ) نظر رتلل	(puh) nazar rātlal	To come into sight.
(پۀ) مېښه راتلل	(puh) makha rātlal	To meet.
(پۀ-بانډې) تبه راتلل	(puh bāndé) taba rātlal	To catch fever.

134. The following nouns take خوړل = *khwaral* to eat as :—

قسم خوړل	*qasam khwaral*	To take an oath.
دوکه خوړل	*dōka khwaral*	To be deceived.
شکست خوړل	*shikast khwaral*	To be defeated
تیندک خوړل	*tindak khwaral*	To stumble.

135. څۀ = *suh* What, is sometimes put at the end of a sentence to form a question as :—

ما خپل کار نۀ دی کړی څۀ	*mā khpal kār nuh day karay suh ?*	Have I not done my work ?

136. The following nouns are commonly met with as collective numerals :—

جوړه	*jōra*	Pair, couple.
درزن	*darzan*	Dozen.
کوړئ	*kaurai*	Score.
سیکړه	*saikara*	Hundred (percent).

137. By adding وارۀ = *wāra* all, to any numerals, with the exception of یو = *yau* one. totality is shown as :—

دوارۀ	*dwāra*	Both.
دری وارۀ	*dré wāra*	All three.
څلور وارۀ	*salōr wāra*	All four
پنځۀ وارۀ	*pinzuh wāra*	All five.

Similarly پۀ = *puh* before and گونه = *gūna*, after the numerals are used :—

پۀ سلګونو	*puh sulgūmo*	Hundreds of.
پۀ زرګونو	*puh zargūno*	Thousands of.
پۀ لکونو	*puh lakūno*	Lakhs of.

*

138. The multiplicative numerals are formed by adding چند—*chand*. after any numeral or by prefixing یو پۀ—*yau puh* to it as :—

دو چند	*dō chand*	twice more.
دری چند	*dré chand*	thrice more.
څلور چند	*salōr chand*	four times more.
پنځۀ چند	*pinzuh chand*	five times more.

or

یو پۀ دوه	*yau puh dwa*	twice.
یو پۀ دری	*yau puh dré*	thrice.

---

* NOTE.—On account of *puh* or *puh bānde*, they are put into the oblique plural.

یو پۀ څلور *yau puh salōr* four times more.
یو پۀ پنځۀ *yau puh pinzuh* five times more.

139. The adverbial numerals once, twice, thrice etc. are formed by adding څل—*zal* = time, in the singular. څلَ—*zala*, in the plural which is inflected to څلو—*zalō*, in the oblique plural as :—

یو څل	*yau zal*	once.
دوه څلَ	*dwa zala*	twice.
دری څلَ	*dré zala*	thrice.
څلور څلَ	*salōr zala*	four times.
لۀ څلورو څلو	*luh salōro*	
نه زیات	*zalō na ziāt*	More than four times.

140. The fractional numerals are :—

نیم	*nim*	half.
پاؤ	*pāw*	quarter.
دری پاوَ	*dré pāwa*	three quarters.
پاؤ کم دوه	*pāw kam dwa*	one and three quarters $1\frac{3}{4}$.

141. دَ = *da* = is sometimes used instead of لۀ = *luh,* the first half of the ablative case as :—

دَ کور نه *da kōr na* or دَ کورَ *da kora* from the house, instead of :—

لۀ کورنه *luh kōr na* or لۀ کورَ *luh kōra* from the house.

142. لیکن = *léken* خو = *kho* مګر = *magar* ولی = *walé* all mean "But" مګر = *magar* and ولی = *walé* are used in the case of expressing exceptions and بلکه = *balké* means on the other hand or instead of as :—

ما ورنه تپوس وکړو چه کور دَ چرته دی لیکن یا خو جواب یی رانهٔ کړ	*mā war na tapōs wo krō chi kōr dé charta day lekén* (or) *khō jawāb yé rā nuh kar.*

I asked him where his house was but he did not answer.

ټول کلیوال ښهٔ دی مګر یو په کښې ښهٔ نهٔ دیَ	*tōl kali wāl khuh di magar* (or *walé*) *yau pa ké khuh nuh day*

All the villagers are good except one who is not good.

زهٔ نهٔ صرف دَ هغهٔ ورور یم بلکه نوکر یی هم یم	*zuh nuh sirf da haghuh vrōr yam balké naukar yé hum yam*

I am not only his brother but (or on the other hand) I am his servant as well.

143. The past tense is used to express past conjunctive as :—

چه کابل ته ورسیدم نو ستا دوست مِ ولیدلو یا ستا دوست راته ملاؤشو	*chi Kābal ta wo rasédam no stā dōst mé wo lidalo* or *stā dōst rā ta milāo sho*

Having arrived in Kabul I met your friend.

144. The simple present is idiomatically used to express desire of a person, wish and present continous as :—

زۀ ځم *zuh zam.*
- I want to go.
- I like to go.
- I wish to go.
- I am going.
- I go.

145. ملاست = *mlāst* Lying is only used for animate objects acting of their own accord, while پروت = *prōt* prostrate or lying, is used for inanimate objects and an animate objects with any kind of disease or helplessness.

زۀ پۀ کټ باندې ملاست یم *zuh puh kat bāndé mlāst yam*

I am lying on the bed.

زۀ درې ورځې ناجوړ پروت وم *zuh dré vrazé nājora prōt wam*

I was lying ill for three days.

کتاب پۀ میز باندې پروت دی *kitāb puh méz bāndé prōt day*

The book is lying on the table

146. حاضر = *hāzir* = Present or at the service of. while موجود = *maujūd* = present is used for superiors or in the case of inanimate objects denoting existing or available etc. as :—

ټول نوکران حاضر دي *tōl naukarān hāzir di*

All the servants are present.

خان پہ موقعہ مو جوُد وہ *khān puh mōqa maujūd woh*

The Khan was present at the spot.

دا حکایت پۂ کتاب کښں مو جوُد دی *dā hikāyat puh kitāb ké maujūd day*

This story is (present) in the book.

NOTE :—خدای حاضر دی—=*khudāi hāzir day*= God is present.

147. It is not polite to address the following persons without using the word صاحب = *sāhib* =

مُنشی	*munshi*	Munshi, teacher, writer.
با بوُ	*bābu*	Clerk.
جمعدار	*jamādār*	Lieut. (Indian rank.)
صو بیدار	*subédār*	Captain (Indian rank.)
سردار	*sardār*	Indian officer in the Army.
حکیم	*hakim*	Physician.
ډاڼګټر	*dāngtar*	Doctor.
مولوی	*maulvi*	Priest, learned.
قاضی	*qāzi*	Judge.

148. بعضی = *bazé* = Some, implies some out of a certain number and خینی—*ziné*—Some. implies some out of a certain number. Also it is a substitute for سخه = *sakha* = (Post position) as :—

بعضی خلق ښۀ دي *bazé khalq khuh di*

Some people are good.

پۀ بعضو کتابونو کښې راغلي دي *puh bazō kītabūno ké rāghali di*

It is written (lit : come) in some books.

ځينې پۀ رسالة کښې نوکری کوي *ziné puh résāla ké naukari kawī*

Some of them serve in the Cavalry.

تا ځينې چاقو شته *tā ziné chāqū shta* Have you a pen knife.

149. مه = *ma* = is the sign of prohibition and is used at the end of a sentence to express fear or force as :—

تۀ نن ځه مه = *tuh nan za ma* = You must not go today (or else you will get into trouble).

150. In the present conditional, the past tense is sometimes used in the first clause to express definite action as :—

کۀ دا کار دِ وکړو نو مړ به دِ کړم *kuh dā kār dé wo kro, nō mar ba dé kram*

I will kill you if you do this.

151. ما وې = *mā wé* or ما وويل = *ma wo wayal* I said, spoke or told has a secondary idiomatic meaning "I meant" as :—

ما ويل زۀ به پۀ رسالة کښې نوکري کوم *mā wayal zuh ba puh resāla ké naukari kawam*__

I meant to serve in the Cavalry.

152. In the following examples it will be noticed that the use of different prepositions is highly idiomatic. Sometimes a change of preposition completely changes the meaning not only of the whole sentence but of the nouns and verbs used as :—

هغه پهٔ سپین آس باندِ سوردې	*hagha puh spin āss bāndé sōr day*	He is riding on a white horse.
هغه پهٔ سپین اس کښن سوردی	*hagha puh spin āss ké sōr day*	He is riding in a trap with a white horse in the shafts.
هغه مورته تلی دی	*hagha mōr ta talay day*	He takes after his mother.
هغه مور باندی تلی دی	*hagha mōr bāndé talay day*	Lit: He has gone back into his mother (term of abuse).
هغه موټر ته پریوتو	*hagha mōtar ta préwato*	He threw himself in front of a motor car.
هغه موټر باند پریوتو	*hagha mōtar bāndé préwato*	He bumped into a stationery motor car.
هغه کورته ننوتو	*hagha kōr ta nanawato*	He went into his house.
هغه پهٔ کور باند ننوتو	*hagha puh kōr bāndé nanawato*	He went into someone else's house.
هغه باغ ته ننوت	*hagha bāgh ta nanawat*	He went into a Garden.

هغه پهٔ باغ ورننوت	*hagha puh bāgh war nanawat*	He went into someone else's garden (because of fear) or he was chased into a garden.
هغه پهٔ پیښور کښې دی	*hagha puh pékhawar ké day*	He is in Peshawar.
هغه پهٔ پیښور باندې دی	*hagha puh pékhawar bāndé day*	He is in charge of Peshawar.
هغهٔ ته اواز وکړه	*haghuh ta awāz wo kra*	Call him.
هغهٔ باندې اواز وکړه	*haghuh bāndé awāz wo kra*	Challenge him.

153. Use the word ځان = *zān* = self, or خپل‌ځان = *khapal zān* = oneself, with the Dative case before a compound transitive verb formed from an adjective to express "pretended to be", e.g :—

هغهٔ ورته ځان مړ کړ	*haghuh war ta zān mar kar*	He pretended to be dead.
هغهٔ ورته خپل ځان اودهٔ کړ	*haghuh war ta khpal zān ūduh kar*	He pretended to be asleep.
ما ورته خپل ځان لیونی کړ	*mā war ta khpal zān léwanay kar*	I pretended to be mad.

154. Note the following idioms dealing with the use of څومره چه = *sōmra chi* = as much, before

the first clause and دومره = *dōmra* = so much, before the second clause, e. g. :—

خومره چه دَ وسَ مِ کیږي دومره کوشش به کوم	*sōmra chi dā wasā mé kégee, dōmra kōshish ba kawam*

I will try my best.

خومره چه دَ وَس دِ کیږي دومره زر هلته لاړشه	*sōmra chi da wasa dė kėgee, dōmra zar halta lārsha,*

Go there as soon as you can.

خومره چه دَ وسَ مِ کیدل دومره جوار مِ ور کړل	*sōmra chi da wasa mé kėdal, dōmra jowār mé war kral.*

I gave him as much maize as I could afford.

خومره چه دَ وسَ مِ کیدلی دومرهٔ روپیۍ مِ ور کړلې	*sōmra chi da wasa mé kédalé, dōmra rūpai mé war kralé*

I gave him as much money as I could afford.

155. When animals and birds are counted use سَر = *sara* = Heads, before them as :—

شل سرَه مال	*shal sara māl*	twenty head of cattle
دیرش سرَ	*dérsh sarā*	
مرغابیۍ	*marghābai*	Thirty geese.

156. In the following idiom "with" the English preposition is not translated as :—

تهٔ خپل طلب	*tuh khpal talab*	What do you do
څهٔ کوې	*sūh kawé*	with your pay ?

157 تا لاش کول = *tālāsh kawal* = to search for. takes indirect object while لټول = *latawal* = to search, takes direct object.

ما دَ کتاب تالاش وکړلو *mā dā kitāb tālāsh wo kralo*

or

ما کتاب دَ پاره تالاش وکړلو *mā kitāb da pāra tālāsh wo kralo*.

I searched for the book.

ما کور و لټو لو *mā kōr wo latawalō* I searched the house.

158. ډک = *dak* = Full, is always governed by ablative case.

تلاؤ لهٔ اوبو نه ډک *talāw luh obo na dak* A tank full of water.

بېړۍ لهٔ سړو نه ډکه *bérai luh saro na daka* A boat full of men

کمرې لهٔ کرسو نه ډکې *kamré luh kursō na daké* Rooms full of chairs.

159. نه رشتیا = *na rishtiā* = Lit. what I said is not right and the following is correct, is used to express "As you were or "I mean."

دَ کور خاوند احمد خان نه رشتیا محمد خان دَی *da kōr khāwand Ahmad Khan na rishtiā Mohmad Khān day*

The owner of the house is Ahmed Khan-as you were-it is Mohamad Khan.

160. Adjectives denoting "belonging to" or native of a place, country etc. are formed by adding ي = *ay* as :—

پنجاب	*punjāb* Punjab.	پنجابی	*punjābay*	from Punjab.
کابل	*kābal* Kabul.	کابلی	*kābalay*	from Kabul.
پیښور	*pékha-war* Peshawar.	پیښوری	*pékha-wray*	from Peshawar

161. Note the following forms :—

سپینه ګیره	*spīna gira*	White beard.
سپین ګیری	*spīn giray*	White bearded.
سره لکئ	*sra lakai*	Red tail.
سوُر لکی	*sūr lakay*	Red tailed.
توره غاړه	*tōra ghāra*	Black neck.
تور غاړی	*tōr ghāray*	Black necked.
سرکوُز	*sar kūz*	Head hanging.
سرکوُزی	*sar kūzay*	Pig.
پيي مخ	*pai makh*	Milk face.
پيي مخی	*pai makhay*	Milk faced.

162. Note the force of repetition of tense in the following examples :—

کهٔ لاړو لاړو *kuh lāro lāro*

If he has gone by his own wish let him go ! I don't care !

کهٔ کوي کوي کهٔ نهٔ کوي نهٔ کوي *kuh kawī kawī kuh nuh kawī nuh kawī*

If he means to do it let him do it, if he does not mean to do it let him not do it, it makes no difference to me.

163. Note the following suffixes :—

ور *war*	زړور *zrawar*	Bold.
	ښکرور *khkarawar*	Horned (term of abuse).
	بختور *bakhtawar*	Lucky.
وان *wān*	باغوان *bāghwān*	Gardener, mali.
	جاله وان *jālawān*	Th[illegible] owner of the r[illegible]
	کاروان *kārwān*	Caravan.
چي *chī*	نشانچي *néshānchī*	Standard bearer.
	توپچي *tōpchī*	Marksman.
	ډنډورچي *dandōrchī*	Halerd, proclaimer.
دان *dān*	زندان *zandān*	Prison.
	خاندان *khānadān*	Family.
	نمکدان *namakdān*	Salt cellar.
دار *dār*	سردار *sardār*	Indian Officer, leader.
	دوکاندار *dūkāndār*	Shopkeeper.
	تانړيدار *tānrédār*	Sub-Inspector of Police.
	ديندار *dindār*	Pious.
	وفادار *wafādār*	Faithful.
	زميندار *zamīndār*	Farmer.

گار	*gār*	خدمتگار	*khidmatgār*	Servant.
		مدد گار	*madadgār*	Helper.
		گناهگار	*gunāhgār*	Sinful, guilty.
داري	*dāri*	خبرداري	*khabardāri*	Care.
		لمبرداري	*lambardāri*	Headman's job.
		څوکيداري	*saukidāri*	Watchman's job.
گر	*gar*	زر گر	*zargar*	Goldsmith.
		جا دو گر	*jādugar*	Juggler.
		کيميا گر	*kimiāgar*	Gold aud silver maker
		کاريگر	*kārigar*	Blacksmith.
کار	*kār*	زنا کار	*zanā kār*	Adulterer.
		بد کار	*bad kār*	Licentious.
		جفا کار	*jafākār*	Tyrannical.
گي	*gi*	مهربانگي	*méhrabān gi*	Kindness.
		روانگي	*rawāngi*	Departure.
		پيشگی	*péshgi*	An advance (of money).
گين	*gin*	غمگين	*ghamgin*	Sorrowful.
		مالگين	*mālgin*	Saltish or salt mine.
مند or من	*mand* or *man*	درد مند	*dārdmand*	Painful.
		شتهٔ مند	*shtuhmand*	Rich.
		فکر مند	*fikarmand*	Anxious,
		سوُد مند	*sūdmand*	Profitable.

ناک	*nāk*	حرصناک	*harasnāk*	Greedy.
		صبر ناک	*sabar nāk*	Patient.
		شرمناک	*sharam nāk*	Shameful.
ستان	*stān*	گلستان	*gulistān*	Place of flowers.
		وزیرستان	*waziristān*	Waziristan, Country of Waziris.
		کفرستان	*kufaristān*	Country of unbelievers.
وار	*wār*	اُمید وار	*umaidwār*	Hopeful, candidate.
		پیدا وار	*paidāwār*	Produce.
		سزا وار	*sazāwār*	Punished.
ژن	*jhan*	دروغژن	*darōgh jhan*	Liar.
		کبر ژن	*kabar jhan*	Proud.
		غمژن	*ghamjhan*	Full of grief.
زن	*zan*	تورزن	*tūrzan*	Brave.
		لاپزن	*lāpzan*	Boaster.
		لانبوزن	*lānbōzan*	Swimmer.
وال	*wāl*	هینډیوال	*handiwāl*	Mess mate.
		کلیوال	*kaliwāl*	Villager.
		بنیروال	*bunérwāl*	Man of Buner.
		تیراوال	*tiruwāl*	Man of Tirah.

164. The following particles are used with adjectives to express quite, very, entirely, absolutely.

تک *tak*	تک سوُر *tak sūr*	Quite red.
	تک سپین *tak spin*	Quite white
	تک شین *tak shin*	Quite green
ټپ *tap*	ټپ ټور *tap tōr*	Very decrepit.
	ټپ ړوند *tap rūnd* or یا پۀ ټپو ړوند *puh tapo rūnd*	Quite blind / Stone blind
ګړب *grab*	زوړ ګړب *zōr grab*	Very old. (applied to a person)
پړ *par*	خړ پړ *khar par*	Quite grey, full of dust.
	غوړ پړ *ghwar par*	Very greasy
پشت *pusht*	خوشت پشت *khusht pusht*	Quite wet.
خوشت *khusht*	لوند خوشت *lūnd khusht*	Very wet.
غوټ *ghut*	غوټ پرېکړې *ghut prékari*	Clear or quite cut off
پټ *pat*	غټ پټ *ghat pat*	Very fat.
روغ *rōgh*	روغ جوړ *rōgh jōr*	Quite well.
تکنړه *takanra*	تکنړه غرمه *takanra gharma*	Blazing noon.
تم *tam*	تورتم *tōr tam*	Quite dark.
لغړ *laghar*	بر بنډ لغړ *barband laghar*	Stark naked
پخ *pakh*	یخ پخ *yakh pakh*	Very cold.
نوزی *nūzāy*	نوی نوزی *nāway nūzay*	Absolutely-new.
پوړ *pōr*	زوړ پوړ *zōr pōr*	Very old. (applied to things worn out)

	شوړ پوړ *shōr pōr*	Very greasy
کپر *kapar*	کنډ کپر *kand kapar*	Destroyed
ووږ *wōg*	کوږ ووږ *kōg wōg*	Entirely crooked:
چوُر *chūr*	چپ چوُر *chap chūr*	Badly shuttered.
وډ *wad*	ګډ وډ *gad wad*	Mixed up.
سمخ *samakh*	سوړ سمخ *sōr samakh*	Very cold.
وور *wōr*	خور وور *khōr wōr*	Scattered.
پنګ *pang*	رنګ پنګ *rang pang*	Smeared (with blood etc.)
جک *jak*	جک جوړ *jak jōr*	Quite well
چُنباق *chunbāq*	چاق چُنباق *chāq chunbāq*	Very energetic.
پنړ *panr*	چنړ پنړ *chanr panr*	Noise of birds.
پل *pal*	دل پل *dal pal*	Absolutely crushed.
ګوُم *gūm*	ګم ګوم *gūm gūm*	Entirely last
تروش *trush*	تنګ تروش *tang trush*	Very Tight. ,, small. ,, narrow.

Section 11.

PARTS OF SPEECH.

ADVERBS.

زر *zur*	Soon.

زر زر	*zur zur*	Quickly.
ولی	*walé*	Why.
هسی	*hasé*	Thus.
ناصا په	*nāsāpa*	By chance.
ناګها نه	*nāghāna*	By chance.
لا	*lā*	Yet.
خو	*kho*	But, at least.
سره	*sara*	Together.
لکه	*laka*	Like, as.
ورو ورو	*vrō vrō*	Slowly.
تل	*tal*	Always.
مُدام	*mūdām*	Always.
همیشه	*hamésha*	Always.

ADVERBS OF PLACE.

بهر	*bahar*	Outside.
چرته	*charta*	Where.
دلته	*dalta* or	Here.
دلی	*dalé*	Here.
هلته	*halta*	There.
بیرته	*biarta*	Back.
پورته	*pōrta*	Above.
هر چرته	*harcharta*	Everywhere.
دننه	*danana*	Inside.
نیزدی	*nizdé*	Near.
بل چرته	*bal charta*	Some where else.

هچرته	*hicharta*	No where.
ښکته	*khkatā*	Below.
لاندِ	*lāndé*	
لاندِ باندِ	*lāndé bāndé*	Upside down.
چاپېره	*chāpéra* or	Around.
گير چاپيره	*gér chāpéra*	
لهٔ لرى نه	*luh laré na*	From a distance.
دَ ورايه	*da vrāya*	
ورستو	*vrōsto*	Behind.
وړاندِ	*vrāndé*	Before.

THE ADVERBS OF TIME.

آخر	*ākhér*	At last, in the end.
بيا	*biā*	Again.
پخوا	*pakhwā*	Formerly.
اوس	*ōss*	Now.
زر زر	*zar zar*	Quickly.
ورو ورو	*vro vro*	Slowly.
وړمبى	*vrumbay*	Firstly.
وار پهٔ وار	*wār puh wār*	In time.
هاله	*hāla*	Then.
كله نه كله	*kala na kala*	Occasionally.
تر كله پورى	*tar kala pōré*	Until when.
كله	*kala*	When.
كله كله	*kala kala*	Sometimes.
پهٔ دى شپو ورځو كښ	*puh dé shpo vrazo ké*	Now a days.

چری چری	*charé charé*	Now and then.
تر اوس پوری	*tar osa poré*	Until now.
لا تر اوس	*lā tar osa*	Even until now.
بیگاه	*bégāh*	Last night.
پرون	*parūn*	Yesterday.
صبا یا صباله	*sabā* or *sabāla*	Tomorrow.
بل صبا	*bal sabā*	Day after tomorrow.
سحر	*sahar*	Morning.
ماښام	*mākhām*	Evening.
نن سحر	*nan sahar*	This morning.
لا بل صبا	*lā bal sabā*	The second day after tomorrow.
نن	*nan*	To-day.
سږ کال	*sag kāl*	This year.
مښی کال	*makhé kāl*	Next year.
پروسکال	*parösa kāl*	Last year.
اورم کال	*oram kāl*	Year before last.
پس	*pas*	After.
هر کله	*har kala*	Ever, at any time.
هر کله چه	*har kala chi*	Whenever.
مدام	*mudām*	Always.
وختی	*wakhti*	Early.
نا وخته	*nāwakhta*	Late.
یو ځل	*yau zal*	Once.
دوه ځله	*dwa zala*	Twice.
څو ځله	*so zala*	How often ?
ډیر ځله	*dér zala*	Many times.

THE ADVERBS OF QUANTITY.

ډېر	*dér*	Much.
څومره	*sōmra*	Howmuch, how many.
دومره	*dōmra*	This much.
هرڅومره	*har sōmra*	How ever much.
لږکوټي	*lūkūti*	A little.
زيات	*ziāt*	More.
هر	*har*	Every.
څۀ	*suh*	Some.
هر څو	*har so*	How ever many.
هر څۀ	*har suh*	Whatever.
هر يو	*har yau*	Everyone.
هر څوک	*har sōk*	Everyone.
تر حدَ پورې	*tar hada pōré*	To the utmost extent.
تر حدَ زيات	*tar hada ziāt*	Beyond degree.
له حدَ زيات	*luh hada ziāt*	,, ,,
بيحدَ	*béhada*	Unlimited.

CONJUNCTIONS.

او	*aw*	And.
چه	*chi*	That.
کۀ	*kuh*	If.
ولې چه	*walé chi*	Because.
بلکه	*balké*	More over.
خو	*kho*	But.
ځکه	*zakā*	Therefore.

خکه چه	*zaka chi*	Because.
هم	*hum*	Also.
یا	*yā*	Or.
سره دَ دی	*sara da dé*	Not withstanding.

PREPOSITIONS.

See Page No. 14.

INTERJECTIONS.

ای	*ay*	Oh.
آفرین	*āfrin*	Bravo.
وائي وائ	*wāi wāi*	Oh dear.
توبه	*tōba*	Fie.
واه واه	*wāh wāh*	Bravo, Oh (To express extreme surprise).
آخ	*akh*	Oh (To express extreme surprise).
چښی	*chakha*	Get away, (to a dog).
کوری	*kuré*	Get away, (to a dog).
رښتیا	*rikhtiā*	Indeed.
افسوس	*afsōs*	Alas.
ها ی ها ی	*hāi hāi*	Alas.
وائي وائي	*wāi wāi*	Alas.
ارمان ارمان	*armān armān*	Alas.
امان	*amān*	Mercy.
شاباش	*shābāsh*	Bravo.

PART II.

PROSE COMPOSITION.

Section 12.

This section of Part II contains sixty short English into Pushtu and Pushtu into English Exercises with Vocabularies, beginning with simple sentences and working upto the standard required for the Higher Standard Examination. The beginner who is taking the Lower Standard Examination is advised to learn the words first and do one or two exercises a day.

VOCABULARY I.

څوک *sōk*	Who.
نُوم *nūm*	Name.
سړی *saray*	A man.
ښځه *khaza*	Woman or wife.
هلک *halak*	Boy.
جنۍ *jinai*	Girl.
ځوی *zōi*	Son.
لُور *lūr*	Daughter.
ورور *vrōr*	Brother.
خور *khōr*	Sister.
چرته *charta*	Where ?
دلته *dalta*	Here.
هلته *halta*	There.

کور *kōr* — Home, House.

کلی *kalay* — Village.

څو یا څومره *sō* or *sōmra* — How many or how much.

څومره لری *sōmra laré* — How far.

لری *laré* — Far.

نیز دی *nizdé* — Near.

چاونړي *chāwnrai* — Station or Cantonment

نوکر *naukar* — Servant.

نوکري *naukari* — Service.

دُشمن یا دښمن *dushman* or *dukhman* — Enemy.

دوست *dōst* — Friend.

چوتي *chuti* — Leave.

ولی *walé* — Why?

حاضر *hāzér* — Present.

غیر حاضر *ghair hāzér* — Absent.

نن *nan* — To day.

پرون *parūn* — Yesterday.

صبا یا صباله *sabā* or *sabāla* — To-morrow.

بل صبا *bal sabā* — Day after to-morrow

بیگاه *bégah* — Last night.

بیگاله *bégāla* — To-night.

ماښام *mākhām* — Evening or p. m.

سحر *sahar* — Morning or a. m.

غرمه *gharma* — Noon.

نن سحر *nan sahar* — This morning.

NOTES :—*(a)* In Pushtù the 2nd person singular is normally used in address i. e., تۀ = *tuh* = thou, instead of تاسو = *tāso* = you, and ستا = *stā* = they, instead of ستاسو = *stāso* = your.

The 2nd person plural is occasionally used for extreme politeness.

(b) The order of the sentence in Pushtu is usually subject, object, verb.

EXERCISE 1.

1. Who are you ? 2. What is your name ? 3. Who is that man ? 4. Where is your house ? 5. How far is it from the Cantonment ? 6. I am his servant. 7. My name is Ahmad. 8. He is my friend. 9. What is his name ? 10. How many men are on leave ? 11. Why were you absent ? 12. What time is it ?

EXERCISE 2.

1. دا سړیَ څوک دی = *dā saray sōk day ?* 2. دَ هغهٔ نوُم څۀ دیَ = *da haghuh nūm suh day ?* 3. کورونه ئی چرته دي = *kōrūna yé charta di ?* 4. ستاسو کورونه څو مره لری دي = *stāso kōrūna sōmra laré di ?* 5. چاونړئ څومره لریَ ده = *chāwnrai sōmra laré dah ?* 6. دَ چا نوکر ئی = *da chā naukar yé ?* 7. تۀ ځما نوکر نۀ ئی = *tuh zamā naukar nuh yé.*

8. خومره سړی غیر حاضر دی = *sōmra sari ghair hāzér di?* 9. پرون زه حاضر نهٔ وم = *prūn zuh hāzér nuh wam.* 10. هغه ستا دوست دی کهٔ نه = *hagha stā dōst day kuh na?* 11. صاحب پهٔ چوټۍ باندې دی = *sāhib puh chūtai bāndé day.* 12. څهٔ وخت وو = *suh wakht woh ?.*

VOCABULARY II.

Common salutions and expressions used by Pathans.

Q.	ستړی مهٔ شې	*staray muh shé?*	May you not get tired?
A.	خوار مهٔ شې یا or تهٔ ستړی مهٔ شې	*khwār muh shé* or *tuh staray muh shé*	May you not become poor!
Q.	پهٔ خیر راغلې	*puh khér rāghlé ?*	You are welcome ?
A.	پهٔ خیر اوسې	*puh khér osé*	May you live happily! (or in peace)
Q.	هر کله راشه یا or راشه هر کله	*har kala rāsha?* or *rāsha har kala?*	You are always welcome ?
A.	هر کله اوسی	*har kala osé*	May you live for ever!
Q.	ښه چارې	*kha chāré ?*	Good luck to you ?
A.	چار د ښه شه	*chār dé kha sha*	May your luck be good!
Q.	په مښه د ښه	*puh makha dé kha ?*	Good bye ?

A.	آمین تا سره	*āmin tā sara*	Same to you. (*amin* = so be it).
A.	خدای د مل شه	*khudāi dé mal sha*	May God be with you.
A.	خدای د وبخښه	*khudāi dé wo bakha*	May God forgive you.
Q.	خدای ته سپارلی ئي	*khudāi ta spā-ralay yé ?*	You are entrusted to God ?
A.	خدای د اباد لره	*khudāi dé abād lara*	May God keep you prosperous.
Q.	څۀ حال دی	*suh hāl day ?*	How are you ?
A.	ښۀ حال دی د خدای فضل دی	*khuh hāl day da khudāi fazal day*	I am all right by the grace of God.

حال	*hāl*	Condition.
جوړ	*jōr*	Well.
ناجوړ	*nā jōr*	Ill.
جک جوړ	*jak jōr*	Quite well. (جک = *jak* is only used with جوړ = *jōr*)
تکړه	*takra*	Strong.
خوشحال	*khushhāl*	Happy.
څنګه	*sunga*	How.
فصل	*fasal*	Grop.
فصلونه	*faslūna*	Crops,
غنم	*ghanam*	Wheat.
جوار	*jowār*	Maize.
اوربشي	*orbashé*	Barley.
پنبه	*punba*	Cotton.

شوتل	*shautal*	Clover.
شولی	*shōlé*	Rice (Crop).
نری جوار	*nari jowār*	Charri, cattle fodder.
کال	*kāl*	Year.
میاشت	*miāsht*	Month, Moon.
جمعه	*juma*	Week or Friday.
سږ کال	*sagkāl*	This year.
پروسکال	*parōsakāl*	Last year.
اورم کال	*oram kāl*	Year before last.
مښی کال	*makhé kāl*	Next year.
دولت	*daulat*	Wealth.
دولت مند	*daulatmand*	Wealthy.
غریب	*gharīb*	Poor.
ښهٔ	*khuh*	Good.
خراپ	*hharāp*	Bad.
ملک	*malak*	Head man.
خان	*khan*	Chief.
فوځ	*fauz*	Troop, Army.
پلټن	*paltan*	Regiment.
رساله	*risāla*	Cavalry.
حوالدار	*havāldār*	Sergeant (infantry)
دفعدار	*dafédār*	Sergeant (Cavalry).
سپاهي	*spāhi*	Soldier.
لیس	*lais*	Corporal.
لیس نائک	*lais naik*	Lance Corporal.

EXERCISE 3.

1. May you not get tired, Malak Sahib! 2. How are you? (lit, what condition is) 3. Are you well? 4. Yes, I am quite well. 5. Are you strong? 6. Yes, I am strong. 7. Are you happy? 8. Yes, I am happy. 9. Who is the Khan of this village? 10. Is he a wealthy man? 11. What is the name of this village? 12. The name of this village is Mardan. 13. Are there any troops in Mardan? 14. Yes, there are two Infantry and three Cavalry Regiments there.

NOTE:—The inflected form of دا = *dā* This is:— دي = *dé* as:—

دَ دی کلي	*da dé kali*	Of this village.
لۀ دی کلي نه	*luh dé kali na*	From this village.

VOCABULARY III.

ځکه	*zaka*	Therefore.
ځکه چه	*zaka chi*	Because.
خو - مګر	*kho, magar,*	But.
ليکن - ولی	*lekan, walé*	But.
باران	*bārān*	Rain.
لږ	*lag*	Little.
ډېر	*dér*	Very, many, much, plenty.

مُلک یا وطن	*mulk* or *watan*	Country.
ښهر	*khahar*	City.
قحط	*qahat*	Famine.
خلق	*khalq*	People.
ټول	*tōl*	All.
دواړه	*dwāra*	Both.
معلوٗم	*mālūm*	Known.
ما ته یا را ته معلوٗم دی	*mā ta* or *rā ta mālūm day*	I know it.
سور	*sōr*	Rider, Horseman.
عهده	*uhda*	Rank.
عهده دار	*uhda dār*	Non-Commissioned Officer.
پهٔ کښې	*pa ké*	In it.
مزدوري	*mazdūri*	Labour, work, wages.
تنګ	*tang*	Oppressed, worried.
اوس	*oss*	Now.
کهٔ	*kuh*	If or or
ځاي	*zāi*	Place.
کله	*kala*	When ?
کله کله	*kala kala*	Sometimes.

Exercise 4.

۱ دَ فصلونو دِ ښهٔ حال دی ؟ ۲ سږ کال فصلونه ښهٔ نهٔ
دی ـ ځکه چه باران لږ ووٗه ۳ کله کله پهٔ باړه کښې اوبهٔ وی او کله
نهٔ وي ۴ تهٔ عهده داری کهٔ سپاهيِ ؟ زه دَ رسالی سوریم

۵ دَ دې کلي نوُم در ته معلوم دئ؟ ۶ ټول فوځ اوس پهٔ
چاونړئ کښې دی ۷ تهٔ پهٔ نوکرئ کښې خوشحال يئ کهٔ نه
۸ دَ کلو خلق دولتمند نهٔ وي[1] ۹ بارانو نه لږ وُو ځکه پهٔ وطن
کښې قحط دی ۱۰ ستا پهٔ پلټن کښې څومره سپاهيان دي
۱۱ دَ هغهٔ دوه ورو نوکران پهٔ نوکرئ کښې تنګ دي ۱۲ دَ هغه
ځائ نوم ورته معلوم نهٔ دی ۱۳ پروسکال دَ غنمو او جوارو فصلونه
خراب وُو ۱۴ چاونړئ لويه ده خو په کښې مزدوري لږ وي -
د خان څلور[2] خامن په پهٔ فوځ کښې دي -

1: See syntax rule No. 23.
2. Learn the numerals on Page 41.

VOCABULARY IV.

دَ چا	*da chā*	Whose ?
کتاب	*kitāb*	Book.
دا	*dā*	This or these.
کتاب چه	*kitab chi*	The book which.
ميز	*méz*	Table.
کُرسئ	*kursai*	Chair.
صاحب چه	*sāhīb chi*	The sahib who.
جرنيل صاحب	*jarnail sāhib*	General.
د پهٔ مينځ کښې	*da-puh mianz ké*	Between, through.
هلک چه نوُم يئ	*halak chi nūm yé*	The boy whose name.
ترېوُر	*tarbūr*	Cousin.
ترُهٔ	*truh*	Uncle.
لار چه	*lār chi*	The road which.

ځي	*zee*	Goes.
ګرم	*garam*	Hot, warm.
ګرمي	*garmī*	Heat.
يخ	*yakh*	Cold. (adj.)
يخني	*yakhni*	Cold (noun.)
اوړی	*oray*	Summer.
منی	*manay*	Autumn.
ژمی	*jhamay*	Winter.
سپرلی	*sparlay*	Spring.
موسم	*mōsam*	Season.
سيند	*sind*	River.
خوړ	*khwar*	Ravine.
غاړه	*ghāra*	Bank (river)
بيړئ	*bérai*	Boat.
ماڼړګی	*mānrgay*	Boat man.
ښکار	*khkār*	Shooting, Hunting
کب	*kab*	Fish.
کبان	*kabān*	Fish (plural.)
يا	*yā*	or
دَ کبانو ښکار	*da kabāno khkār*	Fishing.

چغتې	*chaghaté*	Snipe	(Sing. چغته *chaghata*)
هيلئ	*hilai*	Duck	(Sing. هيلي *hilai*)
بطې	*baté*	Geese	(Sing. بطه *bata*)
تنزرې	*tanzari*	Partridges	(Sing تنزری *tanzary*)
زرکې	*zarké*	Chikor	(Sing زرکه *zarka*)
مړزې	*marzé*	Quails	(Sing مړز *maraz*)

سوی *sawé*	Hares	(Sing سوه *sawa*)
اوسئ *osai*	Deer	(Sing اوسئ *osai*)
اوچ *och*	Dry	

EXERCISE 5.

1. [1] Have you a book? 2. Yes, I have a book, 3. No, I have not a book. 4. Whose book is this?. 5. It is not my book. 6 The books [2] which are on the table are not mine. 7. The sahib who was here this morning is the General's brother. 8. The country between Peshawar and Kabul is dry and bad. 9. The boy whose name is Ahmad, is my uncle's son. 10. The road which goes through Mardan is not a good one 11. I [3] like Peshawar, but my brother does not like it. 12. Why don't, you like Peshawar?. 13. The heat is great in summer 14. There is little water in this country.

NOTES—1. شته = *shta* = Is there or are there? Look up syntax rule No. 45. 2. چه = *ché* = that (conjunction) makes any interrogation relative i. e. څوک چه = *sōk chi* = He who. 3. خوښ *khwakh* = pleasant or liked See syntax rule No. 28.

VOCABULARY V.

تماکو *tamākū*	Tobacco.
چیلم *chilam*	Pipe.

تیلی	*tilay*	Match.
هم	*hum*	Also.
خایئسته	*khāista*	Beautiful or handsome
بدرنګ	*badrang*	Ugly.
هوښیار	*hukhyār*	Clever.
کم عقل	*kam aqal*	Foolish.
وړوکی یا	*warūkay* or	Small.
ورکوټی	*warkōtay*	
لوی	*loi*	Big or Large.
هسپتال	*haspatāl*	Hospital.
په خوا زمانه کښې	*puh khwā zamāna ké*	Formerly.
جبه	*jaba*	Marsh.
چینه	*china*	Spring (of water).
ټوپک	*tōpak*	Rifle.
کونیز ټوپک	*kūniz tōpak* ?	Snider Rifle.
ګورئیز ټوپک	*gōraiz tōpak*	A Martini Henry Rifle.
اوه ډزی ټوپک	*owuh dazay tōpak*	Lee Metford Rifle.
دری‌وال ټوپک	*daréwāl tōpak*	Pass-made Rifle.
بندری ټوپک	*bandari tōpak*	Persian Gulf made Rifle.
چقمقی ټوپک	*chaqmapi tōpak*	A flint lock gun.
باتیدار ټوپک	*bātidar tōpak*	A match lock gun.
د چرو ټوپک	*da charo tōpak*	A Shot gun.
یا	or	
چری دار ټوپک	*charidār tōpak.*	
یا	or	
ښکاری ټوپک	*khkāri tōpak*	

چري *charé*	Shots.
ګولئ *gōlai*	Bullet.
دارؤ *dārū*	Gun Powder or Medicine.
اوس اوس *oss oss*	Presently, Recently.
اوسنئ *osanay*	Recent.
کارتوس *kārtūs*	Cartridge.
ګټه *gata*	Packet of 10 Cartridges.
نښه *nakha*	Mark.
رنګ *rang*	Colour.
سپین *spin*	White.

Exercise 6.

١ تا سخه تماکؤ شته ؟ ٢ ما سخه تماکؤ نشته او تیلئ شته
٣ هغهٔ سخه څلور کتابونه دي مګر ښهٔ نهٔ دي ٤ تا سخه څومره
روپئ دي . خما ترهٔ سخه ډیر دولت وه ٥ خما یو ورور دئ هغه
هم په هسپتال کښں دئ ٦ ستا څومره خامن دي ؟ ٧ خما
یو آس دئ چه رنګ یې سپین دئ ٨ خما د ورور پهٔ ښهر
کښں پنځهٔ کورونه وو ٩ خما یو الس دئ ١٠ دا جنګئ د
هلک خور ده ١١ هغوی دواړه خائیسته دي ١٢ د هغوی
پلار ښهٔ سړئ وه او د هغوی مور هوښیاره ښځه ده ١٣ په خوا
زمانه کښں په دی وطن کښں ښکار وه مګر اوس نیشته ١٤ ځموږ
کلي ته نیږدی جبه شته خو ما سخه د ښکار ټوپک نشته

VOCABULARY VI.

څوکیدار *ṣaukidār*	Watchman. Chaukidar.

څوکئ	*saukai*	Post.
جماعت	*jumait*	Mosque.
حُجره	*hūjra*	Guest house.
ميلمهٔ	*mélma*	Guest.
ميلما نهٔ	*mélmānuh*	Guests.
غريب	*gharib*	Poor.
دولتمند	*daulatmand*	Rich.
دَ-طرف ته	*da-taraf ta*	Towards.
طرف-خوا-ډډه-پلو	*taraf*, *khwā*, *dada*, *palau*	Side or direction.
نور پريواتهٔ يا قبله	*nwar préwātuh* or *qablā*	West.
قبله	*qabla*	Polite word for west
نور خاتهٔ	*nwar khātuh*	East.
سُهيل	*suhail*	South.
قُطب	*qutab*	North.
لاس	*lās*	Hand.
ښیّ لاس	*khay lās*	Right hand.
ګس لاس يا	*gas lās* or	Left hand.
کينړ لاس	*kinr lās*	(Left hand.)
غر	*ghar*	Hill.
اُوچت	*ūchat*	High.
مندرىَ	*mandray*	Short.
زوړ	*zōr*	Old (Thing or person.
سپين ګيرى	*spin giray*	Old, grey bearded man.

نا ست	*nāst*	Sitting	Take the Verb "to be."
ولاړ	*walār*	Standing	
اُوده	*ūduh*	Sleeping	
ملاست	*mlāst*	Lying	

Exercise 7.

1. This man's house is in the city. 2. This boy's father was my servant. 3. These girls' mother was in the house. 4. When I was in Kohat I had two chaukidars. 5. When I was at home (in the house) my horse was not ill. 6. The khan's house is this side of the Mosque. 7. The guest house is beyond the Malak's house. 8. My uncle had much wealth, but now he is poor. 9. What is your father's name ?. 10. There are many hills towards the west of Peshawar. 11. That is the Afridis' country. 12 Where is your Regiment ? 13. What is your Colonel's name ? 14. The old man was sitting on the chair.

VOCABULARY VII.

خاوند	*khāwand*	Owner.
ماليه	*mālia*	Land Tax.
آبيانه	*abiāna*	Water Tax.
محصول	*mahsool*	Tax on property.
زمکه	*zmaka*	Land or ground.
آوي زمکه	*āvi zmaka*	Irrigated land.

للمه زمکه	*lalma zmaka*	Unirrigated land.
سا دین	*sādin*	Ploughed land.
وتره	*watra*	Land ready for sowing.
شاړه زمکه	*shāra zmaka*	Barren land.
ویجاړه زمکه	*wijāra zmaka*	Waste land.
شولګره	*shōlgara*	Rice land.
دَ ازغو تار	*da azgho tār*	Barbed wire.
تار	*tār*	Wire, telegram, thread.
ښینی ښینی	*ziné ziné*	Some.
نه-نه	*na-na*	Neither-nor.
ژوندیَ	*jhwanday*	Alive.
ګینټه	*gainta*	An hour.
پس	*pas*	After (time.)
پسی	*pasé*	After (person.) or business)
روان	*rawān*	Going on. (in the act of going.)
دروازه	*darwāza*	Gate.
ور	*war*	Door.

EXERCISE 8.

۱ دَ دی کور خاوند ښوک دَی ۲ د هغهٔ ملک نوم څهٔ دیَ
۳ مالیهٔیی څومره دهَ ۴ کله چه زهٔ پهٔ دفتر کښی وم نو نوکرِم با هر
ناست وُهٔ ۵ ستا پلارِ ژوندیَ دیَ؟ــــتهٔ کله هلته وی ۶ دوه ګینټی
پس زهٔ به پهٔ دفتر کښی یم ۷ له چاونړیٔ نه ګیر چاپیره د ازغو تار
دیَ ۸ یو سړیَ خان پسی روان دیَ ۹ قبلی طرف تهٔ دَښهر

لويه دروازه دَه ۱۰ اوس څموږ پهٔ پلټن کښې دوه کرنيلان دي ۱۱
د اپريدو ملک ټول غرونه غرونه دي ۱۲ ځينې ځينې پهٔ کښې
ډير هوښيار دي ۱۳ پهٔ دې کلي کښې نهٔ حُجره شته نهٔ جُماعت
۱۴ زمکه يې ټوله اوې دَه—

Short Sentences
and
VOCABULARY VIII.

پوه شوې	*pōh shwé*	Did you understand ?
هو زهٔ پوه شم	*ho zuh pōh shwam*	Yes I understood.
پو هيږې	*pōhégé*	Do you understand ?
هو زهٔ پو هيږم	*ho zuh pōhégam*	Yes I understand.
بيا و وايه	*biā wo wāya*	Say it again.
ورو ورو و وايه	*vro vro wo wāya*	Say it slowly.
زهٔ خبر نهٔ يم	*zuh hhabar nuh yam*	I don't know.
دا رښتيا خبره دَه	*dā rikhtiā khabara dah*	This is true.
ډيره ښه دَه	*déra kha dah*	That is all right.
هوښيار	*hukhyār*	Intelligent.
سر کار	*sarkār*	Government.
سر کاری	*sarkāri*	Belongs to Govt. (Adj.)
قلا	*qalā*	Fort.
تعليم	*talim*	Education.

تعليم يا فته	*talim yāfta*	Educated.
بی تعليم	*be talim*	Uneducated.
رنګروټ	*rangūt*	Recruit.
کمزورئ	*kamzōray*	Weak.
نوئ	*naway*	New.
خټه	*khata*	Mud or muddy.
ګران	*garān*	Dear or difficult.
اسان	*asān*	Easy.
ارزان	*arzān*	Cheap.
ژبه	*jhuba*	Tongue or Language.
اوردي	*urdi*	Uniform.
خيرن	*khiran*	Dirty.
پاک	*pāk*	Clean.
رڼې اوبۀ	*ranré obuh*	Clear water.
خړې اوبۀ	*kharé obuh*	Dirty water.
بندوبست	*bāndubast*	Arrangement.
عمر	*umar*	Age.
ژور	*jhawar*	Deep.
پاياؤ	*payāw*	Shallow.
ګناه يا قصور	*gunāh* or *qasūr*	Fault.
غُزان	*ghuzān*	Walnuts. (غُز *ghuz* S.)
بادام	*bādām*	Almonds. (S. and P.)
خټکی	*khatakay*	Melon.
ايندوانه	*indwāna*	Water Melon.
کيله	*kéla*	Banana.
سمتره	*samtara*	Sweet Orange.

لهٔ نه ډک	*luh-na dak*	Full of.
بیشکه	*béshaka*	Certainly.
ګُندِ یا شاید	*gundé or shāyad*	Perhaps.
کار	*kār*	Work.
ذمه	*zema*	Responsibility.
ذمهٔوار	*zema wār*	Responsible.
مشر	*mashar*	Older.
کشر	*kashar*	Younger.
پنسن	*pensan*	Pension.
دستوُر	*dastūr*	Custom.
مغرور	*maghrūr*	Proud.
پټکی	*patkay*	Turban.
ټوپئ	*topai*	Topi.
کورته	*kōrta*	Shirt.
پرتوُګ	*partūg*	Trousers.
پڼړی	*panré*	Shoes (F. P.)
څپلئ	*saplai*	Grass sandals.
کیړئ	*kérai*	Leather sandals.
څادر	*sādar*	Sheet.
سینه	*sina*	Chest.
پوُره	*pūra*	Complete or up to the standard.
روُند	*rūnd*	Blind.
ګُډ	*gud*	Lame.
ګوُنګ	*gūng*	Dumb.
کوڼ	*kūnr*	Deaf.
حمله	*hamla*	An attack.

ښه خبره نۀ ده	*kha khabara nuh dah*	It is not a good thing.
خبره	*khabara*	Word, speech, matter.

EXERCISE 9.

1. She is an intelligent woman. 2. Is he your son ? 3. It is a big station. 4. That is the Afridis' Fort and not a Government Post 5. Is it true ? 6. How many educated soldiers are there in your Regiment ? 7. He is ill today. 8. All these recruits are weak. 9. Owing to the rain all the roads are very muddy. 10 Pushtu is not a difficult language. 11. Your uniform is dirty. 12. Whose arrangement is this ? 13. How old are you (what is your age) ? 14. How deep is this river ? 15. Whose fault is this ? 16. How many years' service have you (Thou of how many years servant art) ?.

VOCABULARY IX.

ورځ	*vraz*	Day.
شپه	*shpa*	Night.
نیمه شپه	*nima shpa*	Midnight.
شومه قلاره	*shūma qalāra*	Still night.
قلاره قلاری	*qalāra qalāri*	Quiet.
بادشاه	*bādshāh*	King.
لږ	*lag*	Little.

باغ	*bāgh*	Garden.
میوه	*méwa*	Fruit.
انار	*anār*	Pomegranates (M.S. & Plu.)
سیوان	*séwān*	Apples (Sing. سیوُ *séw*).
انګور	*angūr*	Grapes (M. Plu.)
شلتالان	*shaltālān*	Peaches (M.P.) (Sing. شلتالو *shaltālū*)
ناک یا ناشپاتي	*nāk* or *nāshpātai*	Pears.
نارنجان	*nāranjān*	Oranges. (*nāranj* S.)
بیهي	*behai*	Quinces. (F.S. & P.)
پوُره	*pūra*	Complete.
خبری	*khabaré*	Conversation (F.P.)
خبر	*khabar*	Message or news.
ترکاری	*tarkāri*	Vegetables.
تیپر	*taipar*	Turnips.
مولي	*mūlai*	Radish.
ګازری	*gāzaré*	Carrots.
متر	*matar*	Peas.
الوُ ګان	*alūgān*	Potatoes. (M. P.)
ساګ	*sāg*	Spinach.
زورَ ور باران	*zōrawar bārān*	Heavy rain.

EXERCISE 10.

یوه ورځ چه زهٔ پهٔ دفتر کښې وم نو زورَور باران وُه ۲ پهٔ
هندوستان کښې یو بادشاه وُه چه نوُم يې اکبر وُه ۳ زهٔ پهٔ پښتو پوهیږم
مګر لږ لږ ۴ ځما نوکر په پښتو نهٔ پو هیږي ۵ هغه دَ ونې لاندَ
په کښې ملاست دیَ ۶ باغ دَ میوو له ونونه ډک دیَ ۷ ښشکه داستاکارَ

دَی نهٔ ذمه واریږي ۸ ښما مشر ورور په رساله کښې جمعدار ده مګر
اوس په پنسن باندِ دَی ۹ دا دَ دې ملک دستور دَی ۱۰ ستا
پټکی ولې خیرن دَی ۱۱ دَ دې رنګوټ سینه پوره نهٔ دهٔ دا خو
پونډ نهٔ دَی هغه دوه ګز دي او دا ډېر کمزورې دي ۱۲ سینډ ژور
نهٔ دَی ۱۳ په دې حمله کښې یوه رساله او ډېر پلټنِ وې
۱۴ کهٔ دا دهغهٔ قصور وي نو ښه خبره نهٔ ده——

VOCABULARY X.

لهٔ دې ځای نه	*luh dé zāi na*	From here.
ځای	*zāi*	Place.
څومره مُده کیږي	*sōmra mūda kégee*	How long ago.
څومره مُده پس	*sōmra mūda pas*	How long after.
څومره مُده راسې	*sōmra mūda rāsé*	Since how long.
چُټي	*chūtī*	Leave.
پلن	*plan*	Broad.
اوږد	*ūgad*	Long.
مورچه	*mōrcha*	Trench.
پټی	*patay*	Field.
سوُر	*sūr*	Red.
شین	*shin*	Green.
تور	*tōr*	Black.
زیړ	*ziar*	Yellow.
آبی	*ābi*	Blue.
دَ ننه	*danana*	Inside.

باهر *bāhar*	Outside.
خپل *khpal*	Own, relative.
خپلوان *khpalwān*	Relations.
کرائيې *karāyeé*	Rent, hire.
څومره لوي *somra loi ?*	How big ?

MISCELLANEOUS COLLOQUIAL SENTENCES I.

Is there anyone there ?	*sōk shta ?*
Who are you ?	*tuh sōk yé ?*
What is your name ?	*stā nūm suh day ?*
What is your father's name ?	*da plār nūm dé suh day ?*
Where is your houe ?	*kōr dé charta day ?*
How far is it from here?	*luh dé zāi na sōmra laré day ?*
Is that your village ?	*dagha stā kallay day ?*
How wide is the trench?	*mōrcha sōmra plana dah ?*
How deep is the river ?	*sind sōmra jhawar day?*
Whose fields are these ?	*dā da chā pati dee ?*
Where is my gun ?	*tōpak mé charta day ?*
This colour is red	*dā sūr rang day.*
Is my servant inside ?	*zamā naukar danana day ?*
Is he a relation of yours ?	*hagha dé khpal day ?*
Are you the owner of this house ?	*tuh da dé kōr khāwand yé ?*
What is the rent of this house ?	*dā dé kōr karāyee sōmra dah ?*

How big is your house ?	*stā kōr sōmra loi day ?*
I don't know who is your servant.	*zuh khabar nuh yam chi stā naukar sōk day.*

VOCABULARY XI.

اسٹیشن	*istaishan*	Station.
مور پلار	*mōr plār*	Parents.
مړ	*mar*	Dead.
ژوندی	*jhwanday*	Alive.
څنګه	*sunga*	How.
سپاهی توب	*spāhi tōb.*	Soldiering.
فوځ	*fauz*	Troops, Army.
اباد	*abād*	Populated, cultivated.
ابادي	*abādi*	Population, cultivation.
کپني	*kapnai*	Company.
پښتون	*pukhtūn*	Pathan.
طلب	*talab,*	
تنخواه	*tankhwāh*	Pay.
تغمه	*taghma*	Medal.
لنډه لار	*landa lār*	Short road.
ناجوړ تیا	*nājōrtiā*	Sickness.
چري	*charé*	Ever.
هیچري	*hicharé*	Never.

EXERCISE 11.

1. What is the name of your village ? 2. In what direction is it ? 3. How far is your village from the Railway Station ? 4. What

is the Railway fare? 5. How many brothers have you? 6. Are your parents alive? 7. No, they are both dead. 8. How much land have you? 9. How are the crops in your country? 10. Do you like soldiering? 11. Have you any relations in the Army? 12. Is there a river near your village? 13. What is the population of your village? 14. Are you a private or N.C.O.? 15. How many Pathan companies are there in your Regiment? 16. What Regiment are you in? 17. Where is your Regiment? 18. Who is the Officer Commanding of your Regiment? 19. What is your pay? 20. Have you a medal? 21. Which is the shortest way? 22. Whose horses are these? 23. I don't like him.

VOCABULARY XII.

چرته	*charta*	Anywhere or where?
څهٔ	*suh*	Any, some, what?
څهٔ قسم	*suh qisam*	What kind of?
تا وادهٔ کړی دی	*tā wāduh karay day*	Are you married?
تږی	*tagay*	Thirsty.
تنده	*tanda*	Thirst.
اوږی	*ogay*	Hungry.
لوږه	*lwaga*	Hunger.
کوم	*kum*	Which?

کوم ځاي	*kum zāi*	Where, in which place ?
په دې شپو ورځو کښې	*pa dé shpō vrazo ké*	Now-a-days.
مُونډلی شيِ	*múndalay shee*	Can be had, can be obtained, can be received.

بيعه	*baya*	Price	ځنګل	*zangal*	Forest
په کښې	*pa ké*	In it	راسې	*rāsé*	Since
چه په کښې	*chi pa ké*	In which	لوی	*lōi*	Great big, large
لرګی	*largay*	Wood, stick	خدای	*khudāi*	God
			خبر	*khabar*	news
لرګيِ	*largi*	Wood (Plural)	اکثر	*aksar*	Generally
سکارهٔ	*skāruh*	Charcoal (M. P.)	قسمت	*qismat*	Luck
دَ کاڼړيِ سکارهٔ	*da kānri skāruh*	Coal	نصيب	*nasīb*	Fate
خشاک	*khashāk*	Firewood	غله	*ghala*	Grain
کاڼړی	*kānray*	Stone	دومرهٔ	*dōmra*	this much or as much so much
			داسې	*dāsé*	thus, such.

Exercise 12.

١ پهٔ کلي کښې دِ ډيره ناجوړ تيا دهٔ ؟ ٢ ستا کلي ته نيږدې
چرته ښکار مونډلی شي ؟ ٣ څهٔ قسم ښکار دې ؟ ٤ تا واده کړې
دې ؟ ٥ دَ دې سکارو بيعه څهٔ دَه ٦ خما اس تږی دی اوبهٔ

کوم ځائي دي ۷ په دې ښپو ورځو کښې په بازار کښې څهٔ قسم
ميوه موندلی شي ۸ دلته غله ارزانه ده که ګرانه ۹ افغانستان
ښهٔ وطن دی مګر په کښې يخني ډيره وي ۱۰ دَ ښهر خلق
ښهٔ دي ۱۱ ښهر ته نيز دی د لرګو يو لوی ځنګل دی ۱۲
هغه لوی سړی دی ولی هوښيار نهٔ دی ۱۳ پښتو اسانه ژبه
ده ۱۴ څومره مده راسی تهٔ په فوځ کښې يی ۱۵ عهده
داران ټول په دفتر کښې دي ۱۶ ولې د نن رنګ زيړ دی ۱۷
خدای خبر چه ولی دلته تر کاري دومره ارزانه ده ۱۸ دَ دولتمند
سړی دوستان ډير وي ۱۹ زهٔ غريب يم ځکه دوست م نشته ۲۰
اکثر دَ هوښيار سړي قسمت خراب وي—

VOCABULARY XIII.

راشه	*rāsha*	Come !
لاړشه	*lārsha*	Go !
کينه	*kéna*	Sit !
څمله	*samla*	Lie down !
(ته) و وايه	*(ta) wo wāya*	Say, speak, tell !
راوړه	*rāwra*	Bring ! (inanimate)
راوله	*rāwala*	Lead ! (animate)
يوسه	*yausa*	Take away ! (animate)
بوزه	*bōza*	Lead away ! (animate)
وبله	*wo bala*	Call !
وليکه	*wō lika*	Write !
ايسار شه	*isār sha*	Wait !
لري کړه	*laré kar*	Open !
پوري کړه	*pōré kra*	Shut !

کیږده	*kégda*	Place, put !
کړه	*kra*	Do !
شه	*sha*	Become, be !
راوغواړه	*rā wo ghwāra*	Send for ! (thing)
راوبله	*rā wo bala*	Call for ! (person)
ګوره	*gōrā*	Look !
مهٔ ویښوه	*muh wikhawa*	Don't wake up !
بل	*bal*	Next or other.
نور	*nōr*	More, or others.
چټئی	*chitai*	Letter.
خوراک	*khurāk*	Food.
ډوډئ	*dōdai*	Bread.
دفتر	*daftar*	Office or landed property.
سائس	*sāis*	Syce.
کلف	*kalaf*	Club.
جواب	*jawāb*	An auswer.
موټر	*mōtar*	Motor.
بائیسکل	*bāisekal*	Bicycle.
لینړ	*lainr*	Lines.
بیرته	*biarta*	Back.
بیا	*biā*	Again.
دَ سکلو اوبهٔ	*da skalo obuh*	Drinking water.
کاغذ	*kāghaz*	Paper.
قلم	*qalam*	Pen.
مشوانړئ	*mashwānrai*	Ink pot.
سیاهی	*syāhi*	Ink.

اخبار	*akhbār*	Newspaper.
سمدستي	*samdasti*	At once.
صاف صاف	*sāf sāf*	Distinctly.
ورو ورو	*vro vro*	Slowly.
مرمت	*muramat*	Repair.
سم يا نيغ	*sam* or *négh*	Straight.
ګل زيرۍ	*gul ziarai*	Target.
مهرباني ده	*mehrabāni dah*	Thank you.
ډيره مهرباني ده	*déra mehrabāni dah*	Thank you very much.
لوکوټي	*lūkūti*	Little or just.

Exercise 13.

1. Come inside, sit on the chair and tell me some thing about your regiment. 2. Call my servant. 3. Tell him to come to the office. 4. Tell the syce to take my horse to the Club and wait for me there. 5. Shut the door. 6. Take this letter to the Adjutant and bring an answer. 7. Take the Sahib's motor to the lines. 8. Bring the bicycle back. 9. Tell my bearer to bring me some water. 10. Is this water fit to drink ? 11. Take these papers at once to the office and then tell the mali to bring water for this field. 12. Speak distinctly and slowly. 13. Send for the jemadar; Why is he not here ? 14. Take my boots for repair.

15. Look straight towards the target. 16. Don't wake me up before 9 o'clock. 17. Please write him another letter. 18. Just call the head man of this village. 19. Bring food for the dogs. 20. Is there any letter for me?

NOTE:—Wheeled vehicles and irrigation water are treated as moveable objects and take the verbs "*biwal*" and "*rāwastal*".

VOCABULARY XIV.

راکړه	*rā kra*	Give me or give us.
ورکړه	*war kra*	Give him, them, her it.
و لیږه یا	*wo légā* or	Send.
واستوه	*wāstawa*	
واچوه	*wāchawa*	Put.
مهٔ ایسا رېږه	*muh isāréga*	Don't wait.
اسپه	*aspa*	Mare.
میدان	*maidān*	Plain.
یو خوا بل خوا	*yaw khwā bal hhwā*	Hither and thither.
مهٔ ګوره	*ma gōra*	Don't look.
لهٔ نه اول یا	*luh-na awal*	Before in time.
لهٔ نه وړمبی	*luh na vrumbay*	
بالکل	*bilkul*	Quite, absolutely.
پنځهٔ نیمې بجې	*pinzanimé bajé*	Half past five.

پاؤ باندِ پنځهٔ بجې	*pāw bāadé pinzuh bajé*	Quarter past five.
پاؤ کم پنځهٔ بجې	*pāw kam pinzuh bajé*	Quarter to five.
لس مِلټهَ باندِ	*las mélata bāndé*	10 minutes past.
لس مِلټهَ کم	*las mélata kam*	10 minutes to.
درُوند	*drūnd*	Heavy.
سپک	*spak*	Light.

NOTE :—For څهٔ دیِ = *suh di*, look up Syntax rule No. 52. For ورته و وایه چه دَننه راشيِ یا راشه = *warta wo wāya chi danana rāshee* or *rāsha* look up syntax rule No. 16.

EXERCISE 14.

۱ ټول کتا بونه راوړه او په میز باندِ ئې کیږده ۲ یوه بله
کُرسئ راوړه او په برنډهٔ کښې ئې واچوه ۳ ټولو سپاهیانو ته
و وایه چه دَننه راشيِ ۴ ور ته و وایه چه زر جواب راوړه ۵ نوکرانو
ته و وایه چه په کُرسو باندِ نهٔ کینيِ ۶ مالي ته و وایه چه
صبا څما دَ باغ دَ پاره اوبهٔ راوليِ ۷ میز پورې دوه کرسئ هم
کیږده ۸ څما موټر د لته راوله او بائیسکل مِ کور ته بوزه ۹ پهٔ
پاؤ باندِ شپږ بجې را ته نوکر راواستوه ۱۰ دا چټهئ دفتر ته یو سه
خو جواب دَ پاره مهٔ ایسا رېږه ۱۱ ټول اسونه او سپيِ هسپتال
ته بوزه ۱۲ ما ته سم ګوره یو خوا بل خوا مهٔ ګوره ۱۳ له دریؤ
بجو نه اول راشه او ما وینښ کړه ۱۴ له دفتر نه یو بل داسې
کتاب هم راوړه ۱۵ مهر بانی وکړه دا خبره بیا وکړه ۲۶ دَا اوبهٔ دَ
څکلو دَ پاره ښې دی که نه ۱۷ خپل کار وکړه نو دفتر ته راشه ۱۸!

ملک ته سلام وز کړه او ورته و وئیه چه صاحب په حُجره کښې ناست
دیَ ۱۹ داخهٔ دیِ او دغه څوک دیَ ۲۰ دَ دی کلیِ مالیه
درنه ده—

VOCABULARY XV-

اول	*awal*	First, at first.
بیشکه	*béshaka*	Certainly.
ما و ویل	*mā wo wayal*	I said spoke or told.
هیڅ	*hiss*	Nothing (takes tense in negative.)
داسی	*dāsé*	So, such or thus.
څهٔ	*suh*	Any thing.
څنګه	*sanga*	How.
خپل	*khpal*	Own, (used for reflexive pro.)
جوار	*jowār*	Maize, Indian Corn.
تُخم	*tukhum*	Seed.
ټانټې	*tānté*	Stalks.
مال	*māl*	Cattle, property.
حکم	*hukum*	Order.
ګلداڼګ سپَی	*guldāng spay*	Bull dog.
شراب	*sharāp*	Wine.

EXERCIE 15.

1. I beat him, because he beat me first. 2. Certainly he beat me yesterday, but I said nothing. 3. You beat me yesterday and you are beating me again to day. 4. I struck the owner of the house because he had struck all my

dogs. 5. The dog is so ill that he does not eat food. 6. Will you drink any thing ?. 7. I will write a letter to his father, 8. Please write another letter for me. 9. How can I write ?. 10. Tell my servant to keep this dog in his house. 11. We have sown some maize, the grain is very good, but the stalks are so hard that the cattle will not eat them. 12. This man does not obey my orders. 13. We used to keep a bulldog in our house. 14. I wrote a letter to his Colonel at Cherat. 15. The dog bit the man therefore the man beat the dog. 16. I will also send him a message. 17. Can you call my servant ?. 18. I was so ill that I could not drink water. 19. This Darzi cannot sew well so call the Jemadar to arrange for a better one. 20. Don't drink wine.

VOCABULARY XVI.

واښهٔ	*wākhuh*	Grass.
ځاي ځائيگئ يا پته	*zāi zaigay* or *pata*	Address.
خاوند	*khāwand*	Owner.
کله	*kala*	When.
کله کله	*kala kala*	Some times.
سر	*sar*	Head.
پړی يا رسئ	*paray or rasai*	Rope.
ونهٔ	*wana*	Tree.

روټئ	*rōtai*	Bread, food.
مهٔ ورکوه	*muh warkawa*	Don't give him !
گنډل	*gandal*	To sew, sewing.
خپل ځان	*khpal zān*	Oneself.
پهٔ ليکلو کښې	*puh likalō ké*	In writing.
زر	*zar*	Soon.
زر زر	*zar zar*	Quickly.
پخپله	*pakhpala*	Myself, yourself, herself, itself etc.
ويل	*wayal*	To say, speak, tell.
مياشت	*miāsht*	Month, moon.
دَ دې مياشتې پهٔ شلم تاريخ	*da dé miāshté puh shalam tārikh*	On the 20th of this month.
ماجب	*mājeb*	Pay.
ټيپن	*tepan*	Lunch.
غوښه	*ghwakha*	Meat.
پردَی مال	*praday māl*	Others' property.
گُناه	*gunāh*	Sin.
گُنهگار	*gunahgār*	Sinner, guilty.
بې گناه	*bé gunah*	Not guilty.
موقعه	*moqa*	Chance, spot, opportunity.
موجۇد	*maujūd*	Present.
غل	*ghal*	Thief (غلهٔ *ghluh* Plu.)
ځان	*zān*	self.

EXERCISE 16.

اس م ناجوړ دی څکه نهٔ واښهٔ خوري او نهٔ اوبهٔ سکي ۲ په

دې کاغذ باندِ خپله نامه او دَ پلار نامه او ځاې ځائيګې وليکه ۳ هغه
ښهٔ نوکر نه وې چه دَ مالک خبره نهٔ منيِ ۴ کله کله راته چټيَ
رالېږه ۵ اوس ټول فصلونه کرلیَ شوې دې ۶ ما په نايې باندِ
سر خرئيلو پهٔ موقعه موجوُد نه وم ځکه راته معلومه نه دَه چه چا
وهلیَ دې ۷ ما غل په پوړې باندِ وني پوزې وتړلو او خپل نوکر ته مِ
وويل چه روټيَ او اوبهٔ مهٔ ورکوه ۸ کوټ ګنډل داسې اسان
کار نهٔ دې هغه خپل ځان لوی ګڼيِ مګر داښهَ خبره نهٔ دَه ۹
ما درته چټيَ ليکله چه ستا خبر راورسيدلو ۱۰ کهٔ ما ورته چټيَ
ليکلیَ نهٔ وې نو هغهٔ به زهٔ بللیَ نه وم ۱۱ ما ورته تار ولېږلو او په کښې مِ
وليکل چه پلار دِ نا جوړ دې زر راشه ۱۲ هغهٔ راته خبر راولېږلو
چه زهٔ پخپله هم ناجوړ يم او کرنيل صاحب پهٔ چوټيَ دې ځکه اوس
هيڅ ويلیَ نه شم ۱۳ دَ دې مياشتې په شلم تاريخ ماورته يوه چټيَ
وليکله ۱۴ کهٔ خوږې خوره که نهٔ خوږې مهٔ خوره ۱۵ هغه لهٔ
سر کار نه دوه سوَ روپيَ ماجب خوريِ ۱۶ ډيره مهر باني دَه هيڅ
نهٔ خورم ځکه چه ما اوس ټپن خوړلیَ دې ۱۷ ځينې ځينې
هندوان بالکل غوښه نهٔ خوريِ ۱۸ پرَ دې مال خوړل ګناه دَه ۱۹
دا وړوکیَ هلک ماله راکړه زهٔ پهٔ خپل کور کښې به يې ساتم ۹۰
ما ورته وليکل چه ښما دَ کليِ مال ټول ناجوړ دې—

VOCABULARY XVII.

دَ-پهٔ مينځ کښې	*da-puh mianz ké*	Through.
ديوال	*dēwāl*	Wall.
غير علاقه	*ghair alāqa*	Independent. territory.
رعيت	*rait*	British territory, subject.

دَ اور گاډي	*da aur gāday*	Train.
کتل	*katal*	To look, examine.
گورم	*gōram*	I examine (present)
زخم يا پرهر	*zakham or parhar*	Wound.
زخمی يا ژوبل	*zakhmi or jhōbal*	Wounded.
پهٔ وخت	*puh wakht*	In time
اسمان غورېږي	*asmān ghurégee*	It is thundering.
غالب گمان	*ghālib gumān day*	Probably.
باران وريدل	*bārān warédal*	To rain.
واوره وريدل	*wāwra warédal*	To snow.
واوره	*wāwra*	Snow, ice.
داړه	*dāra*	Raid, Raiding party.
داړه مار	*dāra mār*	Raider.
لهٔ ټولونه نيزدي	*luh tōlo na nizde*	The nearest.
تور	*tōr*	Black.
دوکان	*dukān*	Shop.
دوکاندار	*dukāndār*	Shop keeper.
زهٔ ځم	*zuh zam*	I go.
زهٔ را ځم	*znh rāzam*	I come
کهٔ تهٔ لاړشی	*kuh tuh lārshé*	If you go.
لواړګی	*lwārgay*	Landi Kotal.
جم	*jam*	Jamrud.

داسې	*dāse*	Like this, so, such or thus.
هم پهٔ هغه شپه	*hum puh hagha shp̣a*	On the same night.
هم پهٔ هغه ورځ يا امروزه	*hum puh hagha vraz* or *amrōza*	On the same day.
لښکر	*lakhkar*	Party of tribesmen.
گرزيدل	*garzédal*	To walk or wander.
بيرته	*biarta*	Back.
پړاؤ	*parāw*	Camp.
رسد يا راسن	*rasad* or *rāsan*	Supplies, rations.
کله چه	*kala chi*	When (Relative).
وختي	*wakhti*	Early or earlier.
نا وخته	*nā wakhta*	Late.
کليوال	*kaliwāl*	Villagers (S & P).
(ته) نقصان رسيدل	*(tz) nuqsān rasédāl*	To suffer loss.
اوسنی	*osanay*	Recent.
جنګ	*jang*	War or battle.

EXERCISE 17.

1. Where do you live ? I am not living in the village. 2. I am living in Peshawar City, my brother lives in Kohat and after two months we shall live in Cherat. 3. The water of the river flows through my garden. 4. As we reached the wall of the village, the villagers fled towards the mosque. 5. This boy can run

faster than this girl. 6. All the thieves fled towards independent territory. 7. The train arrives at the Station at 2-30 p. m. 8. Don't move, I am going to examine your wound. 9. If you had arrived earlier, you would have seen the king of this country. 10. It is thundering now, it will probably rain tonight. 11. As we saw the raiding party we ran to the nearest village. 12. In the recent war we have suffered a great loss. 13. If you go now you will reach Landi Kotal at 4 p.m. 15. Has your brother arrived from Lahore ? 16. Yes, he arrived before 5 a. m. 17. All my servants cannot live in a small house like this. 18. We arrived there the same night, but the lashkar had run away to the hills. 19. I [1] must go to the office now. 20. When did your regiment arrive in this station ? 21. Has your Colonel arrived back from the camp ?

VOCABULARY XVIII.

خالی	*khāli*	Empty, only, Saturday.
پروت	*prōt*	Lying.
هڅوک	*hisōk*	Nobody (takes tense in negative.)

NOTE:—1. For "must" or "should", see syntax rules Nos. 21 & 22.

کُوځه	*kūsa*	Street.
وینې	*winé*	Blood (Feminine plural.)
سره دَ	*sara da*	With.
څهٔ داسې یا	*suh dāsé* or	
داسې	*dāsé*	So.
هر	*har*	Every.
وار پهٔ وار	*wār puh wār*	Turn by turn.
کثرت	*kasrat*	Bodily exercise.
فقیر	*faqir*	Beggar.
شپه او ورځ	*shpa aw vraz*	Day and night.
شهزاده	*shāhzāda*	Prince.
شهزادګئ	*shāhzādgai*	Princes.
خلاص	*khlās*	Free, finished.
اسمان پړکیږي	*asmān parkégee*	It is lightning.
باران به وشي	*bārān ba wo shee*	It will rain (lit the rain will become.)
وخت پهٔ وخت	*wakht puh wakht*	Time to time.
پیاده	*pyāda*	On foot.
خط	*khat*	Letter,
ګیډه یا خیټه	*géda* or *khéta*	Stomach.
درد	*dard*	Pain,
څرب	*surb*	Fat.
اِتوار	*itwār*	Sunday.
پیر یا ګُل	*pir*	Monday.
نهې	*nahé*	Tuesday.
چار شنبه	*chārshanba*	Wednesday,

پانشنبه	*pānshanba*	Thursday.
یا	or	
دَ زیارت ورځ	*da ziārat vraz*	
جُمعه	*jūma*	Friday.
خالی	*khāli*	Saturday.
دَ اتوار پهٔ ورځ	*da itwār pūh vraz*	On Sunday.
ځوان	*zwān*	Youngman or soldier.
مورچه	*mōrcha*	Breastwork.

EXERCISE 18.

۱ نهٔ هغه را ورسید او نهٔ د هغهٔ نوکر ۲ چه مُوږ ور ورسیدُو
نو کلیَ خالیِ پروت وُه ټول خلق ترِ تښتیدلیِ وُو ۳ نهٔ زهٔ په خپل
وطن کښې اوسم او نهٔ ځما وروز ۴ داسی جنګ وُه چه د کلیِ
په کُوڅو کښې ویښی بهیدلی ۵ پولټیکل صاحب ته خبر ورکړه چه
ځما نوکر سره دَ سلو روپو تښتیدلیَ دیَ ۶ دَ هغهٔ کور ته رسیدل
څهٔ داسی آسان کار نهٔ وُه ۷ چه وخوَ زیدلو نو زهٔ پوه شوم چه
ژوندیَ دیَ ۷ دَ کمان افسر صاحب حکم دَی چه سپاهیان دِ هر
سحر وار په وار دَ کثرت دَ پاره زغليِ ۹ فقیر شپه او ورځ په دی غم
کښې کړیدلو چه پس لهٔ مانه به ځما دَ ښای مانک څوک ویِ ۱۰
یوه ورځ زهٔ خپل نوکر سره وګړیدلم ۱۱ نهٔ زهٔ رار سیدلیَ نهٔ ویَ نو
غل به تښتیدلیَ نهٔ وُه ۱۲ اسمان غوړیږیِ او پړکیږیِ باران به وشيِ
۱۳ چه پلټنی ته ور ورسیږی نو صوبیدار صاحب ته ځما سلام ورکړه
۱۴ چه ځما چټی در ورسیږیِ نو جواب راکړه ۱۵ کوټ ماسټر
صاحب ته و وایه چه واښهٔ او نور دَ خوراک څیزونه پهٔ وخت راورسيِ
۱۶ زهٔ پوه شوم چه په یوه ګیډیهٔ کښې پیاده رسیدلیَ نهٔ شم
۱۷ بیږه مهربانيِ دَه ستا خط راته په تیراه کښې را رسیدلیَ وُه ۱۸

زهٔ زغايدلیَ نهٔ شم خکه چه پهٔ ګيډه کښې م درد دیَ ۱۹ دَ جيټن
صاحب پهٔ حکم بانِد ټول خوانان خپلو خپلو مورچوته بيرته وتښتيدل
۲۰ جمعدار صاحبَ ډير خوړب دیَ خکه سپاهيانو پسی نه شو رسيدلیَ

VOCABULARY XIX.

کټ	*kat*	Bed.
دا هغه سړیَ دیَ	*dā hagha saray day*	This is the man.
سپين	*sṗin*	White.
صُندق	*sunduq*	Box.
ښيل	*khayāl*	To show, direct.
قالين	*qālin*	Rug.
دری	*darai*	Carpet.
تر-پوری	*tar-ṗoré*	Till, upto.
دوره	*daura*	Tour.
چای	*chāi*	Tea.
پهٔ يو مِلټ کښې	*ṗuh yaw melat ké*	In a minute.
سرشته دار	*sarishtadar*	Reader (of the court)
کمره يا کوټه	*kamra or kōta*	Room.
ډاکي	*dāgi*	Postman.
آئنده دَ پاره	*ainda da ṗāra*	In future.
د-په مخ کښې	*da-ṗa makh ké*	In the presence of, infront of.
بيعه	*baya*	Price.
مدام.تل.هميشه	*mudām, tal, hamésha*	Always.
څوک نه څوک	*sōk na sōk*	Someone or other.
ځان سره	*zān sarā*	With me, with him etc.

پکار دې چه اصلی پښتون وي	*pakār di chi asli pukhtūn wi*	He must be a real Pathan.
اصلی پښتون	*asli pukhtūn*	Real Pathan.
ضلع	*zela*	District.
کم ذات	*kam zāt*	Low class, menial.
اُستکار	*ustakār*	Village workman.
برنده	*baranda*	Vranda.

EXERCISE 19.

1. Bring a bed and put it in the vranda. 2. This is the man who brings horses from Afghanistan. 3. I brought a letter from your Colonel. 4. Tell the syce to bring my white horse to the Club and wait for me if I am not there. 5. Where did you put my gun ? I put it under the box. 6. The servants used to bring our food from the city. 7. I will take you to the city and will show you all kinds of carpets. 8. Take away the dogs and don't bring them till the day after tomorrow as I shall be on tour. 9. Bring tea for four men who are coming in a minute. 10. Take my servant to the city and show him my reader's house. 11. [1] He said his name was Ahmad and he said he was a good man. 12. Yesterday my father told me I was a good man. 13. He said his room was smaller than my office. 14. Tell the Postman to bring my letters to the office

in future 15. He brought 20 rupees and put them before the owner of the house saying that it was the price of his food. 16. He always brings someone or other with him. 17. How can I bring the head-man with me ? 18. All whom you bring in [2] must be real Pathans of the Peshawar District. 19. Menials and the village workmen will not do. 20. Can you take my servant's son with you.?

VOCABULARY XX.

لهٔ نن تاریخ نه	*luh nan tārikh na*	From this day.
یو ځل	*yaw zal*	Once.
دوه ځلَ	*dwa zala*	Twice.
درې ځلَ	*dré zalā*	Thrice.
دا ځل	*dā zal*	This time.
ویل	*wayal*	To say, speak, tell.
ضروری	*zarūri*	Important, necessary, urgent.
ضرورې ضرورې	*zarūri zarūri*	Very important ones.
معمؤلی	*māmūli*	Ordinary.
عرضی	*arzi*	Petition.
عرضې	*arzai*	Petitions.
درخواست	*darkhwāst*	Ordinary petition, request.

NOTE :—1. Direct speech.
2. In syntax rule No. 22.

کچهرئ	*kacharai*	Court.
جمع کول	*jama kawal*	To collect.
ښۀ غوندې	*khuh ghundé*	Somewhat good.
خرڅ دَ پاره	*khars da pāra*	For sale.
لۀ بدَ نصيبَ	*luh bada nasiba*	Unfortunately.
لۀ ښۀ نصيبَ	*luh khuh nasiba*	Fortunately.
هره ورځ	*hara vraz*	Every day.
وزګار	*wōzgār*	At leisure.
نا وزګار	*nā wōzgār*	Busy.
مفرور	*mafrūr*	An outlaw.
إنعام	*inām*	Reward.
مؤندل	*mūndal*	To get, obtain, receive, find.
زۀ مؤمم	*zuh mūmam*	I get, etc. (present).
ټګي	*tagi*	Deceit.
اسان	*asān*	Easy.
ربړ	*rabar*	Trouble.
لرګَی	*largay*	Stick, wood.
لالۀ	*lāla*	To me or for me.
را بانديِ ډير کار دیَ	*rā bāndé dér kār day*	I have plenty to do.
پۀ دې شپو ورځو کښې	*pa dé shpo vrazo ké*	Now a days.
يوا ځې	*yawāzé*	Alone.
باران کوټ	*bārān kōt*	Overcoat, water proof coat.
بونګه	*bōnga*	Ransom.

EXERCISE 20.

۱ یو سړی یئ لۀ خذمتل نه راوست او ورته یی ووِ چه لۀ نن
تاریخ نه تۀ خموږ بادشاه یی ۲ ښه مِرزاصاحب څۀ دِ راو ړیِ دیِ؟
ما در ته ویلیِ دیِ چه ضروریِ ضروریِ کاغذونه راو ړه او معمولی
عرضیِٔ او درخواستونه په کچهرئ کښې جمع کوه ۳ زۀ به دِ دَ ملک
حجرې له بوزم ۴ نن څویم تاریخ دیَ . پرون دَ څۀ ورځ وَه - بل
صبا دَ پیر ورځ دَه ۵ ما له یو ښۀ غوندې نوکر راوله ۲ دَ دې
وطن خلق لۀ خذمتل نه وانښۀ او لرګیِ راوړیِ او په ښهر کښې یئ
خرڅویِ ۷ موږ خرڅ دَ پاره سکارۀ هم راوړو ۸ کۀ تا مغرور څما
بنګلی ته راوستیَ ویَ نو ما به ډیر لوی انعام درکړیَ وه ۹ نوکر ته
مِ و وایه چه څما ټیپن هره ورځ دفتر ته راوړیِ ځکه چه را باندِ ډیر
کار دیَ ۱۰ بی لۀ ټکټِ نه دَ مغرورانو راوستل اسان کار نۀ دیَ
۱۱ بیا هیچرې څما چائ په دې میز کښې نه ږدې ۱۲ څما آس
غلو بیولیَ وه دَ اپرید و یو ملک لا له پۀ بونګه راوست ۱۳ ما ته یی
ووِ چه ستا آس مِ په ډیر ربړ سره راوستیَ دیَ ۱۴ لږې نورې اوبۀ
په ګلاس کښې راوړه ۵ پرون مالی دَ دې ټټیِ دَ پاره اوبۀ
راوستی وې ۱۶ رایې وله چه انعام ورکړم ۱۷ زۀ څۀ وکړم په
دې شپو ورځو کښې زۀ ډیر ناوزګاریم ۱۸ دا کار ما یواځې کولی نۀ
شو ۱۹ څما نوکر ته و وایه چه دفتر ته را پسی باران کوټ مِ راوړیِ
۲۰ ټول ټوپکونه راوړه او دَ صاحب پۀ مخ کښې یئ و شماره -

VOCABULARY XXI.

څرخه و ګرځه *garza* Turn !

گس لاس	*gas lās*	Left hand.
ښی لاس	*khay lās*	Right hand.
پیش کړه	*pésh kra*	Bring before or produce.
قدم	*qadam*	Pace.
پونده	*pūnda*	Heel.
سمدستی	*samdāsti*	At once.
لګول	*lagawāl*	To fix, apply, and arrange (Flowers etc.)
سنګین	*sangin*	Bayonet.
مهٔ ځه	*muh za*	Do not go.
مهٔ را ځه	*muh rāza*	Do not come.
شور	*shōr*	Noise.
چُپ	*chup*	Silent.
ویستل	*wistal*	To take out, take off.
وباسم	*wō bāsam*	I take off (present.)
جامې	*jāmé*	Clothes.
آدریدل	*odrédal*	To stand.
نیغ	*négh*	Straight.
کوږ	*kōg*	Crooked.
لږ یا لوکوټی	*lag* or *lūkūti*	Little or please
ګرمی	*garmi*	Heat.
یخنی	*yakni*	Cold.
ناراست	*nārāst, sust*	Lazy.

Miscellaneous Colloquial Sentences II.

Why did you strike him ?	*walé dé hagha wo wahalo*

Turn to the right.	*khī lās ta wō garza.*
Bring him before the C. O.	*kamān afsar ta yé pésh kra.*
Turn to the left.	*gus lās ta wo garza.*
Where do you live ?	*charta osé ?*
When did you arrive here ?	*dalé kala rā wo rasédé ?*
Keep in step.	*qadam melāo kra.*
Heels together	*pūndé yaū zāī kra.*
Bring him at once	*zar yé rāwala.*
Fix bayonet	*sangin wo lagawa.*
Pull vigorously	*puh zōr sara yé rā wobāsa*
Come here	*dalé rasha* or *dalta rāsha.*
Do not go there	*halta muh za.*
Hurry up	*zar sha.*
Tell the sepoys not to make a noise	*spāhyāno ta wo wāya chi shōr nuh kawee.*
Keep quiet.	*chup sha.*
Take the horse to the house	*ass kōr ta bōza.*
Take off your clothes	*jāmé dé wo bāsa.*
Stand up straight	*négh wodréga.*
Lie down	*sumla.*
Wait a little	*lūkūti sabar wo kra*, or *wār wo kra.*
Take this letter to the Adjutant	*dā chitaī jitan sāhib ta yāusa.*

Bring an answer quickly	*zar jawāb rāwra.*
It is very hot today	*nan déra garmi dah*
Owing to the rain it is cold	*da bārān puh sabab yakhni dah.*
You are very lazy	*tuh dér nārāst yé.*
Do not bring all the papers	*tōl kāgazūna muh rāwra.*
Put them in the office	*puh daftar ké yé kégda.*

VOCABULARY XXII.

قصه	*qisa*	Story.
اخستل	*akhistal*	To take or buy. آخلم = *akhlam* I take (present).
خرڅ	*khars kawal*	To sell, spend.
مجرم	*mujrem*	Accused or offender
جرم	*juram*	Crime.
قتل یا خون	*qatal* or *khūn*	Murder.
قاتل یا خونی	*qātél* or *khūni*	Murderer.
وژلیَ شویَ	*wajhalay*	
سړیَ یا مړیَ	*shaway saray* or *maray*	Murdered man.
ما خبر کړه	*mā khabar kra*	Let me know
مدرسه	*madrasa*	School.
تیار شه	*tayār sha*	Get ready.
ضروری	*zarūri*	Necessary, urgent.
کار	*kār*	Work.

ناوخته	*nā wakhta*	Late.
وختی	*wakhti*	Early.
خما پهٔ فکر کښې	*zamā puh fikar ké*	I think, I am afraid, In my opinion.
قریب	*qarib*	About, nearly.
لیدل	*lidal*	To see.
بیرته	*biarta*	Back.
بیا	*bia*	Again.
تګ را تګ	*tag rā tag*	Coming and Going.

EXERCISE 21.

1. When will you go back ? 2. He came inside, sat on the chair and told me to tell him my father's story. 3. When did your brother come from Lahore ? 4. We went to the City but did not see Mahabat Khan's Mosque. 5. The people of the city come to my garden to buy fruit. 6. When you first saw the accused, was he coming to his house or had he arrived there ? 7. Where did you come from ? 8. Let me know wher my servant arrives. 9. I will sit on this chair, you can lie down on that carpet and the village people will come to us. 10. I go at 10 in the morning and come back at 4 p. m. 11. Get ready! We will go to the cantonment at 2-30 p. m. 12. Come to my house every day and do the necessary work. 13. It is very late now, I think you had better

go tomorrow. 14. My servant has gone to the bazar and will be back in about an hour. 15. Yes, the Khan had come, but I did not see him. 16. My regiment was in Pindi but it has now come to Peshawar. 17. Ahmad went to his house and did not come back again. 18. If he had come, you would have seen him. 19. We used to sit on the bank of that river. 20. I went to the hill without seeing anyone coming or going.

VOCABULARY XXIII.

راځه چه	*rāza chi*	Let us.
(ته) نقصان رسول	*(ta) nuqsān rasawal*	To cause damage.
ناراستي	*nārāsti*	Idleness.
نيستي	*nésti*	Poverty.
تخم	*tukhum*	Seed.
(ته) نقصان رسيدل	*(ta) nuqsān rasédal*	To suffer loss,
پريټ	*parait*	Parade
اخبار	*akhbār*	Newspaper.
د پهٔ ځاى كښې	*da puh zāi ké*	Instead of
وينځل	*winzal*	To wash.
بندول	*bandawal*	To close.
کنجي	*kunji*	Key.
ناظر	*nāzer*	Manager.
کار	*kār*	Work.

ملاحظه کول	*mulāheza kawal*	To inspect.
ورته به معلومه شي	*warta ba malūma shi*	He will find.
ضرور	*zarūr*	Certainly.
معافوَل (معاف کول)	*muāfawal (muāf kawal)*	To remit, forgive.
په يو مخ	*puh yau makh*	All in one time.
هله يا حمله	*hala* or *hamla*	Attack.
نۀ صرف...بلکه	*nuh serf..balké*	Not only...but
سيزل يا سوزوَل	*sézal* or *swazawal*	To burn.
سوزيدل	*swazédal*	To be burnt.
(ته) شکست ورکول	*(ta) shikast warkawal*	To defeat.
شکست خوړل	*shikast khwaral*	To be defeated.
بدرگه	*badraga*	Escort.
قام	*qām*	Tribe.
(سره) شپه کول	*(sara) shpa kawal*	To stay the night with.
وخت راته نۀ وه	*wakht rā ta nuh woh*	I had no time.
خرڅ دَ پاره	*khars da pāra*	For sale.
تر اوسَ پورې	*tar osa pōré*	Up to the present. till now.
تير کول	*tér kawal*	To pass (time).
هيلۍ	*hilai*	Duck.
جبه	*jaba*	Marsh.

ګشت	*gasht*	Rounds, patrol
د چرو ټوپک	*da charō tōpak*	Shot gun.
څوکئی کول	*saukai kawal*	To guard.
ملا بانګ مالی	*mulā bāng mālé*	At dawn.
نښه	*nakha*	Sign, mark.
نوی	*naway*	New.
زوړ	*zōr*	Old.

EXERCISE 22.

۱ راځه چه هغه کلي ته لاړشو او د کلي ملک سره د رسد
بندوبست وکړو ۲ صاحب يو خان راغلی دی او تا سره ليدل غواړي
۳ يو کم عقل سړی خپل دښمن ته دومره نقصان نه شي رسولی
لکه چه خپل ځان ته ئي رسوي ۴ دا رښتيا خبره ده چه ناراستي
د نيستي تخم دی ۵ نن دوه ځل شه. ته لاړم او راغلم مګر ستا
ورور م و نه ليد ۶ ما هغه دفتر ته رغوښتلو او ورته م تپوس وکړ
چه پرون چه ته په پريښ باندِ وی نو چا پوری د خندلی ؤو ۷ صبا
سحر په پنځه بجی زه به ښکار له ځم ته به راسره ځی که نه ۸ پرون
م په اخبار کښ ولوستل چه ستا سو پلټن به کوهاټ ته ځي او بيرته
به نه راځي ۹ که ته پخپله نه شی راتلی نو ورور د په خپل ځای
کښ راواستوه ۱۰ قلمونه وينځل او د دي کمری ټولی کرسئي او
ميزونه صافول او پنځه بجی دفتر بندول او بيا کنجي ناظر ته ورکول
ستا کار دی ۱۱ که تحصيلدار د فصلونو ملاحظی د پاره راشي نو
ورته به معلومه شي چه فصلونه ښه نه دي او ضرور به د
ماليی معافولو د پاره رپوټ وکړي ۱۲ که ټول برګيډ
په يو مخ په دښمن باندِ حمله کړی وی نو نه صرف

ورته شکست به ئی ورکړی وه بلکه د هغو کلي به ئی هم سیزلي وُ
۱۳ کهٔ زهٔ راتلی شوی نو پخپله به راغلی وم اوقام بدر ګی سره به م
د وطن دوره کړی وه اوشپه به م تاسره کوله مګر وخت راته نه وه
۱۴ اسونه لهٔ افغانستان نه راوستلی کیږي او پهٔ پیښورکښې پهٔ
ګرانه بیعه خرخیږي کله کله دا اسونه پنجاب ته هم د خرخ د پاره
بیولی کیږي ۱۵ هغه پاڅیدو روان شو ویی و چه صبا به بیا راشم
مګر تراوسه پوری را نهٔ غی ۱۶ موږ دوه د څرو ټوپکونه ځان
سره واخستل او د ښکار د پاره روان شو خلقو راته و چه پهٔ جبو کښې
ډیری هیلۍ راغلی دی موږ ټوله ورځ تیره کړه مګر یوه هم ونهٔ لیدلی
شوه ۱۷ زهٔ خبر[2] درکولو د پاره راغلی یم چه کهٔ تن ستاسو ګشت
د لاری څوکۍ ټولو د پاره لا نهٔ ړو نو پهٔ قلا باند به د قطب له ډیری
نه حمله وشي ۱۸ ځلویښت تن ځوانان ځان سره واخله او لس
لس کس ځائ په ځائ په لار کینوه تر ملا بانګ مالی د په خپلو
خپلو ځایونو ناست وي ۱۹ که تر ځلورو بجو د دشمن نښه نه وي
نو راځي د ۲۰ ته د لکهٔ نوکر ښما ئی او کار د د بل کوی —

NOTE:—1. For *rāza chi* look up syntax rule No. 30.

2. For the infinitive of purpose see syntax rule No. 12.

VOCABULARY XXIV.

روان کیدل	*rawān kédal*	To start.
پوری کول	*pōré kawal*	To shut.
ما ور نه تپوس	*mā war na tapōs*	
وکړو	*wɔ kro*	I asked him.
کوم	*kum*	Which.

پس لۀ هغه	*pas luh hagha*	After that, later on, afterwards.
هم پۀ هغه ورځ	*hum puh hagha vraz*	On the very day.
لام	*lām*	Expedition.
جنګ	*jang*	Fight, war, battle.
تیره میاشت	*téra miāsht*	Last month.
تیندک خوړل	*tindak khwaral*	To stumble.
خوږ کیدل	*khūg kédal*	To hurt.
ښپه	*khpa*	Foot, leg.
لالټین	*lāltain*	Lamp.
پۀ غلا تلل	*puh ghlā tlal*	To be stolen.
غلا	*ghlā*	Theft.
غل	*ghal*	Thief.
غلۀ	*ghluh*	Thieves
غلا کول	*ghlā kawal*	To Steal.
توره	*tūra*	Sword.
پیشقوزه	*peshqauza*	Killing knife.
توره پۀ لاس	*tūra puh lās*	With a sword in hand.
لختی	*lakhtay*	Water cut.
برتی کول	*barti kawal*	To enlist.
قافیله	*qāfela*	Caravan.
ماشی	*māshay*	A mosquito.
کټمل	*kātmal*	Bug.
وروږه	*vraga*	A flea.
میزری	*mézaray*	Dwarf palm.
بوږ	*būnr*	String made of dworf palm.

منجور	*manjawar*	Shrine keeper.
امام	*imām*	Leader in prayer.
سيّد	*sayad*	Descendent of prophet.
ميان	*miān*	Descendent of any religious person.
سپږه	*spaga*	Louce.
پاتی کيدل	*pāté kédal*	To remain.
تير	*tér*	Last.
ميله	*maila*	Fair.
زيارت	*ziārat*	Shrine.
بل کول	*bal kawal*	To light.
مړ کول	*mar kawal*	To put out.

EXERCISE 23.

1. I gave him an order to go to that village in the plain. 2. He started but an hour later sent me a message that he could not go. 3 Please shut the door. 4. I asked him what village he came from (Thou of which village art?) 5. He said his name was Ahmad but afterwards said it was Mohammad. 6. He died on the same night. 7. All the crops have been harvested. 8. Two of my sons had been wounded in the Tirah expedition. 9. He became a Jamadar on the 15th of last month. 10. The Colonel's horse stumbled this morning but the Sahib was not hurt. 11. We fell off the

motor and I broke my leg (my leg was broken). 12. Light the lamp and do not put it out till 11 o'clock. 13. My house was burgled and all my clothes were stolen. 14. As we opened the door of the house I saw a man standing near the tree with a sword in his hand. 15. The land of the village is irrigated from this river by a small water cut. 16. I am glad that the Adjutant enlisted me on the very day. 17. I cannot shut the door as I am ill. 18. In the winter and spring the caravans go on Tuesdays and Fridays ; in the hot weather and rains they only go on Fridays. 19. The jirga came to thé Political Agent on Sunday last, but as the Sahib was out on tour, they had to stay in the city for the night. 20. A fair is held every year at the shrine of Kaka Sahib at Nowshera.

VOCABULARY XXV.

اوښ	*ūkh*	Camel.
ساروان	*sārwān*	Camelman.
ګنی	*ganay*	Sugar cane.
هیڅ فائده نشته	*hiss fāida nishta*	There is no use.
شولی	*shōlé*	Rice (Crop)
زمیندار	*zamindār*	Land owner, farmer.
چلی کار	*chalé kār*	Cultivator.
مالیه	*māliya*	Land revenue.
زیات	*ziāt*	Excessive.

ګوړه	*gura*	Brown sugar (gurh)
خرڅول یا خرڅ کول	*kharsawal* or *khars kawal*	To sell, spend.
خرڅېدل یا خرڅ کېدل	*kharsédal* or *khars kédal*	To be sold, to be spent.
پُنبه	*punba*	Cotton.
علاج	*ilāj*	Remedy, Cure.
روژه	*rōjha*	Fast or fasting.
ور	*war*	Door.
دَ روپو تیلۍ	*da rūpo télai*	Bag of money
پاتی کیدل	*pāté kédal*	To remain.
نیمه لار	*nima lār*	Half way.
کوز کول	*kūz kawal*	To take down, take off.
کوز کیدل	*kūz kédal*	To get down, dismount.
حُجره	*hujra*	Guest house.
سلام اچول	*salām achawal*	To say salam to.
پهٔ-باندِ خوَرول	*puh-bāndé khurawal*	To cause to eat.
پهٔ-باند سکَول	*puh-bāndé skawal*	To cause to drink or smoke.
خدمت	*khizmāt*	Service.
غرق اودهٔ	*gharq ūduh*	Fast asleep.
هینړهار	*henrahār*	Neighing of horses.
خبر	*khabar*	Message or news.
کم	*kam*	Less, deficient.
دارو	*dārū*	Medicine.

پیښنمی یا پیشمنی	*péshnamay* or *péshmany*	The time of first meal before dawn in month of Ramzan.
ګاډی	*gāday*	Cart, car.
دُعا	*dūaā*	Prayer.
مونځ کول	*mūnz kawal*	To pray.
اغوستل	*aghustal*	To wear etc.
اغوندم	*aghundam*	I wear (present.)
پیغمبر	*péghambar*	Prophet.
کوچ کول	*kōch kawal*	To march.
افسوس کول	*afsōs kawal*	To be sorry.
سینتری	*séntri*	Sentry.
پهره	*pehra*	Sentry-go.
ناګهانه	*nāgahāna*	By chance.
ناساپه	*nāsāpuh*	Suddenly.
چپاؤ	*chapāo*	Surprise attack.
پهٔ باندِ ورختل	*puh-bāndé warkhatal*	To invade.
(سره) مقابله کول	*(sara) muqābela kawal*	To withstand.
هم هغسې	*hum haghasé*	Still, in the same manner.
تخت	*takht*	Throne.
فقیر	*faqir*	Beggar.
عبادت	*ibādat*	Worship.
پهٔ باندِ لاس پورې کول	*puh bāndé lās pōré kawal*	To start, commence.
ساړ فصلونه	*sār faslūna*	Withering crops.

مینه	*maina*	House.
سترګه	*starga*	An eye.
سر	*sar*	Head.
مخ	*makh*	Face.
خوله	*khuluh*	Mouth.
مرئ	*marai*	Throat.
څټ	*sat*	Back of neck.
تندیَ	*tanday*	Forehead.
غوږ	*ghwag*	Ear.
ویښته	*wékhtuh*	Hair (M. S. and P.)
لاس	*lās*	Hand.
ښپه	*khpa*	Foot or leg.
ګوته	*gōta*	Finger.
پوزه	*pōza*	Nose.
زړه	*zruh*	Heart.
تیز	*téz*	Fast, sharp.
پۀ-باندِ اواز کول	*puh-bāndé awāz kawal*	To challenge.
(ته) اواز کول	*(ta) awāz kawal*	To call out to.
پۀ-باند ډز کول	*puh-bāndé daz kawal*	To fire at.
پۀ تکی	*puh taki*	Instantly.
ګیر کول	*gér kawal*	To surround.
مدت راغو ښتل	*madat rāghukhtal*	To call for help (re-inforcements).
تار	*tār*	Wire, telegram.
شیشه	*shisha*	Helio.

جنډئ	*jandai*	Flag, signalling.
مُخبر	*mukhber*	Informer, spy.
ضمانت	*zamānat*	Security.
ضامن	*zāman*	Surety.
منظور کول	*manzūr kawal*	To sanction.

Exercise 24.

۱ ساروان نا جوړ شو قافلې پسې ونهٔ رسيدلی شو ۲ اوس
دَ ږمنو پهٔ فصل، کښې هيڅ فائيده نشته ځکه چه ماليه يې ډېره زياته دَه
او ګوړه ډېره ارزانه دَه ۳ موټر له پکار دی چه هغه فصلونه وکړو چه ګران
ګران خرڅېږي پکار ږو چه موټر سکال پنبه کرلی وی ۴ موټر يې
ډېر علاج وکړو مګر دَ روژې دَ مياشتې پهٔ دريمه ورځ مړ شو ۵ دَ
دوکان ور يئ پورې کړه چه تلو نو دَ روپو تيلئي ورنه هم پهٔ هغه ځائ
پاتې شوه ۶ چه نيمې لارې ته ورسيدم نو له ګاډي نه ئې کوز
کړم ځکه چه ځما ټکس خالي تر پېښو پورې وُه هلته يوې حجرې ته
ورغلم سلام مې وا چاوه کيڼا ستم دَ حجرې خاوند را باندې ډوډئ وخوړوله
چلم ئې را باندې وسکولو نو راته ئې ويل چه کهٔ ما ته نور څهٔ خدمت
وي نو هم زهٔ ورته تيار يم ۷ کهٔ دَ کلي خلق غرق اودهٔ نهٔ وی نو
ځموږ دَ اسونو هيڅ هار به ئې اوريدلی وُه ۸ صاحب کهٔ دا انعام
دِ پهٔ ما پيروز وی نو راته به دِ دَ داړې دَ راتلو خبر راکړی وُه
۹ بادشاه لهٔ تخت نه کوز شو او فقير ته ئې وو چه راځه ځما پهٔ ځای
اوس تهٔ کېنه پخپله يې دَ فقيرانو جامې واغوستې پهٔ جماعت کښې
کېناست دَ خدای پاک پهٔ عبادت ئې الس پورې کړه ۱۰ زهٔ نوکرئ
پسې لهٔ وطن نه راغلی يم مګر اوس ځموږ دَ علاقې برتی بنده دَه
۱۱ کله چه ډوډئ وخورم نو ستا چټئ به واخلم ۱۲ کهٔ ډپټی
کمشنر صاحب دَ فصلونه ملاحظې کولو دَ پاره راتلی نو تر اوس به

راغلیَ ؤه ارمان دیَ چه یوځل خو ئې ، څمونږ دا ساړ فصلونه لیدلیَ
ویَ ۱۳ کار را باند دومره زیات دی چه کام ناکام م دوه چلی
کاران وسائل او خوا مخوا به وزله میدنی هم د اوسیدلو د پاره ورکوم
۱۴ ملک سخه یوه اسپه دهَ چه یو سترګه یې دهَ (یا پۀ یوه سترګۀ ړنده
دهَ) ولی داسی تیزه ده چه په دری سوَ ئې هم نۀ ورکوي ما خپل
آس پۀ ملک باند پۀ سل روپیې خرڅ کړ ۱۵ اول سنتری پۀ غل
باندِ اواز وکړ او بیایې وویشت پۀ ټکیِ ئې مړ کړ ۱۶ ستا خر
څامن دیِ لۀ ټولونه مشر څوی دِ دَ څو کالو دیَ او تۀ دَ څو کالو
نوکر ئی ۱۷ ناګهانه دَ سرکار فوځ پۀ قلا باندِ حمله وکړه او دَ جرمن
فوځ ئې په کښې ګیر کړ فوځ مدت راغوښتلو دَ پاره ټیلیفون ورکړ مګر
دَ سرکار فوځ ټول تارونه پری کړيِ ؤو بیایې زر شیشه ورکړه او جنډیې
یې هم ورته ووهله ۱۸ مونږ خپل مُخبر ته ویل چه منځ کښې منځ کښې
څه مګر هغه پۀ یوه سترګه مغذور ؤه نۀ شو تلیَ ۱۹ کرنیل صاحب یو
پښتون سړیَ دیَ مُدام پۀ خپلو سپاهیانو ولاړ ويِ ۲۰ که ورشی
او وګوری نو صاحب به راغلیَ ويِ او ستا ضمانت به یې منظور
کړيَ وي

VOCABULARY XXVI.

بی لۀ طلب نۀ	*bé luh talab na*	Without pay.
دَ-شفارس کول	*da-shafāras kawal*	To recommend.
کمان افسر	*kaman afsar*	Officer Commanding
(سره) اتفاق کول	*(sara) ittefāq kawal* or *manal*	To agree.

هغهٔ وليدل	*haghuh wo lidal*	He saw.
ما تهٔ معلومه شوه	*mā ta mālūma shwa*	I found out.
ختل	*khatal*	To climb.
پوره كول	*pūra kawal*	To complete.
سر	*sar*	Head, top, end.
گټل	*gatal*	To win.
بيلل	*bélal*	To lose.
هاكي	*hāki*	Hockey.
لوبې كول	*lōbé kawal*	To play.
لوبه	*lōba*	Game.
كوټ گارت	*kōt gārat*	Quarter Guard.
تماچه	*tamācha*	Pistol or revolver.
بدي	*badi*	Feud.
اوړم كال	*ōram kāl*	Year before last.
پهٔ خهٔ شان سره	*puh khuh shān sara*	Well, satisfactorily.
پورې غاړه	*pōré ghāra*	Far bank.
راپورې غاړه	*rā pōré ghāra*	Near bank.
ساتل	*sātal*	To engage, (servant) keep.
نيول	*niwal*	To engage (barrister).
كيږي	*kégee*	Ago, becomes (present of *kédal*
غوږ دې دی	*ghwag dé day*	Are you listening ?
تيريدل	*térédal*	To pass by.
اغوستلی وهٔ	*aghustalay woh*	Was wearing (lit : had worn.)

خاکی یا خړ	*khāki* or *khar*	Khaki, grey.
ځان پټ کول	*zān pat kawal*	To take cover.
تر بلَ حکمَ پوری	*tar bala hukma pōré*	Till next order.
وادهٔ	*wāduh*	Marriage.
وعده کول	*wada kawal*	To promise.
مال	*māl*	Cattle.
څرَول	*sarawal*	To graze (transitive.)
ورشو	*warsho*	Grazing ground.
ګوره	*gora !*	Look here !
یو څو	*yau so*	A few,
دامان	*dāmān*	Summer pasture ground.
منډۍ	*mandai*	Market.
ګانړۍ	*gānrai*	Sugar cane press.

EXERCISE 25.

1. What do you want? 2. I want ten days leave, without pay. 3. I will recommend you to the Commanding Officer and will send for you if he agrees. 4. The boy fell into the well and saw that he could not climb up. 5. Can you go across the river? 6. There is no boat, the river is deep so how can I cross? 7. Can you recognise this man? Yes he is the man whom I saw in the bazar yesterday. 8. Sultan Mahmud went to Ghazni and left his sardars to complete the necessary work, 9. We found

that the enemy were on the top of the hill. 10. Every one of the boys got 50/- rupees as a reward for winning the hockey match. 11. A thief was running towards the Guard Room and the sentry shot him dead with a revolver. 12 He had a feud with Mohmands, because they killed his father the year before last. 13. Can you read and write ? 14. I cannot read but in two months I shall be able to read well. 15. Do you see that big tree on the near bank of the river ? That is our camp. 16. Look here, young man I engaged you as Mali on 15/- rupees a month, a few months ago. 17. Do you hear ? 18. I saw a man passing by here wearing a khaki coat. 19. The sepoys will have to dig trenches and take cover till next order. 20. I have heard that the King of Afghanistan is coming to Peshawar.

VOCABULARY XXVII.

ښه ټوپک ويشتل	*khuh tōpak wishtal*	To shoot (well.)
نښه	*nakha*	Mark.
ډزکول	*daz kawal*	To fire.
سيلاب	*sélab*	Flood.
نُقصان	*nuqsān*	Loss.
(ته) بد بد کتل	*(ta) bad bad katal*	To stare at.

بی خودَ	*bé khuda*	Senseless.
پهٔ خود	*puh khud*	In senses
سترګی غړول	*stargé gharawal*	To open eyes.
سترګی پټی کړه	*stargé paté kra*	Shut your eyes !
خولهٔ وازه کړه	*khuluh wāza kra*	Open your mouth !
خولهٔ پیچی کړه	*khuluh piché kra*	Shut your mouth !
غوږ کیږده	*ghwag kégda*	Lit. place ear. } Listen !
پروت	*prōt*	Lying.
خپل خپلوان	*khpal khpalwān*	Relations.
ګیر چاپیره	*gérchāpéra*	All round.
پیشکی	*péshki*	Advance (of money)
پټکی پهٔ سر کول	*patkay puh sar kawal*	To wear a pagri.
پڼی پهٔ خپو کول	*panré puh khpo kawal*	To wear shoes.
دستانی پهٔ لاس کول	*dastāné puh lās kawal*	To wear gloves.
سور کیدل	*sōr kédal*	To mount.
خیر خیریت	*khér kheriat*	All well.
بالکل	*bélkul*	Absolutely, entirely
تباه کول یا برباد کول	*tabāh kawal* or *barbād kawal*	To ruin.

پۀ-باندِ اعتبار کول	*puh-bāndé ittebār kawal*	To trust.
پۀ-باندِ يقين کول	*puh-bāndé yaqin kawal*	
پۀ-باندِ باور کول	*puh-bāndé bāwar kawal*	
رشتيا	*rishtiā*	Truth.
دروغ	*darōgh*	Lie.
غلط فهمی	*ghalat fahmi*	Misunderstanding.
پۀ کلیِ باندِ داړه پريوتله	*puh kali bāndé dāra préwatala*	The village was raided.
پۀ کلیِ باندِ جُرم پريوت	*puh kali bāndé jurm préwat*	The village was fined.
چغه	*chagha*	Pursuit party.
مازديګر	*māzdigar*	Early evening (between 3 o'clock and sunset).
ماښپښين	*māspakhin*	Afternoon.
ما ښښتن	*māskhutan*	Night prayer time (between 8 o'clock and midnight.
پۀ لاس راتلل	*puh lās rātlal*	To come in hand, procure.
تحقيقات کول	*tahqiqāt kawal*	To enquire.
تفتيش	*taftish*	Police enquiries.
معلومه شوه	*malūma shwa*	It turned out.
کليوال	*kaliwāl*	Villager.
غفلت	*ghaflat*	Negligence.

(تۀ) لار نیول	*ta lār niwal*	To ambush.
خرا په خبره ده	*kharāpa khabara dah*	It is a bad bussiness.
ډیر ځلَ	*dér zal*	Many times.
د-پرواه کول	*da-parwāh kawal*	To take notice of.
هیڅ پروا نشته	*hés parawāh nishta*	Never mind.
هیڅ باک نشته	*hés bāk nishta*	Never mind.
پهم کولَ	*paham kawal*	To take care.
سپین سری ښځه	*spin saré khaza*	White headed woman, old woman.
(پوری) خندل	*pōré khandal*	To laugh at.
لۀ-نه-روان کیدل	*luh-na rawān kédal*	To start, leave, set out from.

Exercise 26.

۱ ما دَکلي ملک ګواهئ دَپاره ډير ځلَ راوغوښت مګر
زانۀ غیَ ۲ افریدیان ډیر ښۀ ټوپک ولي هغوئ هره ورځ پۀ خپل خپل
کلي کښې پۀ نښو باندِ ډزی کوي ۳ پۀ جنګ کښې ځموږ
څلور تنَ سپاهیان ووژلیَ شول ۴ دکور خاوند وِ چه ما دری تنَ
داړه ماران پیژندلي دي ۵ پۀ سیند کښې سیلاب دیَ ځکه ورنه
پوریوتل ګران کاردیَ ۶ دَدی کتاب پۀ لوستلو کښې ستا څۀ
نقصان دیَ ۷ ولی بدبد ګوری ۸ لۀ اس نه پریوتم ښپه ِم ماته
شوه بی خودَ شوم چه پۀ خود شوم اوسترګی ِم وغړولی نوپۀ هسپتال
کښې پۀ یو کټ باندِ پروت وم اوخپل خپلوان زانه ګیر چاپیره ناست وو
اوبی ژړل ۱۰ داس روپیٔ پیشکی واخله اونوری بۀ بیادرکړم.

١١ آرډی ئې وسوسه پټکئ ئی په سر ډېرو بوټونه ئی په ښپوکړل
دستانی یی په لاس کړی اوبه اس سورشه لاړ ١٢ ته وائی چه فصلونه
موسم کال ښه شوه دی په باره کښې اوبه کمی دی د سکلو دپاره هم
نه راځی مګر پرون خان راغلی وه هغه خو ویل چه ټول خیرخیریت دی
فصلونه بالکل ښه دی اوبه ډیری دی ١٣ صاحب موږ خه ووایو
چه ناږی موږ روی نو ټول کلی موږ روی نو ١٤ په کلی داړه پریوته
دوه کوروڼه یی لوټ کړل چغه ورپسی ووته خو مازدیګر بیرته راغله
خکه چه داړه ماران په لاس ورنه رغلل ١٥ پولس تحقیقات وکړ
معلومه شوه چه دا د کلیوالو غفلت دی خکه ور باندې دوه زر روپئ جرم
پریوت ١٦ هغه په ډیر ربړ سره له کور نه را ووتلو ١٧ خلوروتنو اپریدو
ورته لار نیولی وه ټولی جامی ئی ، ترې واخستی ١٨ صوبیدار صاحب
دا د دی داړو ډیره خرابه خبره ده ـ ما ته ډیر خل پوه کړی ئی چه
هره شپه د خپلی کیږدۍ سره په وطن کښې ګشت کوه ـ مګر ته خما د
خبری هیڅ پرواه نه کوی ١٩ سپین سری ښځی تانړه دار پوری
وخندل او ترې روانه شوه ٢٠ صاحب که ته راغلی نه وی نو زه به ئی
وژلی وم ـ

VOCABULARY XXVIII.

لیونی	*léwanay*	Mad.
لیونی سپی	*léwanay spay*	Mad dog.
اوچ کول	*ūch kawal*	To dry.
لوند	*lūnd*	Wet.
نور	*nwar*	Sun, sunshine.
سپوږمۍ	*spōgmai*	Moon
تروږمۍ	*tarōgmai*	Moonless.

ستوری	*stōray*	A star.
ډیر ساعت	*dér sāat*	Much longer, for a long time.
دومره ساعت	*dōmra sāat*	So much longer.
نیول یا گرفتار کول	*niwal* or *géréftār kawal*	To arrest.
په موقعه باند	*puh mōqa bāndé*	On the spot.
پاڅیدل	*pāsédal*	To get up.
هسی تازهیروي	*hasé tā zāhirawee*	They are only pulling your leg !
ټوقی کول	*tōqé kawal*	To joke.
مږه	*maga*	Rat.
ټکړه	*tukra*	Piece.
پریږده چه لاړ شی	*prégda chi lārshee*	Let him go !
چمن	*chaman*	Grass lawn.
کله چه	*kala chi*	As soon as.
اواز	*awāz*	Sound, voice.
بیګل	*bigal*	Bugle.
فوځ	*fauz*	Troops, Army.
(ته) چوټی ورکول یا شړل	*ta chuti war-kawal* or *sharal*	To dismiss.
جواری کول	*jawāri kawal*	To gamble.
جوارګر	*jawārgar*	Gambler.
له نه قرض اخستل	*luh-na qarz akhistal*	To borrow.
ته قرض ورکول	*ta qarz war-kawal*	To lend.

ځما پۀ هغۀ باندې لس روپئی دی	*zamā puh haghuh bāndé las rupai di*	He owes me ten rupees.
دَ هغۀ پۀ ما باندې لس روپئی دی	*da haghuh puh mā bāndé las rupai di*	I owe him ten rupees.
بنیا	*bania*	Bunia.
اُمید دی	*omaid day*	I hope.
دَ کټ جامې	*da kat jāmé*	Sleeping suit.
فرش	*farsh*	Floor.
شړل	*sharal*	To drive out, turn out.
جرمانه کول	*jarmāna kawal*	To fine.
ویښ کول	*wikh kawal*	To wake up (transitive.)
تر هغه وخته پورې	*tar hagha wakhta pōré*	Then, till that time
اودۀ کیدل	*úduh kédal*	To sleep.
خوب	*khōb*	Sleep.
خوب لیدل	*khōb lidal*	To dream.
غُسل	*ghusal*	Bath.
وینځل	*winzal*	To wash.
ټوله رښتیا خبره	*tōla rikhtia khabara*	The whole truth.

EXERCISE 27.

1. He came out of the door and ordered me to shoot the mad dog 2. Take all the

tables and chairs out of this room and dry them in the sun. 3. The jamadar went into the room and did not stay any longer. 4. Do not laugh at him 5. A boy was sitting on the road-side crying, a man came up on him and asked him why was he weeping. 6. The Police arrested him on the spot ond produced him before the Magistrate. 7. He got up and went out, saying that he would come again tomorrow 8. The old man wrapped the rat in the piece of cloth and took it to the house. 9. Untie the horse and let it go to that grass field. 10. As soon as the horse heard the sound of the bugle he ran towards our troops. 11, I dismissed my servant, because he had lost 200/- rupees in gambling, which he had borrowed from the regimental Bania. 12. I hope you did not mind seeing me in my sleeping suit. 13. The Colonel found a sentry sleeping on guard, and shot him dead with his revolver. 14. Jemadar! tell these people that if any one spits on the floor I shall certainly turn him out and fine him five rupees. 15. Wake me at 7 o'clock if I am still asleep. 16. I could not sleep the whole night, because the old man was coughing all the time. 17. The sepoys used to bathe in the spring near the fort. 18. If you had sent for the bearer, he would have told you the whole truth. 19. Turn to the left. 20. What a fool you are!

VOCABULARY XXIX

ځینی	*ziné*	From, some.
ورو	*vro*	Slow.
ډاک	*dāg*	Post, mail.
هوائي جهاز	*hawāī jehāz*	Airship, aeroplane.
پښتو	*pukhtu*	Modesty, Pushtu.
پښتون	*pukhtūn*	Modest, Pathan.
پهٔ.باندِ اودریدل	*puh-bāndé odrédal*	To take the side of.
مُدام پهٔ خپلو سپاهیانو باندِ ولاړ ویِ	*mudām puh khpalo spāhiyāno bāndé wlār wi*	He always takes the side of his soldiers.
تیښته	*tékhtā*	Flight.
خلاصیدل	*khlāsédal*	To escape.
معلومیدل	*malūmédal*	To be seen.
پهٔ پهم سره	*puh paham sara*	Carefully.
کتل	*katal*	To look, examine.
ملاحظه کول	*mulāhéza kawal*	To inspect.
ما ته یاد دیِ	*mā ta yād dee*	I remember.
بهانه	*bahāna*	Pretence.
(ته) تندی تریؤ کول	*(ta) tanday triw kawal*	To frown at.
لرل	*laral*	To have.

دنیا	*dunia*	World. wealth.
آخِرت	*ākherat*	The day of judgement.
بدله	*badala*	Revenge.
غضب	*ghazab*	Rage.
پهٔ ټوقو ټوقو کښی	*puh tōqo tōqo ké*	Jokingly.
قربان دِ شم	*qurbān dé sham*	May I be sacrificed !
بار	*bār*	Load.
قچره	*qachara*	Mule.
په دی حساب سره	*pa dé hisab sara*	At this rate.
نور پریواتهٔ	*nwar prewātuh*	Sunset, west.
نور خاته	*nwar khātuh*	Sunrise, East.
دره	*dara*	Valley (over mountain).
غاښیَ	*ghākhay*	Pass.
پهٔ-باندِ ګمان کول	*puh-bāndé gumān kawal*	To suspect.

EXERCISE 28.

۱ یو مارغهٔ دَ بل مارغهٔ ښینی لوُر غواړِی ولی هغه ترِ دَ مرغانو دستوُر غواړی ۲ دا سړیَ پیژنه کله چه زهٔ پهٔ جذمت کښی اپریدو و بیولیَ وم نو ښما یی ډیر خدمت کړیَ وهٔ ۳ صاحبَ تا ته خو معلومه نه چه زهٔ پهٔ لیکلو لوستلو نهٔ پوهیږم نو ستا چټهٔی راته یو بل سړیِ ولوسته ۴ کهٔ تا ټوخلیَ نهٔ ویَ نو نور مرغان به د هم ویشتلیِ ؤو مګر بیا هم تهٔ ډیر ښهٔ ټوپک ولی ۵ کهٔ رښتیا وایم دَ

هر چا بدې شم که دروغ وایم نو د ملک م شړې ۶ زهٔ لوکوټی پهٔ
غوږو دروند یم ورو خبره نه اورم ۷ اوس ټاګ په هوائی جهاز
کښې څې راځې ۸ زهٔ پهٔ رساله کښې برتی کیدل غواړم د رنګروټ
افسر دفتر ورته وښیه ۹ زهٔ پوه شوم چه پهٔ تیښته نهٔ خلاصیږم
۱۰ دا آس م پهٔ شکل خوښ دی خو ګډ ښکاریږی ۱۱ جرنیل
صاحب راغلو ټول څیزونه ئې پهٔ پښم سره وکتل ډیر خوشحال شهٔ چه
تلو نو وئې لیکل چه هر شی ډیر ښهٔ اوصاف دی پهٔ دریمه میاشت
به بیا ملاحظه کوم ۱۲ ولی چوټۍ اخلې؟ مدام ستا پلار مړ وی
ستا هیر دې ولی ما ته ښهٔ یاد دی چه د تېر اکتوبر پهٔ پنځلسم
تاریخ د هم یهٔ دی بهانه چوټۍ اخستې وه ۱۳ غوږونه بهٔ
د وباسم ۱۴ پښتون له شاباشی ورکوه نو کار به درله پهٔ ښهٔ شان
سره کوی ۱۵ او کهٔ تندی د ورته ترېو کړ نو د ښهٔ کار امید ترمهٔ کوه
۱۶ کله سړی خاندی او کله ژاړی ۱۷ بادشاه د غضب جامی
واغوستې په تخت کیناست ۱۸ وزیر په ټوقو ټوقو کښې بادشاه ته
ووې چه قربان د شم نن یخنی وای چه بیځاله به د فوځ داسی
خدمت وکړم چه صبا له به بادشاه او وزیران د خپلو خپلو اسونو
خدمتونه پخپله کوی ۱۹ نو اوس زرشه دا باروونه له اوښانو نه
کوز کړه پهٔ قچرو یی واچوه پهٔ دی حساب به تر نور پریواتهٔ پوری
لهٔ دری نه و نهٔ څو ۲۰ تانړهدار د کور لهٔ خاوند نه تپوس وکړ چه
چاژوبل کړی ئی او په چا باند ستا ګمان دی -

VOCABULARY XXX.

پهٔ یو کلي کښې	*puh yau kali ké*	In a certain village.
تر اوسه پوری	*tar osa pōré*	Up to the present, so far.

زما ښکار خوښ دی	*zamā khkār khwakh day*	I am fond of shooting.
په خطا	*pūh khatā*	Accidentally.
له قصدَ	*luh qasda*	On purpose.
قسم خوړل	*qasam khwaral*	To take oath.
سوګند خوړل	*saugand khwaral*	To take oath.
ایران	*Irān*	Persia.
سیلاب	*sélāb*	Flood.
تناؤ	*tanāw*	Boat rope.
بېړئ په تناؤ ده	*bérai puh tanāw dah*	The boat is pulled by a rope.
چا ئي	*chāi*	Tea.
پئ	*pai*	Milk.
چینی	*chini*, *misri*	Sugar.
هګی یا ها	*hagai* or *hā*	Egg, Eggs.
ها سپینول	*hā spinawal*	To shell an egg.
ختل	*khatal*	To climb.
داړه مار	*dāra mār*	Raider, dacoit.
شوکه کول	*shūka kawal*	To loot, rob.
شوکمار	*shūkmār*	Robber.
خوا و شا	*khwā-o-shā*	Neighbourhood, vicinity.
ګنړ ځنګل	*ganr zangal*	Dense jungle.
رنګی واښهٔ	*rangay wākhuh*	Thin grass.
ویرېدل	*veyarédal*	To fear.

که ستا نصیب ښه وي	*kuh stā nasib khuh wī*	If you are lucky.
رنګی باران	*rangay bārān*	Slight rain.
را ګرزیدل	*rā garzédal*	To return.
بیرته راتلل	*biarta rātlal*	To come back.
ساده	*sāda*	Simple.
غلطي کول	*ghalati kawal*	To make a mistake.
رسید	*rasid*	Receipt.

EXERCISE 29.

1. In a certain village there was a clever boy, who was so clever that his father said that up to the present such a clever boy had never been. 2. He used to read books and newspapers and never played with bad boys. 3. In the city of Peshawar there was a king who had two sons and three daughters. 4. The younger son was fond of shooting. 5. One day he went out shooting to Adam Khel pass and was accidently shot by his own gun. 6. His father took an oath that he would kill all the servants who came with him from Persia. 7. The Kabul river was in flood (in the river of Kabul flood was) and people crossed in a boat which was pulled across by a rope. 8. On the 15th of June of that year I was enlisted as a Jemadar and three years afterwards I became a Subadar. 9. Will you drink tea? 10. I will eat some

eggs, shell one for me. 11. Put very little sugar in the tea. 12. No, do not put in any milk, I do not like it. 13. Subadar Sahib! take your company and climb the hill. 14. The dacoits appeared to be in great fear of the Indian troops and whenever they heard of any in the vicinity, they at-once moved away to dense jungle or jowar crops. 15. His father died when he was only three years old. 16. When he was very young, he used to drive birds from the field. 17. If you are lucky the raiding gang will probably return on that road this morning. 18. The people of this country are very simple. 19. They are ruined by their Khans and Maliks. 20. You made a great mistake in that you did not take any receipt from him.

VOCABULARY XXXI.

دربار	*darbār*	Darbar.
دَ بادشاہ پۂ ښپو پریوت	*da bādshāh puh khpo prewat*	Fell at the king's feet.
پۂ ژړا شو	*puh jharā sho*	Began to weep.
موسم	*mōsam*	Season.
اکثر	*aksar*	Generally.
حوالات	*hawālāt*	Custody.

لږ ډیر	*lag dér*	Somewhat.
ټول کول	*tōl kawal*	To collect.
جمع کول	*jama kawal*	To collect.
حاجت	*hājat*	Need.
حاجتمند	*hājatmand*	Needy.
ځنګل ویستل	*zangal wéstal*	To take out weeds.
وړوکی	*wrūkay*	Small.
واړهٔ	*wāruh*	Small (M. Plu).
زیات	*ziāt*	More (in comparison)
بی سببَ	*bé sababa*	Without reason.
مواجب	*mājéb*	Pay, allowance.
ذمه وار	*zémā wār*	Responsible.
ذمه	*zéma*	Responsibility.
پهٔ خوا زمانه کښی	*puh khwā zamāna ké*	Formerly.
مشر	*mashar*	Elder.
سپین ږیرَی	*spin giray*	Grey beard, elder.
پړ	*par*	Loser.
وړ	*war*	Winner.
فریق	*fariq*	Party.
سوره	*swara*	A girl in exchange.
رواج	*rewāj*	Custom.
شاباش	*shābāsh*	Well done.
نمک حلال	*namak halāl*	Loyal.
نمک حرام	*namak harām*	Disloyal.
بال بچ	*bāl bach*	Children, family.
ماشوم	*māshūm*	Child.

زه د هغه د لاسه تنګ یم	*zuh da haghuh da lāsa tang yam*	I am worried by him.
زما لاس تنګ دی	*zamā lās tang day*	I have no money.
د هغه کار جوړ دی	*da haghuh kār jōr day*	He is flourishing.
اوروَل	*aurawal*	To announce, to cause to hear,
سپکوالی	*spakwālay*	An insult, disgrace.
سپک کول	*spak kawal*	To insult.
مرګ	*marg*	Death.
سزا	*sazā*	Punishment.
خپیمانه کیدل	*khpémāna kédal*	To repent.
رعیت	*rait*	Subject (to Govt.)
ارام	*arām*	Rest.
کوشش	*kōshash*	Try.
زلزله	*zalzala*	Earth quake.
لوټې لوټې کول یا بر باد کول	*lūté lūté kawal* or *barbād kawal*	To destroy.
لوټه یا غونډه یا	*lūta* or *ghunda*,	
تیږه	*tiga*	Clod of earth.
بهادر	*bahādar*	Brave.
عمر	*umar*	Age.
نیت	*niat*	Intention.
مسافر	*musāfar*	Traveller.
منت کول	*menat kawal*	To entreat.

ولی	*walé*	But, why.
هیڅ فائده ونهٔ شوه	*hiss fāida wo nuh shwa*	No use.
خیال	*khyāl*	Thought.
خیر خو دیَ؟	*khér kho day*	Is all well ? Can I do anything for you ?
نظر	*nazar*	Sight.
پهٔ باندې نظر لږیدل	*puh-bāndé nazar lagédal*	To see.
پهٔ باندِ مین کیدل	*puh-bāndé main kédal*	To fall in love.
مسکیَ کیدل	*maskay kédal*	To smile.
فائده	*fāida*	Use, benefit.
پهٔ نظر راتلل	*puh nazar rātlal*	To come into sight.
وفادار	*wafādār*	Faithful.
بی وفا	*béwafā*	Faithless.
ویړیا	*wéryā*	Free, gratis.
تنګول	*tangawal*	To worry.
سوال	*swāl*	Question.
کاڼیَ مات کول	*kānray māt kawal*	To declare war, (lit to break stone.)
کاڼیَ کیښودل	*kānray kékhodal*	To make a truce.

EXERCISE 30.

۱ یوه ورځ یو فقیر پهٔ دربار راننوت دَ بادشاه پهٔ ښپو پریوت او پهٔ
ژړا شو ۲ غلو دروازه ما ته کړه او ټول مال ئی بوت ۳ دَ کلو

ملکان اکثر په دې موسم کښې په حوالات کښې وي. د دې
سبب دا دی چه فصلونه ښۀ نۀ کیږي. ځکه خلق مالیه نۀ شي
ورکولی او که څۀ لږه ډیره ټوله کړي نو ملک پخپله ورته حاجتمند
وي وئی خوري. ۴ مالي ته م ووې چه د څټمل ویستو د پاره درې
واړۀ واړۀ هلکان وساته ولې چه طلب ئی د پنځو پنځو روپو نه زیات نۀ
وي. ۵ جرګې پولټکل صاحب ته ووې چه کۀ ته بې سببه څمونږ
مواجب بند وې نو آئینده د پاره دا امید مۀ لره چه مونږ به ستا خدمت
وکړو که په لارو شوکې کیږي یا په کلو داړې پیوځی نو مونږ ذمه وار
نۀ یو او هر رنګ مال چه څمونږ علاقې ته راوستلی شي نو په
بونګه به ئی در نۀ کړو. ۶ په خوا زمانه کښې به چه د ښځو په
سر بدې وشوه نو د قام مشرانو به جرګه وکړه او کوم فریق به چه
ډېرشو نو د وړ فریق د پاره به ئې ور باندې سوره کېښوه مګر دا رواج
اوس کم دی ځکه چه په دې خبره بدې زیاتیږي ۷ چه دا ئی
واوریدل نو نوکر ئی راوبللو او ورته ئی ووې چه شاباش ته ډیر نمک
حلال سړی ئی کۀ ته مړشې نو ستا بال بچ له به زۀ روټئ جامه او
دیرش روپئ میاشت پنسن ورکوم. ۷ افریدیان چه په بدئ کښې تنګ
شي او یا د فصل وخت راشي نو کانړې کیږي. دي ۹ اورنګزیب
د هندوانو د لاس تنګ شو نو حکم ئی واوراوۀ چه کۀ هر هندو د
اسلام سپکوالی وکړ نو د مرګ سزا به ورکړې کیږي ۱۰ بادشاه هغه
دی چه د خپل رعیت د ارام د پاره کوشش کوي ۱۱ دا دا سې زلزله
وه چه په یو ملنګ کښې ئی مېنځ لوټې لوټې کړ سړي ښځې ما شومان
سپي چرګان ټول د خاورو لاندې شول ۱۲ هوښیار سړی هیچرې
بهادر نۀ وي ۱۳ مونږ دعا کوو چه نوي بادشاه له خدائ لوئ
عمر ورکړي او غریب هندوستان ته یې نیت په خیر شي ۱۴ چه د

ښهر دروازې ته ورسېد نو دروانچي دَ ننه پرې نه ښود مساپر ډېر منت
وکړ خو هيڅ فائيده و نهٔ شوه ځکه لاړ دَ سړک خوا ته کیناست
۱۵ دروازه لرې شوه او يوه ښځه راووته او فقير ته يې وِ با نن ولې
ښيې وختي راغلى ۱۶ چه ښما نظر ور باندِ واړېد نو ورباندِ مين
شوم ۱۷ فقير راته وکتل او مسکىَ شو ۱۸ صاحبَ دا وفادار
سپىَ کښې لاندِ اودهٔ وهٔ ۱۹ ګاډىَ په لس نيمى بجې رواندېږي
۲۰ ماښهٔ تذکوه دومره وخت راته نشته چه ستا دَ سوال جواب درکړم۔

MISCELLANEOUS COLLOQUIAL SENTENCES III.

Can you recognize this man?	*Dā saray péjhandalay shé?*
Why cannot you recognize him?	*Walé yé nuh pejhané?*
Do you not know his father?	*Tuh da haghuh plār nuh péjhané?*
What is the latest news to-day?	*Nan suh tāza khabar day?*
How old are you?	*Tuh da so kālo yé?*
Are you married?	*Wāduh dé karay day?*
How long have you been in the service.	*Da so kālo naukar yé?*
Take this recruit to the hospital and tell the doctor to let me know what is wrong with him.	*Dā rangūt haspatāl ta bōza aw dāktar ta wō wāya chi mā khabar kra chi pa duh suh chal shaway day.*
That hill is not within the range of our guns.	*Dagha ghar zaṃūng da tōpo da gōlo lāndé nuh rāzee.*

Let him write another petition and put it on the Sahib's table.	*War ta wō wāya chi bala arzi wo likee, aw da sāhib puh méz bāndé yé kégdee.*
We did not notice, but there was a big forest on our rear.	*Mūng wo nuh lidalo kho zamūng shā tā yau lōi zangal woh.*
Are the roads good? are supplies obtainable?	*Lāré khé dee? rasad múndalay shi?*
I will dine out to-night.	*Bégāla zamā rōtai bāhar dah.*
Why did you kill this man?	*Walé dé dā saray wō wajhalo.*
Who told you to kill him?	*Chā darta wayali woo chi wō yé wajhna?*
Why did you not take revenge on him?	*Walé dé war na badal wā nuh khistalo.*
Can you shoot well?	*Tuh khuh tōpak wōlé; kuh na?*
I did not see him.	*Mā hagha wō nuh lidalo.*
Did you not see me in the motor yesterday afternoon?	*Parūn māspakhin dé puh mōtar ké wō nuh lidalam?*
I greeted you but you did not answer.	*Mā darta salām wo kro kho tā jawab rā nuh kar.*
Have you heard that the Aka Khel are going to attack the fort?	*Aurédali dé di chi Aka khél puh qalā bāndé hala kawee.*
Go out of my house.	*Zamā da kōra wōza.*

You go and find out somewnere else.	*Lārsha aw bal charta yé malūm kra* or *wo mūma.*
Do not laugh at him.	*War pōré muh khānda.*
The dog barked but when I threw a stone at him, he ran towards the lane.	*Spi woghapal, kho chi puh kānri mé wo wishtalo no da kūsé taraf ta wozghalédalo.*
The thief jumped into the street and got up by the ladder	*Ghal kūsé ta wo dangal aw puh andrapāya bāndé woʀhatalo.*
Have you seen him ?	*Tā hagha lidalay day ?*
Why cannot you cross ?	*Walé pōré watalay nuh shé ?*
The Colonel fell off his horse and broke his arm	*Karnail sahib luh ass na préwato aw lās yé māt sho.*
I cannot climb the hill.	*Zuh puh ghar khatalay nuh sham.*
I left the book on the table	*Kitab ra na puh méz pāté sho,*
I left Peshawar on the 20th	*Puh shalam tārikh zuh luh pékhawar na rawān shwam.*
Pull this motor car to that village.	*Dā mōtar dagha kali ta rākāga.*
Whose round was it last night ?	*Bégā da chā gusht woh ?*
I shall stop this custom	*Dā dastūr ba zuh band kram.*
What will the people say ?	*Khalq ba suh wāyee ?*

Why do you not tell me the whole truth ?	*Tōla rishtiā khabara walé nuh kawé ?*
Give me a clean handkerchief.	*Yau pāk rūmāl rākra.*
Thank you for your trouble.	*Zuh stā da rabar da pāra déra shukria adā kawam.*
Every thing is very dear.	*Har shay dér grān day.*
We are paying famine rates.	*Puh mūng bāndé da qahat narkhūna dee.*
Keep it in your house ; I will take it when I come back from the camp.	*Puh khpal kōr ké yé wo sāta chi luh parāw na biarta rāsham, no ba yé wākhlam.*
There will be a big parade tomorrow.	*Sabāla ba yau loi parait wee.*
The General will inspect the Regt.	*Jarnail sāhib ba do paltané mulāhiza kawee.*
It is very cold today, snow will fall on the hills.	*Nan déra yakhnī dah puh ghrūno ba wāwra préwozee.*
Try once more ! I am sure you will do it this time.	*Yau zal biā kōshash wo kra, zamā yaqīn day chi dā zal khuh shān sara ba yé wo kré.*
You mind your business!	*Tuh khpal kār kawa !*
Who has brought this letter ?	*Chā dā chitai rāworé dah ?*
To whom did you take the letter.	*Chā ta dé chitai yaura.*
Can you show me the way to Shahi Bagh ?	*Da shāhi bāgh lār rā ta khayalay shé ?*

I cannot understand what you say.	*Zuh stā puh khabara nuh pōhégam.*
Is there any drinking water near the camp?	*Parāw ta nizdé da skalō obuh shta?*
How do you do?	*Suh hāl day?*
Does this road lead to Pabbi.	*Dā lār pabo ta talé dah?*

VOCABULARY XXXII.

زری	*zaray*	Guide.
خطا کول	*khatā kawal*	To miss.
ورک کول	*vrak kawal*	To lose.
پۀ وخت	*puh wakht*	In time.
منل	*manal*	To obey.
الوځول	*alūzawal*	To blow up to make to fly.
چاودل	*chāudal*	To split, burst.
چوم	*chwam*	(Present.)
فتح موندل	*fatah mūndal*	To gain victory.
بری موندل	*baray mūndal*	To gain victory.
شکست ورکول	*shikast warkawal*	To defeat.
شکست خوړل	*shikast khwaral*	To be defeated.
شکایت کول	*shekāyat kawal*	To complain.
برابر	*barābar*	Proper, reasonable.
پۀ بیعه اخستل	*puh baya akhistal*	To buy.
شفارس کول	*shafāras kawal*	To recommend.
بار کول	*bār kawal*	To load. (animal).

سپک	*spak*	Light.
دروند	*drūnd*	Heavy.
پایه	*pāya*	Wheel.
جُرم	*jurum*	Crime.
سزا ورکول	*sazā warkawal*	To punish.
سزا موندل	*sazā mūndal*	To be punished.
غوښتل	*ghukhtal*	To ask for.
بیان کول	*biān kawal*	To explain.
ټوله قصه	*tōla qisa*	The whole story.
بد ګنړل	*bad ganral*	To feel offended.
همیشه دَ پاره	*hamésha da pāra*	For good, for always, for ever.
کهٔ نهٔ وِی	*kuh nuh wi*	Otherwise.
هسی نهٔ وی	*hasé nuh wi*	Lest.

EXERCISE 31.

1. If he had come, I would have seen him. 2. If you had sent me a letter, I would have answered it. 3. If you had worked hard, you would have passed the examination. 4. Had they been loyal, the Government would have rewarded them. 5. If our guide had not lost his way, we should have reached the hill in time. 6. Had you accepted it, it would have been all right. 7. If the sentry had fired at the outlaw, he would have certainly killed him 8. If we had not blown up the fort, we could

not have gained the victory. 9. If the enemy had crossed the river we would have defeated them. 10. If I had not enlisted in the Army, I should not have become a Subadar. 11. If you had not struck him, he would not have complained to the police. 12. If you had charged (asked for) a reasonable price, I should have bought it from you. 13. If you had done well, I would have recommended you to the Colonel 14. If you had loaded it lightly the wheel would not have broken. 15. If you had not committed this crime, I would not have punished you 16. If you had asked for ten days leave I would have certainly given it to you. 17. Had I seen you in the bazar I would have told you the whole story. 18. If you had not come he would have killed me. 19. If the old man had not laughed, I should not have felt so offended. 20. If I had not felt so offended, I should not have run away, but I did not mean to run away for good, otherwise I should not have come back.

VOCABULARY XXXIII.

عدالت	*adālat*	Court.
وختی	*wakhti*	Early.
ناوخته	*nāwakhta*	Late.
سُستی	*susti*	Laziness.
لُو کوتي	*lūkūti*	Little.

اسانئ سره	*asānai sara*	Easily.
بی لهٔ ربړ نه	*bé lūh rabar na*	Without trouble.
راویښ کیدل	*rāwikh kédal*	To wake up (Intransitive.)
کنډر کول	*kandar kawal*	To burgle.
ارت	*art*	Broad, wide.
لهٔ نه پهٔ لانبو پوریوتل	*luh-na puh lānbo pōré-watal*	To swim across.
دولت	*daulat*	Riches.
متل	*matal*	Proverb.
دوکان کول	*dūkān kawal*	To be a shopkeeper.
دَ باد شاه لوُر به مِ کړی وَه	*da bādshāh lūr ba mé karé wah*	I would have married the king's daughter.
مُتیازی کول	*mutyāzé kawal*	To make water, urinate.
معامله	*māméla*	Affair.

Exercise 32.

١ كهٔ دَ كور خاوند وړ باندِ را غليَ وےَ نو غل به ئی نيوليَ وَهٔ ٢ كهٔ ګرمي زياته نهٔ وےَ نو زهٔ به كشمير ته تليَ نهٔ وم ٣ كهٔ زهٔ ناجوړ شويَ نهٔ وےَ نو زهٔ به پهٔ عدالت كښې حاضر شويَ وم ٤ كهٔ لار خرابه نهٔ وےَ نو موټر به وختي رسيدلې ؤو ٥ كهٔ دَ كلي خلقو سُستي كړيَ نهٔ وےَ نو داړه ماران به ئي ټول نيولې ؤو. ٦ كهٔ تهٔ او كوټي وختي راغليَ وےَ نو ټول انتظام به پهٔ وخت شويَ وهٔ ٧ كهٔ اوبهٔ ډيرې وےَ نو فصلونه به ښهٔ شوي ؤو او موټر به

ما لیه اسانئی سره ورکولی شوه ۸ زهٔ درنه دومره لوی یم چه کهٔ
زهٔ اوښ وی نو تهٔ به خر وی ۹ کهٔ پهٔ نیمه شپه کښې راویښ شوی
نهٔ وی نو غلو به م پهٔ کور کښې کنډر کړی وُهٔ ۱۰ کهٔ سیند ارت
نهٔ وی نو مونږ به ورنه پهٔ لانبو پوریوتی وُو ۱۱ کهٔ یَو نهٔ مړکیدی
نو بل به خهٔ خوړل کهٔ دولت راسخه نهٔ وی نو یو دوست به م هم نهٔ وُه
۱۲ کهٔ باران شوی نه وی نو دَ سکلو اوبهٔ به هم نهٔ وی ۱۳ کهٔ
خمونږ بیټونه پهٔ غرهٔ باندِ ابریدلی نهٔ وی نو دشمن به پهٔ پړاؤ باندِ
حمله کړی وَه ۱۴ کهٔ زه پښتون نهٔ وی نو به م دوکان کړی وُه ۱۵ کهٔ
دولت راسخه وی نو به م دَ بادشاه لوُر کړی وَه ۱۶ کهٔ زهٔ متیازو دَ پاره
باهر وتی نهٔ وی نو دا معامله به م لیدلی نهٔ وَه ۱۷ کهٔ اپریدی م
نیکهٔ قتل کړی نهٔ وی نو ورسره به م داسی سخته بدی نهٔ وَه
۱۸ کهٔ انګریزی م زده کولی نو اوس به لوی بابوُ وم ۱۹ کهٔ زهٔ
لاړ نهٔ شم نوټول مال به م بربادشیِ ۲۰ کهٔ زهٔ پخیله راتلی شوی
نو ډیره ښه به وَه مګر نهٔ شوم راتلی—

VOCABULARY XXXIV.

مړ کیدل	*mar kédal*	To die.
لوږه	*lwaga*	Hunger.
هم پهٔ هغه معامله کښې	*hum puh hagha māméla ké*	In the same case.
قسم خوړل	*qasam khwaral*	To swear.
له ټولو نه لنډه لار	*la tōlō na landa lār*	The shortest road.
پهٔ-بانډِ ورختل	*puh-bāndé warkhatal*	To invade.
نوی	*naway*	New.

خرڅ کول	*khars kawal*	To sell, spend.
بائسکل	*baiskal*	Bicycle.
زهٔ تبی نیولیَ یم	*zuh tabé niwalay yam*	I have caught fever
زهٔ یخنئی وهلیَ یم	*zuh yakhnai wahalay yam*	I have caught cold.
ځما سر خوږ یږی	*zamā sar khūgégee*	I have a headache.
پهٔ هغهٔ باندِ ننکئ ختلی دی	*puh haghuh bāndé nanakai khatalé di*	He has small pox.
ملګریَ	*malgaray*	Companion.
بله میاشت	*bala miāsht*	Next month.
تیره میاشت	*téra miāsht*	Last month.
سر	*sar*	Head
سترګه	*starga*	An eye.
پوزه	*pōza*	Nose.
غاښ	*ghākh*	Tooth.
خولهٔ	*khuluh*	Mouth.
ژبهٔ	*jhuba*	Tongue, language.
مخ	*makh*	Face.
غوږ	*ghwag*	Ear.
مرئ	*marai*	Throat.
څټ	*sat*	Back of neck.
شا	*shā*	Back.
زړهٔ	*zruh*	Heart.
پړ پوس	*parpus*	Lung.
کُناټیَ	*kunātay*	Buttock.

پتوُن *patūn*	Thigh.
ډوډی *dūday*	Hip.
تشی *tashay*	Loin.
ښپه *khpa*	Foot, leg.
زنګون *zangūn*	Knee.
ګوته *gōta*	Finger.
تلی *taḷāy*	Sole of foot, palm of hand.

EXERCISE 33.

1. He said he was going to Persia. 2. They said that they were dying of (from) hunger. 3. The Magistrate answered that he was still enquiring into the same case. 4. He asked me what had become of my dog. 5. I asked him if he was prepared to come with me (to go with me) to the city. 6. He swore that he did not see this man with his own eyes. 7. He asked me which was the shortest way to the city. 8. I asked him why was he staying in the hotel. 9. He thought that he also came to the office on the same day. 10. The general concluded that it was difficult for him to invade the country during the winter. 11. He said his son was cleverer than his daughter. 12. The Major himself said that he would take me with him to Afghanistan. 13. He said his son could not ride my black mare. 14. They

replied that they wanted 10 days leave. 15. Did he say he was new to the country and that he did not know the custom of the village? 16. Did you say you were thirsty and that you wanted to drink some water ? 17. He said he would sell his bicycle. 18. Tell my reader to bring all the papers. 19. The next day I caught fever, I therefore told my companion that I could not go before the 1st, of next month. 20. Every body seems to have a cold, it is bad weather. 21. You must have written this letter, do you not remember ?

VOCABULARY XXXV.

تیارۀ	*tyāruh*	Darkness.
رڼړا	*ranrā*	Light (day.)
رڼړا ورځ	*ranrā vraz*	Broad daylight.
دومره لری	*dōmra laré*	So far.
بادشاهي	*bādshāhi*	Kingdom.
ځموږ فصلونه په باران کیږي	*zāmūng faslūna puh bārān kégee*	Our crops are dependent on the rain fall.
ظلم	*zulum*	Tyranny.
ظالم	*zālém*	Tyrant.
هیرول	*hérawal*	To forget.
باور کول	*bāwar kawal*	To believe.
فیصله-کول	*faisala kawal*	To decide, settle.
ما ښۀ پوه کړ	*mā khuh poh kar*	I made him understand well.

يوه پيسه *yawa paīsa* Single pice.
كوټه روپيۍ *kōta rupi* Bad rupee.

EXERCISE 34.

۱ ار دلي جواب راكړ چه زهٔ ستا نوكر خو نهٔ يم زهٔ دَ سركار
نوكريم ۲ بيائي وو چه پهٔ تيارهٔ كښې ماسړىَ ليدلىَ نهٔ شو ۳ دَ دې
علاقې خلق وائي چه موږ جوار كرلي وُو مگر چه اوبهٔ كمې وې نو ونهٔ
شوُ ۴ كليوالو وو چه تر صبا پورې به موږ دَ ماليئې معافولو دَ پاره
ډپټي كمشنر صاحب ته درخواست وركړوُ ۵ صاحب وو چه زهٔ به
ځلور ورځې پس له دورې نه بيرته راشم ۶ دَ كلو هلكانو وو چه
دومره لرې مدرسې ته تلل موږ دَپاره گران كار دىَ ۷ سليم وو چه زهٔ
دَ بادشاهئ هيڅ پروا نهٔ كوم ۸ دَ دې وطن ټول فصلو نه پهٔ باران
كيږي ۹ ما ته ئې وو چه بيشكه تهٔ ښما وروړئې مگر ستا ظُلم
نهٔ شم هيرولىَ ۱۰ ځوىِ م راته وو چه ښما بائسكل ستا له موټر نه
گړندىَ دىَ ۱۱ ملك وو ښما دَ كلي خلق داسې هوښيار نهٔ دي
چه تا ويپژني چه تهٔ ښموږ تحصيلدار ئې ۱۲ ښما لهٔ رسيدو نه
اول ئې را ته خبر ليږلىَ وُه چه پلارِ د مړشوىَ دىَ ۱۳ ماورته وو
چه زهٔ ستا پهٔ خبره باور نهٔ شم كولىَ ۱۴ خان سلام راليږلىَ دىَ
او وائي چه صبا به زهٔ پخپله ستا ليدلو دَ پاره راشم ۱۵ گل جان
پاڅيد او وئې وِ چه زهٔ پهٔ جرگه فيصله نهٔ كوم ۱۶ آستاذ وويل چه
ما ټولو هلكانو ته وويل چه خپل خپل نوم پهٔ بورډ بلند وليكئىَ
۱۷ رحمت وو چه ښما كلىَ له دې ځائې نه سل ميلَ لرې دىَ
۱۸ پهٔ كرُسئ باند كيناست او را ته ئې وو چه دپلاټن د څهٔ حال دىَ
۱۹ ورته م وو چه زهٔ به ستا پهٔ ځائ كار كوم ۲۰ ما څهٔ پوه كړ چه
كهٔ بيادِ داسې كار وكړ نو يوه پيسه طلب به در نهٔ كړم—

VOCABULARY XXXVI.

پهٔ غلا تلل	*puh ghalā tlal*	To be stolen.
برنډه	*baranda*	Verandah.
مشکل سره	*mushkil sara*	With difficulty.
نيول	*niwal*	To catch, arrest
راضى	*rāzi*	Willing, satisfied.
نوکرى کول	*naukari kawal*	To serve.
هيڅوک	*hésōk*	No one.
تاريخ	*tārikh*	Date.
دا	*dā*	The following, this.
بيان	*bayān*	Explanation, statement.
دانه	*dāna*	Grain.
وسله	*wasla*	Arms.
وسله دار سړى	*wasla dār saray*	Armed man.
ما خبر کړه	*mā khabar kra*	Let me know.
تلاؤ	*talāw*	Tank.
ډنډ	*dand*	Pond of water.
لهٔ نه ډک	*luh-na dak*	Full of.
رڼړى اوبهٔ	*ranré obūh*	Clear water.
خړى اوبهٔ	*kharé obuh*	Muddy water.
دَ هغهٔ مطلب دا وهٔ	*da haghuh matlab dā woh*	He meant.
هوار کول	*howār kawal*	To level
واښهٔ مشين کول	*wākhuh mashin kawal*	To cut grass with a mower.

گوډ کول	*gōd kawal*	To weed.
ځنګل ويستل	*zangal wistal*	To weed.
وسله کيښودل	*wasla kèkhōdal*	To surrender.

EXERCISE 35.

1. My bicycle has been stolen from the veranda, please inform the Police. 2. 10 days leave was granted to him with great difficulty. 3. The letter was written and sent at once. 4. The doctor was sent for, but we could not understand what he was talking about, as he could not speak Pushtu. 5. The father was killed and the son was arrested. 6. Ask him if he is willing to serve in the Cavalry. 7. No one was seen on the spot. 8. I cannot shoot birds and animals flying and running besides I cannot afford to buy a shot gun. 9. Yesterday the Adjutant called me to the office and I made the following statement. 10. At what time do you feed the horses? 11. If you see any armed man let us know. 12. It is all very well for you to bring up recruits of this type, but they will certainly not be passed by me. 13. Tell all the non-commissioned Officers that the Officer Commanding wants to see them at 10 o'clock outside the office. 14. I saw him running

towards the cantonment. 15. This tank is always full of clear water. 16. The doctor asked me if I had bitten his dog. 17. I laughed when he said this, because he really meant to ask whether his dog had bitten me. 18. When a murder is committed in Lahore, do you make all the Nawabs and Sardars responsible? 19. Tell the mali that while I am away he must cut the grass and take out all weeds. 20. Tell him to make tea and put it on the table at 3-30.

VOCABULARY XXXVII

بوڼړ	*būnr*	Dwarf-palm string for making beds.
میزری	*mézaray*	Dwarf palm.
ګذران یا ګذاره	*guzrān* or *guzāra*	Living.
(سره) بدنام کیدل	*(sara) badnām kédal*	To get bad name (with).
ټبر	*tabar*	Family.
هاله	*halā*	Then.
بدی	*badi*	Feud.
خلاص کول	*khlās kawal*	To finish, settle.
لۀ یو بل نه	*la yāu bal na*	From one another.
یو بل سره	*yau bal sara*	With one another.
خشاک	*khashāk*	Firewood.

جرنده	*jranda*	Water mill.
میچن	*méchan*	Hand mill.
کار روزگار	*kār rōzgār*	Work etc.
برج	*braj*	Tower.
یو بل باندې	*yau bal bāndé*	On one another.
(پهٔ-باندې) ډز کول	*(puh-bāndé) daz kawal*	To fire at.
طرف	*taraf*	Side. party.
برابر	*barābar*	Equal.
قام یا قوم	*qām*	Tribe.
مشر	*mashar*	Elder.
جوړه یا روغه یا صلح	*jōra, rōgha, sula*	Peace.
کاڼړی	*kanray*	Stone.
برخلاف	*barkhélāf*	Against.
(پهٔ-باندې) دعوي کول	*(puh-bāndé) dāwa kawal*	To claim, to charge, (against).
مدعی	*mudāi*	Plaintiff.
مدعالیه	*mudālay*	Defendant.
سیزل یا سوزول	*sézal* or *swazawal*	To burn.
سوزیدل	*swazédal*	To be burnt.
مقدمه	*muqadéma*	Case.
ثبوت	*sabūt*	Proof.
ثابت کول	*sābet kawal*	To prove.
منکر کیدل	*munkar kédal*	To deny.
(لهٔ-نه) انکار کول	*(luh-na) inkār kawal*	To refuse.

پهٔ کانړی باندِ ویشتل	*puh kānri bāndé wishtal*	To throw a stone at
جګړه کول	*jagara kawal*	To quarrel.
قاضی	*qāzi*	Judge.
ګانړه کول	*gānra kawal*	To mortgage.
څومره چه دَ وس مِ کیږی دومره کوشش به کوم	*sōmra chi da wasa mé kégee dōmra kōshash ba kawam*	I will try my best.
حق	*haq*	Right.
اسمان شین دی	*asmān shin day*	It is clear (to-day.)
کهٔ دِ خوښه وی	*kuh dé khwakha wi*	If you like.
جوپه	*jōpa*	Trading party.
سختی	*sakhti*	Hardship, Evil day.
پهٔ کار راتلل	*puh kār rātlal*	To be useful to
طبیب	*tabib*	Doctor, a physician
بیماری یا ناجوړتیا	*bimāri* or *nājōrtia*	Disease.
رنځ	*ranz*	Disease.
رنځور	*ranzūr*	Patient (in hospital)
پوزَی	*puzay*	Matting.

EXERCISE 36.

۱ پهٔ ژمیِ کښِں دَ غیر علاقی خلق لرګیِ اومیزریِ او پوزی دَ پیښور پهٔ ښهر کښِں خرڅ دَ پاره راوړیِ او پهٔ دی باندِ ګزران کویِ

۲ څوکیدار وائیِ چه پهٔ دی طلب باندِ څما ګزاره نه کیږیِ یا مِ.

طلب زیات کړه او یا چوټي راکړه ۳ دَ اپریدو دا دستور دےَ چه
یوه ښځه چا سره بدنامه شي نو خپلوان دا ښځه هم هغه سړي ته
ورو شړي او تر هغه به ئې ورسره بدي وي چه دوه سړي ورنه
ونه وژني ۴ کله کله دا بدي تر پېړو پورې چلیږي او دَ یو بل
نه سړي وژني ۵ ښځې ئې دَ خټکَ واښهٔ او خشاک راوړي
جرنده کوي دَ کور ټول کار روزګار کوي او سړي ئې پهٔ برجونو کښې
ناست وي او پهٔ یو بل سره ډزې کوي ۶ پهٔ بدئ کښې ښځې
نهٔ وژلي ۷ چه دواړه طرف پهٔ قتلونو کښې برابر شي نو دَ
قام سپین ږیري را جمع شي جوړه ئې وکړي ۸ کهٔ یو طرف پړ وي
او بل وړ وي نو دَ اړې مډې دَ پاره کاڼي کیږدي چه کارتوسونه
او غله ځان ته واچوي نو پهٔ مقرر وخت کاڼي ئې مات شي
۹ کهٔ پهٔ روغه کښې چا پهٔ یو بل ډز وکړ نو ټول قام ور باندې را جمع
شي کلي ئې وسیزي ۱۰ پهٔ دې مقدمه کښې ثبوت نهٔ وُه ځکه
ټانړه دار هیڅ نهٔ شو کولے ۱۱ مدعي وو چه څلور کال کیږي چه
ما ورته څلوېښت روپئې ورکړې دي ۱۲ مدعا علیه منکر شهٔ
او وئې وې چه زهٔ تا نهٔ پیژنم تهٔ څوک ئې ۱۳ ډیرې جګړې کولو
پس موږ قاضي ته لاړو ۱۴ قاضي ورته وې چه تا دَ دې سړي
مال ولې پټ کړے دے ۱۵ زمکه مې کانړه کړه او څوئ له مې پرې واده
وکړ ۱۶ څومره چه دَ وس مې کیږي دومره کوشش به وکړم چه ستا
حق ثابت شي ۱۷ اسمان شین دے ورځ ښه دهٔ جوپې به راشي
۱۸ دوست هغه دے چه پهٔ سختئ کښې پکار راشي ۱۹ چه
غلائي وشوه نو څوکیدارئې وساتلو ۲۰ طبیب دَ هغې بیمارئ علاج
پهٔ ښهٔ شان سره کولے شي چه ور باندې پخپله تېره شوې وي -

VOCABULARY XXXVIII.

پایاؤ	*pāyāw*	Shallow.
پۀ مخ کښې	*puh makh ké*	Further on, in front.
(سره) خبرې کول	*(sara) khabaré kawal*	To converse with. to talk to.
نو	*no*	So, then.
لواړه ژبه کول	*lwāra jhuba kawal*	To speak indistinctly.
ژور	*jhawar*	Deep..
کُنډه	*kunda*	Widow.
کنډاؤ	*kandāw*	A gap (in wall etc).
کندوُ	*kandū*	Corn bin.
کنده	*kanda*	Abyss.
کنډه	*kand*	A small scale.
کُنډۍ	*kundai*	Wooden cup
(ته) طلاق ور کول	*(ta) talāq warkāwal*	To divorce.
زنا	*zanā*	Adultery.
تربوُر	*tarbūr*	Cousin.
رضا	*razā*	Furlough.
وبا گډه دهَ	*wabā gada dah*	Cholera is prevalent.
اجازت	*ijāzat*	Permission.
مینځ	*mianz*	Middle.
سفر	*safar*	Journey.
پۀ مخه راتلل	*puh makha rātlal*	To meet.
لۀ لاس نه	*luh lās na*	By the hand,

گواه یا شاهد	*gawāh* or *shāhad*	Witness.
گواهی یا شاهدي	*gawāhi* or *shāhdi*	Evidence.
سپینه سپوږمئي	*spina spōgmai*	Bright moonlight.
لهٔ کمری نه وتل	*luh kamrė na watal*	To leave the room.
کوټه	*kōta*	Room.
زورور باران	*zōrawar bārān*	Heavy rain.
سیند ختلی دی	*sind khatalay day*	The river rose, has risen.
وړل	*vral*	To carry.
پُل	*pul*	Bridge.
گودر	*gūdar*	Ferry.
زورور باد	*zōrawar bād*	Strong wind.
(سره) واقف	*sara wāqif*	Acquainted (person.)
لهٔ-نه واقف	*(luh-na) wāqif*	Acquainted (language.)
(پهٔ-کښې) واقف	*(puh-kė) wāqif*	Acquainted (country.)
پهٔ پهم سره	*puh paham sara*	Carefully.
زړهٔ	*zruh*	Heart.
پهٔ زړهٔ سره	*puh zruh sara*	Attentively.
محاوره	*muhāwera*	Idiom.
دَ خبرو سړی	*da khabaro saray*	Converser.
کمَی	*kamay*	Scarcity.

ضلع	*zela*	District.
ويستلى تۆره	*wistalé tūra*	Drawn sword.
ستړى	*staray*	Tired.
اوده کيدل	*ūduh kédal*	To sleep.
ويشل	*wéshal*	To divide.

EXERCISE 37.

1. The water is shallow here, but further on it is very deep. 2. How many sepoys are there who wish to speak to me? 3. You speak so fast and indistinctly that I can not understand a word you say. 4. Her husband is dead she is now a widow. 5. I have heard that he has divorced her. 6. Subadar, how many men of your company are on furlough? Have them all recalled at once. 7. Owing to the prevalence of cholera in the city, the people of the city are not allowed to come into the cantonment. 8. In the middle of our journey we met an old man, whom a little boy was leading by the hand. 9. One witness has stated that the night was dark and another that it was bright moonlight. 10. Ahmad Khan left the room where the Deputy Commissioner was sitting. 11. Owing to the heavy rain in Swat, the Kabul river rose and carried away the bridge. 12. I have come to make a report that at 2-30 last night Jan Mohammad killed his own father. 13. How long

before that were you acquainted with him? 14. How long have you been learning Pushtu? 15. If you study the Pushtu idioms attentively and carefully listen to your converser, you will soon be able to speak the language and understand others. 16. Why did you tell me that my father had arrived? 17. On account of scarcity of rain there is little grass in the District. 18. I saw a man running with a drawn sword in his hand. 19. I am tired, I did not sleep last night. 20. Divide the money among these people.

VOCABULARY XXXIX

لوټ کول	*lūt kawal*	To loot.
ماشوم	*māshūm*	Little child.
بهانه	*bahāna*	Pretence.
پهٔ چغه تلل	*puh chagha tlal*	To pursue.
دَ پاره دَ دې	*da pāra da dé*	In order to, for this purpose.
را خلاص کول	*rā khlās kawal*	To release.
بونګه	*bōnga*	Ransom.
دَ دروغو ګواهي	*da daroghō gawāhi*	False evidence.
نرخ	*narkh*	Rate.
څرول	*sarawal*	To graze.
اګر کهٔ	*agar kuh*	Although.
همسايه	*hamsāya*	Tenant.

همسایه گان *hamsāyagān* Tenants.

میلمستیا *mélmastiā* Hospitality.

میلمه دوست *melma dost* Hospitable.

حج *haj* Pilgrimage.

حاجی *hāji* Pilgrim.

ورته حاجی صاحب وائی *warta hāji sāhib wāyee* He is called pilgrim.

جوړیدل *jōrédal* To be made.

معلومیدل *mālūmédal* To look like, to seem

کارتوس *kārtūs* Cartridge.

پا له اسانه *pā la asāna* Easily.

دَ غره لمن *da ghruh laman* Skirt of the hill.

زرکه *zarka* Chikor.

تنزری *tanzaray* Partridge

کرونده *karwanda* Newly sown crops.

ښهٔ ویشتونکی *khuh wishtūnkay* A good shot.

پهٔ لږ ساعت کښې *puh lag sāat ké* In a short time.

یوی کول *yawé kawal* To plough.

تیریدل *térédal* To pass by.

ناگهانه *nāgahāna* By chance.

خطا کیدل *khatā kédal* To be missed.

عن *an* Right-up to, right down to.

لګیدل *lagédal* To be hit, to be struck against.

چرګ بانګ مالی *charg bāng malé* At dawn.

ملا بانګ مالې	*mulā bāng mālé*	At the time of early call to prayer.
ګنړه یا کنې	*ganṛa* or *kani*	Otherwise.

Exercise 38.

۱ پۀ کلي داړه پریوته دَیو هندو کورئی لوټ کړ او یو ماشوم
څوړ ئی بوت ۲ دَ کلي خلقو هسې بها نه وکړه چه داړې پسې
پۀ چغه تلي یو دَپاره د دې چه پۀ کلي جرم پرې نۀ وشي ۳ کۀ
دا دَچا مسلمان څوئ وې نو کلیوالو به ضرور راخلاص کړې وۀ
مګر اوس دَ دې هلک راخلاصولو دَ پاره یوه لویه بونګه به پکار وي
۵ زۀ به ور باندې پۀ عدالت کښې دعوې وکړم او وکیل به ورله ونیسم
۶ کۀ ګواهان پکارشي نو پۀ ښهر کښې ډیر دي ۷ دَ دروغو ګواهي
وِرکولو دَپاره پنځۀ روپئې نرخ دې ۸ صاحب موږ پۀ خپلو غرونوکښې
مال څرولو او دَ دوئ دَ قام لس سړي رابانده راغلل ټول مال ئی
رانه بوتلو ۹ اګر کۀ موږ هلکان یو خو کۀ ټوپکونه راسره وې نو
مال ئی را نه نۀ شو بیولې ۱۰ هغه مشهور سړی دی او ډیر همسایه
ګان لري او ډیر میلمه دوست سړی دی ۱۱ دوه ځل ئی حج کړی دی،
ځکه ورته خلق حاجی صاحب وائي ۱۲ دروغ خو بالکل نۀ وائي
۱۳ سپي غاپي ګوره چه غل خو نشته ۱۴ دَ کوهاټ پۀ دره کښې
ډیر ښۀ ټوپکونه جوړیږي ۱۵ چه ماښام شي نو دَغرۀ نه زرکې
او تنزرې راکوز شي او پۀ کروندو کښې غنم او اوربشې خوري کۀ
سړی ښۀ ویشتونکی وي نو پۀ لږ ساعت کښې به دیرش څلویښت
مرغان ولي ۱۶ ما یوې کوله او دې پۀ لار تیریدو ناګهانه یئی
رابانده ډز وکړ زۀ خطا شوم ولې غوایئم ولړیدو ۱۷ چه ماپرې ډز
وکړ نو عن پۀ سر ولړیدو را پریوتۀ او مړ شو ۱۸ کۀ هغۀ رابانده اول

ږز کړی نهٔ وی نو زهٔ خو لیونی نهٔ وم چه ما به ور باندِ ږز کاوهٔ
۱۹ چرګ بانګ مالی روانیدل پکار دي ګنړه ګاډی ته به ونه رسی
۲۰ لهٔ دی ځایِ نه تر لواړګي پوری خوړه کرائيِ لګړيِ—

VOCABULARY XL.

جاهل	*jāhel*	Ignorant.
پره جنبه	*para junba*	Faction feeling.
پهٔ خپلو کښِ	*pūh khpalo ké*	Among themselves.
وران کیدل	*vrān kédal*	To be ruined, to go wrong.
مسافر	*musāfar*	Traveller.
سلامت	*salāmat*	Safe.
سلامتِی	*salāmati*	Safety.
ویره	*vyara*	Fear, danger.
ویره ناک	*vyara nāk*	Dangerous.
لهٔ قچری نه بار کوز کول	*luh qacharé na bār kūz kawal*	To unload mule.
ګاډی تش کول	*gāday tash kawal*	To unload cart.
غوا	*ghwa*	Cow.
غوایهٔ	*ghwāyuh*	Bullock (Plural *ghwāyān.*)
پهٔ څو دِ اخستی دی	*puh so dé akhistay day?*	How much did you pay for it?
خیمه یا تنبو	*khéma* or *tanbū*	Tent.
تنبوُ لګول	*tambū lagawal*	To pitch a tent.

دَ اوبو څوکۍ	*da obo saukai*	Picquet on the water supply.
سخت جُرم	*sakht juram*	Serious crime.
متيزه کول	*matiza kawal*	To elope.
کوشش کول	*kōshash kawal*	To try.
پهٔ روپو باندِ فيصله کول	*puh rūpo bāndé faisala kawal*	To make a money settlement.
ونهٔ شو	*wo nuh sho*	Did not become, failed.
بدرګه	*badraga*	Escort.
تاوان ور کول	*tāwān war kawal*	To compensate.
څهٔ وشوٓ	*suh wo shoo ?*	What happened ?
ژبه دِ وباسه	*jhuba dé wo bāsa*	Put out your tongue.
دارُو	*dārū*	Medicine or gun powder.
کهٔ نهٔ وي	*kuh nuh wi*	Otherwise.
تبه به در باندِ بيا راشي	*taba ba dar bāndé biā rāshee*	You will catch fever again.
چاى کار	*chalé kār*	Cultivator.
دَ زمکى خاوند	*da zmaké khāwand*	Land owner.
شپږمه حصه	*shpagama hisa*	1/6th part.
پيدا وار	*paidā wār*	Produce.
لږ لاندِ	*lag lāndé*	Lower down.

کهٔ زر کړې	*kuh zar kré*	If you make haste.
ګړۍ	*garai*	Watch.
ګړی ساز	*gari sāz*	Watch maker.
زما ګړی ورانه ده	*zamā garai vrāna dah*	My watch has gone wrong.
پهٔ چا باندې مرمت کول	*puh chā bāndé muramat kawal*	To have repaired.
پهٔ صبانئی ورځ	*puh sabānai vraz*	Tomorrow week.
پهٔ ننئی ورځ	*puh nananai vraz*	This day week.
پهٔ پرونئی ورځ	*puh parūnai vraz*	Yesterday week.
لاس تړلی	*lās taralay*	Hands tied.
رسئی پهٔ غاړه	*rasai puh ghāra*	With a rope round one's neck.
واښهٔ پهٔ خولې	*wākhuh puh khulé*	Grass in one's mouth.
مریی	*mrayay*	Slave.
وینځه	*winza*	Slave girl
کړکئ	*karkai*	Window.
جمع کیدل	*jama kédal*	To be collected. assemble.
انتظار کول	*intézār kawal*	To wait.
چاندماری	*chāndmārai*	Musketry, range.
دَ ګولو کارتوسونه	*da gōlō kārtūsūna*	Ball cartridges.
شلخی کارتوسونه	*shalkhi kārtūsūna*	Blank cartridges.

هړ سړيِ د پاره يا *har sari da*
دَ هر سړی پۀ سړ *para* or *da har*
sari puh sar For each man.

EXERCISE 39.

1. They are ignorant people and owing to faction feeling and their fighting among themselves, the country is being ruined. 2. Travellers do not go that way now, all the roads being unsafe. 3. Unload the mules first and then unload the carts. 4. Is this cow for sale, how much do you want for it and how much did you pay for it? 5. if the General pitches his camp on that spot, there is danger that the picquet on the water supply will be attacked from the pass. 6. My brother's son has committed a serious crime. 7. He eloped with a malak's wife and ran away to the hills. 8. We tried to make a money settlement, but failed. 9. If these villagers send their cattle to graze without a proper escort and refuse to send out a pursuit party after them when they are stolen, the Govt. will certainly refuse them compensation. 10. What has happened to the old man who killed Sarfaraz? 11. Put out your tongue; you must take this medicine at once otherwise the fever will recur. 12. The cultivator gets 1/6th of the produce from the land owner. 13. The boatman has gone away but there is a ford lower down and if

you make haste you can cross the river before sunset. 14. My watch has gone wrong, tell the bearer to have it repaired. 15. Come tomorrow week, the office will then be open. 16. He came in with his hands tied, with rope round his neck and grass in his mouth and fell at the Deputy Commissioner's feet and said "I am your slave." 17. Open all the windows while I am sitting here. 18. At midnight the troops assembled on the bridge and waited for the next order. 19. Take the recruits to the range tomorrow and have every thing ready there before the Adjutant arrives. 20. Take 10 rounds of ball and 10 rounds of blank for each man.

VOCABULARY XLI.

بلوه	*balwa*	Riot.
ژوبل کېدل	*jhōbal kédal*	To be wounded.
پۀ آخرکښې	*puh ākhér ké*	In the end.
پۀ شروع کښې	*puh shurū ké*	At the beginning.
عمری قید کېدل	*ūmri qéd kédal*	To be sentenced to transportation for life.
پۀ-بانډې دپانسۍ	*puh-bāndé da*	
حکم کېدل	*pānsai hukam kédal*	To be sentenced to death.
إعتبار نۀ دی پکار	*itebār nuh day pakār*	One must not be trusted.
إعتبار	*itébār*	Trust.

ملگری	*malgaray*	Companion.
محصول	*mahsūl*	Toll, custom duty.
سوداگر	*saudāgar*	Merchant.
گټه	*gata*	Profit.
فائده	*fāida*	Benefit.
مزدور	*mazdūr*	Labourer.
مزدوري	*mazdūri*	Labour, wages.
گذاره کول	*guzāra kawal*	To make a living.
زخم یا پرهر	*zakhām* or *parhar*	Wound.
نو یا زوه	*naw* or *zawa*	Pus.
خوار	*khwār*	Poor fellow.
اوږه	*uga*	Shoulder.
چپ چوړ	*chap chúr*	Shattered.
اودس ماتي له	*audas māti la*	
تلل	*tlal*	To go to make water.
اودس کول	*audas kawal*	To wash for prayer.
چينه	*china*	Spring of water.
مونځ کول	*munz kawal*	To pray,
مانځه دپاره	*mānzuh da pāra*	For prayer (Oblique.)
څنکي	*sankai*	Post.
تار	*tār*	Wire, telegram.
باراني زمکه	*bārāni zmaka*	Unirrigated land.
قيد	*qaid*	Locked up, imprisonment.
بدن وجود	*badan, wajūd*	Body.

دَ.دَخاطَر نهٔ تيردل	*da-da khātera nuh térédal*	To displease.
لنګيدل	*langédal*	To give birth to a child.
دَ يو بل ښهٔ ويل	*dā yau bal khuh wayal*	To say good of each other.
خير خيريت	*khér khériat*	Welfare, all well.
معلوم کيدل	*mālūm kédal*	To be found out.
خيرن	*khiran*	Dirty.
کنزل کول	*kanzal kawal*	To abuse.
لهٔ.نه بدل اخستل	*luh-na badal akhistal*	To take revenge.
شرم	*sharam*	Shame.
ښکاريدل	*khkārédal*	To appear.
پردي ژبه	*pradai jhuba*	Foreign language.
زده کول	*zda kawal*	To learn.
ګڼړل	*ganral*	To consider.
يو بل وژل	*yau bal wajhal*	To kill each other.
ژوندون	*jhwandūn*	Life.
پيسي اخستل	*paisé akhistal*	To take bribe.
بډي اخستل	*badé akhistal*	To take bribe.

EXERCISE 40.

۱ په دى بلوه کښں دوه سړى قتل شول او پنځه سخت
ژوبل شول ۲ په آخر کښں يو سړى عمرى شو او په دوهؤ دَ پانسيْ
حکم وشو ۳ پهٔ ښځه پهٔ آس او پهٔ تورهٔ خهٔ اعتبار دىَ ؟ ۴ دلارى
ملګرىَ دَ مور مېړهٔ وى ۵ په دى موسم کښں ډير اسونه لهٔ افغانستان

ده راوستلی کیږي اګر چه پهٔ لار کښې وربانډې ډیر محصول لږي
مګر بیا هم سوداګر په کښې ډیره ګټه کوي ۶ غریب خلق پهٔ چاونړئ
کښې مزدوري کوي او وربانډې ګذاره کوي ۷ ډانګتر ورته ووې چه مهٔ
ویرېږه زخم دې ګوزم بیګا ور نه ښه زوه راوتی وه کهٔ نه . ۸ یو سړی
رانه پهٔ موټر والږید خوار به مړشي ښکه چه اوږهٔئی ماته ده
۹ زهٔ ودس ماتې دَ پاره لهٔ ښوکيږ نه راووتم اودس مې ماتکړ او پهٔ
چینهٔ اودس وکړ مانښهٔ ته اودریدم چه ستا تار راورسید ۱۰ زمکهٔ
ټوله بارانې ده ښکه مدام پهٔ مالیه کښې قید یم ۱۱ داسې وویریدم
چه ټول بدن مې خولې خولې شهٔ ۱۲ ښلور ورځې شوې دي
چه غوا مې لذګه شوې ده ښلور سیر پيئ کوي ۱۳ پښتانهٔ هیڅرې
دَ یو بل ښهٔ نهٔ وائي ۱۴ زهٔ ستا خیر خیریت معلومولو دَ پاره
راغلی یم ۱۵ پښتوُن ښهٔ دوست دی او خطر ناک دشمن دی
پهٔ شاباش ډیر خوشحالیږي پښتوُن کهٔ ډیر غریب وي خو پهٔ وهلو
او کنزلو وربانډې ښوک کا نهٔ شي کولی ۱۶ پښتوُن خپل بدل
هیڅرې نهٔ پرېږدي ۱۷ دَ پښتنو تعلیم خوښ نهٔ وي او دوکان
کول ور ته شرم ښکاري ۱۹ پښتوُن پردئي ژبه زر زده کولی شي
۲۰ په ښځو او پهٔ زمکه مدام پښتانهٔ سره یو بل وژني او بیا مفروران
شي مګر پهٔ غیر علاقه کښې هم دَ مفرور ژوندوُن ګران وي ښکه چه
اپریدیان پرې پیسې واخلي او وئ وژني —

MISCELLANEOUS COLLOQUIAL SENTENCES IV.

Does this road go to the city?	*Dā lār khahar ta talė dah?*
He always tells lies.	*Hagha mudām darōgh wāyee.*

There will be no parade this evening.	*Nan māzdigar ba parét nuh wee.*
Why do you not come in time?	*Walé puh wakht nuh rāzé?*
It is very cold here in the winter.	*Puh jami ké dalé déra yakhni wee.*
These boys are playing the whole day.	*Dā halakān tōla vraz lōbé kawee.*
If your gun is loaded, unload it.	*Kuh tōpak dé dak wī no khāli* or *tash yé kra.*
Please forgive me this time I shall never do it again.	*Méhrabānī wōkra dā zal mé māf kra, biā ba dāsé kār hicharé wo nuh kram.*
We had five hundred women to cook our food.	*Mūng sara pinzuh sawa khazé wé chi zamūng dōdai ba yé pakhawala.*
How long will it take you to reach there?	*Puh sōmra sāat ké ba halta wo rasé?*
We arrived there a little after midday.	*Mūng halta luh gharmé na lūkūtī vrōsto wōrasédaloo.*
He is quite innocent.	*Hagha bilkul bégunāh day.*
What time will the guard change?	*Gārat ba suh wakht badlégee?*
Show me some other samples.	*Suh nōré namūné rā ta wo khaya.*
Keep your accounts always clear.	*Mudām khpal hésāb sāf sāta.*
Is he a relation of the headman?	*Haghada malak khpal day?*

You are young and strong, why do you not enlist in the army.	*Tuh zwān yé aw takra hum yé, walé puh fauz ké nuh barti kégé.*
Are the pass made rifles any good ?	*Daréwāl tōpakūna suh khuh wee ?*
I have forgotten your name.	*Sta nūm rā na hér sho.*
Have you ever been on active service ?	*Tuh charé puh lām talay yé ?*
Tell all Indian Officers that I want to see them tomorrow at 4-30 p.m.	*Tōlo sardārāno ta wo wāya chi saba puh salōr nimé bajé yé lidal ghwāram.*
The ration arrangements were not very good.	*Da rāsan intézām bilkul khuh nuh woh.*
Have you finished your annual musketry ?	*Tā da kāl chāndmārai khlāsa karé dah ?*
I get up at five and after a bath and having had my breakfast I go to the office.	*Zuh puh pinzuh bajé pāsam aw da ghusal aw hāzérai na pas daftar ta zam.*
When did you last go on leave ?	*Tér zala tuh kala puh chūtai bāndé talay wé.*
I do not remember exactly what clothes the man was wearing.	*Mā ta bilkul yād nuh di chi hagha sari sanga jāmé aghustalé wé.*
I walked in from Shabkadar this morning.	*Nan sahar zuh luh Shabkadar na pyāda rāghlam.*
Show me your certificates.	*Chitai dé wō khaya.*

Take this parcel to the post office and bring a receipt.	*Dā pārsal dākkhāné ta yausa aw rasid rāwra.*
Our ration is free but we can't save any money.	*Zamūng rāsan muft day lékin hiss paisa na shoo bach kawalay.*
Whom do you want to see ?	*Tuh sōk lidal ghwāré ?*
The village has two quarters, the upper and the lower ones Sarfarāz is the head man of the upper quarter.	*Puh kalī ké dwa kandi di, bar aw kūz. Sarfarāz da bar kandi malak day.*
The knife and fork are both dirty.	*Charuh aw kānta dwāra khirané di.*
Take this cheque to the treasury and cash it.	*Dā chak khazāné ta yausa aw māt yé kra.*
Bring small change for three rupees.	*Da dréo rūpō māt gud rāwra.*
Do you know where my head clerk lives ?	*Tā ta mālūma dah chi zamā lōi bābū charta ōsee ?*
How many men were absent from rollcall ?	*La géntrai na sōmra sari ghair hāzér woo?*
Why did he go without permission ?	*Walé bé ijāzata lār?*
He said this in my presence "Hide yourself in that thick grass."	*Haghuh dā khabara zamā puh makh ké karé dah, puh hagha ganro wākho ké zān pat kra.*
Where have you been for such a long time ?	*Dōmra dér sat charta wé ?*

Put an anna stamp on this envelope.	*Pa dé lifāfa bāndé da ané tikas wō lagawa.*
When will you fulfil your promise?	*Kala ba khpala wāda pūra kawé?*
We attacked them with our bayonets, but soon returned.	*Mūng puh khpalo sanginūnō bāndé war bāndé hamla wo kra kho zar rā wo jārwatoo.*
Tell the subedar to be back before sunset.	*Subédār sāhib ta wo wāya chi luh nwar préwātuh na awàl rāshee.*
Put picquets on the hills on all sides, for the camp must be protected.	*Puh tōlō tarafo bāndé puh ghrūno pikatūna wo lagawa, zaka chi parāw sātal pakār dī.*
It appears to me that the enemy has retired.	*Malūmégee chi dushman māt shaway day.*
We halted there for three days.	*Mūng dréo vrazō da pāra halta muqām wo kar.*
Here is the list of 11 bad characters living in your village.	*Dā da yawolaso badmāshānō ferest day chi stā puh kali ké osee.*
For each I require a security of Rs. 500/.	*Da har yau da pāra da pinzo pinzo sawo zamānat ghwāram.*
Does the climate of this country suit you?	*Da dé mulk ābō hawā dar bāndé rāsta (muafiqa) dah kuh na?*
How many men have been killed in this riot?	*Pa dé balwa ké sōmra sari wajhalay shawi di?*

Do they bring horses from Afghanistan ?	*Haghui luh Afghānistān na asūna rāwalee?*
Still the merchants make much profit.	*Biā hum saudāgar déra gata kawee.*
I came out of the post and went to pray.	*Zuh luh saukaī na rā wo watam aw mānzuh la lāram.*
Why do travellers not go that way now ?	*Walé musāfar hagha khwā ta os nuh shi tlay ?*
Because all roads are dangerous.	*Zaka chi tōlé lāré khatarnāké dī.*
How much did you pay for this horse ?	*Dā as dé puh so akhistay day ?*
The elders of the tribe tried to make a money settlement but failed.	*Da qām spin giro puh rūpō bāndé da faisalé kōshash wo kar kho wo nuh sho,*
I am a cultivator and live in Yusafzai. I cultivate 10 jaribs of land.	*Zuh chalékār yam aw puh yūsufzo ké osam. lās jariba zmaka karam.*
Why did he come with a rope round his neck?	*Walé rasaī puh ghāra rāghlo ?*
My village was raided.	*Zamā puh kali dāra préwata.*
They carried off Harnam Singh's son.	*Da Harnām Singh zōi yé bōtlō.*
How can I give false evidence ?	*Sanga da darōghō shahdi war kawalay sham ?*
All the sepoys want to see you.	*Tōl spāyān dé lidal ghwāree.*

Why are the people of the city not allowed to come into the cantt?	*Walé da khār khalqō ta da chaunrai da rātlo ijāzat nishta?*
The flood has carried away all the bridges on the Kabul river.	*Sélāb da kābul puh sind bāndé tōl pulūna woree di.*
When I was in the Tirah expedition I was well acquainted with the General.	*Chi zuh da Tirah puh lām bāndé wam, no jarnail sara khuh wāqif wam.*
Owing to the heavy rain in Swat, the Kabul river is in flood.	*Puh Swāt ké da zorāwar bārān puh sabab Da Kabal puh sind ké sélāb rāghalay day.*
Where there is no river or canals the women grind their corn with hand mills.	*Charta chi sindūna yā nehrūna nuh wī no halta khuzé puh mechanō oruh kawee.*
I have a large family, I therefore have to take to service.	*Zamūng lōi tabar .day zaka naukari kawoo.*
Who wrote the letter and sent it back to Delhi?	*Chā chitai wolikala aw Dehli ta yé biarta wo légala?*
Why did the Adjutant call you to the office What did he tell you?	*Walé Ajitan sāhib daftar ta wo balalé suh yé dar ta wo wayal?*
Mind, my dog will bite you.	*Paham kawa zamā spay ba dé wo chīchi.*
He said he would come himself if he wanted to see me.	*Hagha wō wé chi kuh zuh dé winam, nō pakhpala ba darsham.*

VOCABULARY XLII.

جاسوس	*jāsūs*	Spy.
مُخبر	*mukhbér*	Informer.
پټ کول	*pat kawal*	To hide.
خوړ يا ناله	*khwar* or *nāla*	Ravine.
اگرچه	*agarchi*	Although.
دَ شولو پټی	*da shōlo patay*	Rice field.
توئ	*tōi*	Stream.
دَ غر خوا	*da ghar khwā*	Hill side.
ډز کول	*daz kawal*	To fire.
لگيدل	*lagédal*	To be hit.
مقام کول	*muqām kawal*	To halt.
لږ وخت دَ پاره	*lag wakht da pāra*	For a short while.
نړول	*narawal*	To knock down (or building).
ذکر کول	*zikar kawal*	To mention.
تازه	*tāza*	Fresh.
درک	*darak*	Trace clue.
چاپ	*chāp*	Foot print.
ظاهره	*zāhéra*	Evidently.
گډه	*gada*	Sheep.
تلاش کول	*tālāsh kawal*	To look for.
ډزی وشوی	*dazé wo shwé*	Shots were fired.
کمر	*kamar*	Cliff, neck (in hill.)
هم په هغه وخت	*hum puh hagha wakht*	At the same moment.

غائیب کیدل	*ghāib kédal*	To go out of sight.
پناه کیدل	*panāh kédal*	
روان کیدل	*rawān kédal*	To start, set out.
نور پریواتهٔ	*nwar préwātūh*	Sunset.
وریسی کول	*warisé kawal*	To remove.
یو خواته کول	*yau khwā ta kawal*	
ټګی	*tagi*	Trap.
(ته) پهٔ پسوڼی کینی کینا ستل	*ta puh psūni ké kénāstal*	To ambush.
(ته) لارنیو ل	*ta lār niwal*	

Exercise 41.

While the force was encamped on a hill near Kaneguram an informer came and told the Political Officer that the Shabi Khels had all their cattle hidden in a nulla about seven miles away to the north. For this he received a handsome reward. Although it was the middle of the day and very hot we started at once for the place. On the way we passed some rice fields which were irrigated from a small stream flowing down the hill side. Near these fields was a tower from which a shot was fired at us as we approached. No one was hit, and the man who fired the shot fled before we could get up to the tower and escaped among the hills

We halted there for a short while and knocked the tower down. Then we went on, and about three o'clock reached the place mentioned by the informer. There were fresh traces of cattle on every side, but evidently their owners had taken them away for we could not find so much as a single sheep. While we were looking about some shots were fired from a neck between two hills, and at the same moment the informer, whom we had brought with us, fled. Many shots were fired after him, but he was soon out of sight. So we started back to camp and going by a different route reached it just before sunset. It was said afterwards that the informer was himself a Shabi Khel, and that he had taken care to have the cattle removed before the troops started, and that the whole thing was a trap. If we had returned by the same route as we went, the tribesmen, who had collected and made an ambush on the road while we were looking for the cattle, would have given us a very bad time.

VOCABULARY XLIII.

لۀ نن تاریخ نه	*uh nan tarikh na*	From this date.
کنزل کول	*kanzal kawal*	To abuse.
کمزوری	*kamzōray*	Weak.

مضبوط	*mazbūt*	Strong.
ځان	*zān*	Self.
قوت	*quat*	Strength.
مغرور	*maghrūr*	Proud.
پۀ حيرانتيا سره	*puh hairāntiā sara*	With astonishment.
دليل	*dalil*	Reason.
ليونی	*léwanay*	Mad.
اول	*awal*	First.
و ړومبی	*vrūmbay*	First.
ځنګه چه	*sunga chi*	As.
هم دغَسی	*hum dagha sé*	The same way.
خبره دا ده	*khabara dā dah*	The true fact is.
بی ګناه	*bé gunah*	Innocent.
بی هيڅ	*bé hissa*	For nothing.

Exercise 42.

يوه ورځ يوی ښځی خپل خښتن ته ووِ چه لۀ نن تاريخ نه پس
بيا مِ نۀ شی وهلیَ - او نۀ راته کنزل کولیَ شی - خښتن ورته ويل
دا خبره د پۀ څۀ خيال وکړه - زۀ درته کمزوری ښکاره شوم او کۀ خپل
ځان درته مضبوط ښکاره شو او نۀ دَ خپل پلار پۀ قوت مغروره شوی
چه بيا دِ نۀ شم وهلیَ - دې ورته وِ چه بس ما درتۀ و ويل چه
بيا مِ نۀ شی وهلیَ - سړی بيا ورته پۀ حيرانتيا سره تپوس وکړو چه
دا خبره تۀ پۀ کوم دليل سره کوی - ليونۍ خو نۀ ئی چه ليونۍ ئی
ځنګه چه ~~ته اول~~ خدا ښځه وی هم دغَسی اوس ئی او ځنګه چه
زۀ و ړومبیَ سړا خښتن وم هم دغَسی اوس هم يم - نو ځنګه د نۀ

شم وهلیَ - ښځی ورته پهٔ جواب کښې و ویل چه خبره دا دهَ چه هر
څهٔ چه ته وائی هغه به منم - نو چه ټولی خبری د منم نو تهٔ لیونیَ
خو نه ئی چهٔ بیځناه به م وهی - یا بی هیڅ به راته کنزل کوی -
سړیِ و خندل تر روان شو -

VOCABULARY XLIV.

دوه جمعی کیږی	*dwa jumé kégee*	A fortnight ago.
د شپږو اوو بجو پهٔ مینځ کښی	*da shpagō owo bajō puh mianz ké*	Between 6 and 7 o'clock.
اواز	*awāz*	Voice, noise.
کړپهار	*krapahār*	Footsteps, sound of feet.
پهٔ ترات	*puh trāt*	Galloping.
خلاص راتلل یا پهٔ پوره چال راتلل	*khlās rātlal* or *puh pūra chāl rātlal*	To come on at full speed.
سوز	*sōr*	Rider.
ظاهره	*zāhéra*	Evidently.
قابوٗ	*qābū*	Control.
آس يې لهٔ قابوٗ نه و تلی وه	*as yé luh qābū na watalay woh*	He lost control of his horse.
راښکل	*rākhkal*	To tug.
سورلیِ	*swarli*	Riding, passenger
رکاب	*rekāb*	Stirrup.
واږی	*wāgé*	Reins.
گز	*gaz*	Yard.

قدم	*qadam*	Pace.
رغړيدل	*rgharédal*	To roll.
اوږه	*oga*	Shoulder.
بازيگره	*bāzīgara*	Somersault.
بازيگره اړول	*bāzīgara arawal*	To turn a somersault.
ښڼهل	*sandal*	To brush.
گرد	*gard*	Dust (flying).
خاوره	*khāwra*	Earth (lying on the ground).
خټه	*khata*	Mud.
جامې	*jāmé*	Clothes.
لهٔ ښهٔ نصيبه	*luh khuh nasiba*	Fortunately.
لهٔ بدَ نصيبه	*luh bada nasiba*	Unfortunately.
نرم	*naram*	Soft.
بوس	*būs*	Straw, bussa.
خسنړی	*khasanray*	A straw.
ډز	*daz*	A shot (of gun).
دنگل	*dangal*	To bolt.
ياغی کيدل	*yāghi kédal*	To bolt, to run away out of control.
خپل ځان خوزول	*khpal zān khwazawal*	Shake oneself.
يو خوا بل خوا زنگيدو را زنگيدو	*yau khwā bal khwā zangédo rā zangédo*	Swinging from side to side.

EXERCISE 43.

About a fortnight ago when I was walking across the maidan in the early morning between six and seven, I heard the voice of foot steps behind me. Looking round, I saw a horse galloping towards me at full speed. The rider had evidently lost control of his horse, and was leaning back, tugging at the reins and swinging from side to side. His feet were out of the stirrups, and I expected every moment to see him fall. Sure enough he had not gone more than fifty yards or so after passing me when he rolled off and fell on his shoulder, turning a complete somersault. I ran up thinking he might have broken his neck but before I reached him, he was up, and shaking himself began to brush the dust off his clothes Luckily for him he had fallen in a soft place where there was plenty of loose straw and no stones. He told me his horse had taken fright at the firing of a gun and bolted with him.

VOCABULARY XLV.

جولا *jōlā*	A weaver.
اودل *odal*	To weave.
اوم *owam*	I weave (Present.)
پګړۍ یا پټکی *pagrai* or *patkay*	Turban.

حُجره	*hūjra*	Guest house.
میلمه	*melma*	Guest.
عالم	*ālam*	A learned man.
ادب	*adab*	Respect.
(سره) جور پر تازه کول	*(sara) jōr tāza kawal*	To welcome.
مجلس	*majlas*	Assembly, gathering.
دَ-عزت کول	*da-izat kawal*	To respect.
څنګ په څنګ	*sang puh sang*	Side by side, close.
هيڅ ئی نهٔ ويل	*hiss yé nuh wayal*	Saying nothing.
دَ-يقين کيدل	*da-yaqīn kédal*	To believe.
چپ چاپ	*chap chāp*	Silent.
آخر	*ākhér*	At last.
پهٔ آخر کښی	*puh ākhér ké*	In the end.
دَ میاشتی پهٔ آخر کښی	*da miāshté puh ākhir ké*	In the end of month.
دَ میاشتی پهٔ شروع کښی	*da miāshté puh shurū ké*	In the beginning of month.
روژه	*rōjha*	Fast, fasting.
ماتول	*mātawal*	To break.
نور پريواتهٔ	*nwar préwātuh*	Sunset, West.
ساعت	*sāat*	Moment.
ناګهانه	*nāgahāna*	By chance.
بيا به څهٔ چل کيږی	*biā ba suh chal kégee ?*	What will happen then ?

خر	*khar*	An ass, donkey.
کتهٔ	*kata*	Pack saddle.
زین	*zin*	Saddle.

EXERCISE 44.

یو جولا ښځی جامی واغوستی سپینه پټکۍ ئی پهٔ سر کړه او
دَیو قاضی حُجری له ورغیَ - قاضی صاحب چه دا میلمه ولید نو
خیال ئی وکړ چه څوک دَلویٔ کور سړیَ دیَ او عالم هم معلومیږیِ
نو ډیر پهٔ ادب ورته پاڅید او ډیر جوړ تازه ئی ور سره وکړل څکه نور
مجلس هم دَ دهٔ ډیر عزت وکړ جولا قاضی صاحب سره څنګ پهٔ
څنګ کیناست هیڅ ئی نهٔ ویل په دی بانِد نور هم دَ خلقو یقین
وشهٔ چه ډیر هوښیار سړیَ دیَ نو یو ساعت څو ټول مجلس سره
چپ چاپ ناست وۀ هیڅا څهٔ نهٔ ویل آخر یو سړیِ لهٔ قاضی صاحب
نه تپوس وکړ چه روژه پهٔ څهٔ وخت ماتیږیِ قاضی جواب ورکړ
چه لهٔ نور پریواتهٔ نه لږ ساعت پس دَ روژی ماتولو وخت ویِ ناګها نه
جولا پهٔ کښې ویل قاضی صاحبَ کهٔ نور تر نیمی شپی پوری پری
نهٔ وځیِ نو بیا به څهٔ چل کیږیِ پهٔ دی بانِد ټولو وخندل او وئی
ویل چه خر هم هغه دیَ کته ور بانِد بله دَه—

VOCABULARY XLVI.

دَ عربو یو ټولیَ	*da arabō yau tōlay*	A band of Arabs.
ټولیَ یا داړه	*tōlay* or *dāra*	Party, raid.
بندَول	*bandawal*	To block.
دَ وطن خلق	*da watan khalq*	Inhabitants.
ظلم	*zulum*	Tyranny.
بي خبرَ	*bé khabara*	Unwittingly.

(ته) وسله کیښودل	*(ta) wasla kėkhōdal*	Surrender.
وسله	*wasla*	Weapon.
مغلوب یا لاندِ	*maghlūb* or *lāndė*	Overpowered.
مورچه	*mōrcha*	Strong hold.
دَ استوګنې	*da astōgnė*	
ځائی	*zāi*	Fixed residence.
دَ بادشاه مشیر یا صلاح کار	*da bādshāh mashir* or *salāh kār*	Counsellor of the king.
مصلحت کول	*maslahat kawal*	To consult.
سره	*sara*	Together.
لری کول یا	*larė kawal* or	
وریسی کول	*warisė kawal*	To remove.
خپګان	*khapgān*	Grievances.
راج	*rāj*	State.
طاقتور	*tāqatwar*	Powerful.
لاند کیدل	*lāndė kėdal*	To be subdued.
جاسوُس	*jāsūs*	Spy.
مُخبر	*mukhbėr*	Informer.
موقعی ته کتل	*muqė ta katal*	To watch opportunity.
خالی	*khāli*	Evacuated.
خپل ځان پټ کول	*khpal zān pat kawal*	Conceal oneself.
لوُټ	*lūt*	Plunder, loot (noun)
موقعه مؤندل	*mōqa mūndal*	To get a chance.

پسوُنی	*psūnay*	An ambush.
شوُکمار	*shūkmār*	A Robber.
شوُکه کول	*shūka kawal*	To rob.
مړ کول یا وژل	*mar kawal* or *wajhal*	To put to death.
پایه تخت	*pāya takht*	Capital.

EXERCISE 45.

A band of Arabs had collected among the mountains and were in the habit of stopping and looting caravans, as they crossed the pass. The inhabitants of the country around were also in great distress because of the tyranny of these bandits, while the Sultan's troops seemed powerless to deal with them, because of the strength of the position they had taken up in the mountains. The Sultan's counsellors were very anxious to deal effectively with the band which was daily becoming more powerful as it was attracting to its banner all the bad characters of the region. They accordingly sent spies to report on the movements of the robbers. Soon after, news came in from a spy that the band had left their strong hold to raid a tribe some distance away. The counsellors seized this opportunity to despatch a regiment of troops to intercept the robbers on their return with the plunder. The operation was completely successful as the thieves fell unwittingly into the ambush. Many of them were killed and the remainder surrendered to the Sultan's troops and were brought into the capital for trial. The Sultan sentenced most of them to death.

VOCABULARY XLVII.

راکوز کیدل	*rā kūz kédal*	To come down.
خپل خپلوان	*khpal khpalwān*	Relations.
علاج	*ilaj*	Cure, remedy (noun).
دا ښهٔ چل نهٔ دَی	*dā khuh chal nuh day*	This is not a good plan.
سترگی دِ پټی کړی	*stargé dé paté kree*	He should shut his eyes.
خوږ کیدل	*khūg kédal*	To be hurt.
رسول	*rasawal*	To cause to arrive.
مشر	*mashar*	Elder.
پهٔ قهر شهٔ	*puh qahar shuh*	Became enraged.
ژوندی	*jhwanday*	Alive.
ښیل	*khayal*	To show, direct.
رسئ	*rasai*	Rope.
سر	*sar*	The end, head.
پاس	*pās*	Up.
را اچول	*rā achawal*	To throw towards me or us.
ملا	*mlā*	Waist.
کلک	*klak*	Hard, tight.
پهٔ زور سرهٔ	*puh zōr sara*	With force.

را ګذار کول	*rā guzār kawal*	To throw down.
سره دَ راپرېوتو	*sara da rāprêwato*	Immediately on falling.
کمبخته	*kam bakhta !*	O you unlucky one !
دَ خپل لاسه	*da khpala lāsa*	Intentionally.
اجل	*ajal*	Fixed day for death.
ګنړه	*ganra*	Otherwise.
ځان کندن یا ځنکدن	*zān kandan* or *zankadan*	The point of death.
برج	*braj*	Tower.

EXERCISE 45.

یو جولا پهٔ ونه کښې ختلې وهٔ او بیا نهٔ شو راکوزیدې نو خپل
خپلوان ئې راجمع شول پهٔ علاج ئې نهٔ پوهیدل چه څنګه ئې راکوز کړو
چا به ویل راځئ چه داونه پرې کړو نو چه ونه را پرېوځي نو پخپله به
تر راکوز شي بل به ویل نه دا څهٔ چل نهٔ دی دَ ونې پهٔ پریوتو
کښې به سړی مړ شي چا به ویل سترګې د پټې کړي او راټوپ
د کړي پوه به هم نهٔ شي او پهٔ زمکه به ودریږي بل ویل نه دا هم څهٔ
چل نهٔ دی اسړی به خوږ شي چا به ویل راځئ چه یو پهٔ بل
ودریږو او بل پهٔ بل نو پهٔ دې شان به ځان ور ورسوو او راکوز به ئې
کړو نورو ویل دا هم څه خبره نهٔ دَه چا به ویل راځئ چه دَ ونې خواته
یو برج جوړ کړو چه برج ور ورسي نو په آسانۍ به ئې راکوز کړو بل ویل
تر برج تر جوړولو به سړي دَ لوږې او تندې مړ شي پهٔ دوئې کښې
یو مشر وهٔ چه هغه راغې نو ورته ډېر پهٔ قهر شو او ویل ئې چه پهٔ
داسې اسان چل باند هم نهٔ پوهیږئ ؟ ورشئ یوه لوینه رسئ

راو ړيږي چه رسيږئی راوړه نو دَرسيږي يو سړئی جولا ته پاس ورګُذار کړ
ورته ئی وويل چه ملا پوزی ئی کلک وټړه چه هغهٔ دَرسيږي سر
ملا پوری. وټړلو نو دی مشر جولا دَ رسيږي بل سر پهٔ زور سره ښکته
راښکلو لاندِئی راګُذار کړ سړیَ سره دَ را پريوتو مړشو دی نورو جولا
ګانو ورته وِ کم بخت دا دِغهٔ وکړل دَخپلَ لاسَ دِ سړیَ ووژلو دهٔ ورته
پهٔ جواب کښ ووِ چه اجَل ئی وٌه ځکه مړ شو ګنړه ما ډير خلق پهٔ
دی چل سره لهٔ کوهيِ نه راويستليِ دیِ—

VOCABULARY XLVII.

يو ځائی کيدل	*yau zāi kédal*	To join.
تحريک يا شور وشر	*tahrik* or *shōr-o-shar*	Movement.
ظاهره	*zāhéra*	Outwardly.
ځما لهٔ ويرې	*zamā luh veyaré*	Through fear of me
پټ	*pat*	Secretly.
پهٔ جار	*puh jār*	Openly, publicly
اوروَل	*aurawal*	To announce.
اعتبار يا وعده	*itébār* or *wada*	Assurance.
دَ قام مشران	*da qām masharān*	The elders of the tribe.
پهٔ باند يا پهٔ ذريعه دَ	*puh-bandé* or *puh zaria da*	Through, by means of.
سرحد	*sarhad*	Border.
هله ګله	*hala gula*	Disturbances.
فساد	*fasād*	Mischief..

انګریزي سرکار	*angrézi sarkār*	British Government.
لری کول یا رفع کول	*laré kawal* or *rafa kawal*	To dispel.
رفع کیدل	*rafa kédal*	To be dispelled.
دَ پاره دَ دی	*da pāra da dé*	In order to
رعیت	*rait*	Subject.
دَ دشمنئی پهٔ نیت	*da dushmanai puh niat*	With hostile intention.
نیت	*niat*	Intention.
پهٔ زړهٔ زور تیرول یا برداشت کول یا صبر کول	*puh zruh zōr térawal* or *bardāsht kawal* or *sabar kawal*	To tolerate.
گمراه	*gumrāh*	Mis-guided.
بی وجی یا بی هڅَ	*bé waje* or *bé hissa*	Unprovoked.
یقین	*yaqin*	Belief.
ساتل	*sātal*	To keep, watch.
منع کول	*mana kawal*	To prevent.

EXERCISE 47.

You have said my tribesmen can never join in such a movement openly for fear of me. If any one has gone, he must have gone secretly. What I now ask you, in accordance with those assurances of friendship, which you have so readily made, is that you will publicly announce to the tribesmen throngh your local officers that, if they cross the borders and join in disturbances against the British Government, they will incur your displeasure. (Lit: You will be annoyed from them). The belief is entertained by many misguided persons that they will not incur your disapproval by acting in a hostile manner against Government and this belief can be dispelled if your officers will keep watch along the river and at other places in order to prevent your subjects from crossing the Frontier with hostile intentions, whether secretly or openly. I ask you therefore, to issue orders to this effect. By so doing you may put an end to these disturbances, which were wholly unprovoked and cannot be tolerated.

VOCABULARY XLIX.

امزرَیَ یا زمریَ	*amzaray* or *zmaray*	Tiger.
(تہ) نصیحت کول	*(ta) nasihat kawal*	To advise.
گورہ	*gōra*	Look here.
څناور	*zanāwar*	Animal.
خبردار	*khabardār*	Beware, be careful.
جګړہ خلاصول	*jagara khlāsawal*	To settle dispute.
إنصاف	*insāf*	Justice.
خدائی پاک	*khudāi pak*	Pure God.

طاقت	*tāqat*	Power, strength.
مناسب دی	*munāseb di*	It is befitting.
عاجز	*ājaz*	Poor, needy.
غور	*ghōr*	Justice, care.
پهٔ ښهٔ شان سره	*puh khuh shān sara*	Satisfactorily.
بیزو	*bīzō*	Monkey.
شکل	*shakal*	Appearance.
اوږد	*ūgad*	Long.
لهٔ لرې نه	*luh laré na*	From a distance.
لوګےَ	*lūgay*	Smoke.
دَ سړي پهٔ غوږو ډیر بد لګيِ	*da sarı puh ghwagō dér bad lagee*	One can not bear to hear it.
پهٔ بانډِ سرپه کول	*puh bāndé sarpa kawal*	To spare.
که دَلاسَ دِ کیږيِ	*kuh da lāsā dé kégee*	If possible.
پهٔ بانډِ لاس برکیدل	*puh-bāndé lās bar kédal*	To get the better of.
مُنصف	*munséf*	Just (Adjective.)
لږ ډیر	*lag dér*	Some what.
ملاویدل	*melāwédal*	To resemble.

EXERCISE 48.

یو امزري ځپل خوی ته نصیحت کاوهٔ ویل ئی ګوره تهٔ به پس
لهٔ مانه پهٔ دی ځنګل کښې دَ ټولو ځناورو بادشاه ئی او بادشاه نوم
دَ خدايِ دیَ خبردار چه پهٔ چا بیګناه ظلم ونهٔ کړې ډیرِ خلق به
در له دَ جګړو خلاصَولو دَپاره راځيِ ولی تهٔ پهٔ انصاف سره هرهٔ جګړه

فیصله کوهٔ چا له چه خدای پاک طاقت ورکړې نو مناسب دې چه
دَ خوارو عاجزو غوږ پهٔ ښهٔ شان سره کوې مګر یاد لره په دې ځنګل
کښې یو ځناور دے چه پهٔ دوهٔ ښپو ګرځي شکل ئې دَ بیزو سره
لږ ډیر ملاویږي خلق ورته سړے وائي اکثر ورسره یو تور اوږد لرګے
وي هر کله چه مونږ خلق ووینې نو دا لرګے راته نیغ ونسي
دَ دې لرګي نه لوږې راوځي او دَ دې لوږې یو داسې ناکار او
نااشنا واز وشي چه دسړي پهٔ غوږو ډیر بد لږي او دَ دې اواز
پهٔ اوریدو سمدستي سړے زخمي شي پهٔ ځمکه راپریوځي او مړشي
نو ښما خبره واوره چه په دې ځناور هیچری صر په ونهٔ کړې کهٔ ګنهګار
وي کهٔ بیګناه خو چه وئ وینې او کهٔ دَ لاس دَ کیږي نو وژنهٔ ئې
انصاف ور سره مهٔ کوه بچي ورته وِ بابا نوزه پهٔ ښهٔ بادشاه شوم چه
انصاف ورسره نهٔ کوم لمزري ورته ویل بچیَّ پهٔ هر ځناور کښې
انصاف شته ولې په دهٔ کښې خوبالکل نشته او دام هم اوریدلي نهي ؟
چه په خپلو ورونړوئی لاس برشي نو هم ورباندِ صر په نهٔ کوی نو ځکه
ښما نصیحت واوره چه بی انصاف دشمن لهٔ ځان اول وژل
پکار دي —

VOCABULARY L.

بله ورځ *bala vraz* The following day.
جامی اغوستل *jāmé aghustal* To dress.
زر زر *zar zar* Hastily
دَ کبانو ښکار *da kabānō khkār* Fishing
ایله ایله رڼړا *ila ila ranra* Hardly light.
ترَغونی *taraghunė* Dusk.
واقعه *waqea* Mishap, adventure.

ډوغل	*dōghal*	Pit.
ګرب	*grab*	Hole.
ټوپئی	*tōpai*	Cap, hat.
لړزيدل	*larzédal*	To shake or shaking, to tremble.
لړزان	*larzān*	Shaking, trembling.
د وار خطا کيدل	*da-wār khaṭā kédal*	To be dismayed.
وار خطا	*wār khaṭā*	Alarmed, dismayed.
اوتر	*autar*	Alarmed, frightened
هډوکی	*hadūkay*	Bone.
کړ کړ په خندا کيدل	*kar kar puh khandā kédal*	To burst out laughing.
مقام	*muqām*	Halting place.
پړاو	*parāw*	Camp.
ربړ	*rabar*	Adventure.
جښت په وخت يا په ښه وخت	*jukht puh wakht* or *puh khuh wakht*	Just in time.
ښه شروع	*kha shurū*	Satisfactory beginning.
بچ کيدل	*bach kédal*	To be saved.

EXERCISE 49.

The following day my friend and I were up in good time and after dressing hastily mounted our ponies which were in readiness at the door, and started for a twelve miles ride to the river where we were going to fish. It was nearly 3 o'clock when we started. Soon after starting I had a little mishap which might have put an end to my sport for that and many days. In the uncertain light my pony put his foot into a hole and came down with me, throwing me over his head. Luckily my topi saved me and I got up with nothing worse than a shaking. My friend at first was a little alarmed, but when he found there was no bone broken, he burst into a hearty laugh in which I joined. We reached our halting place without any further adventure and just in time to get the best of the early morning. A few minutes afterwards I landed my first mashir, a small one it is true, but a satisfactory beginning.

VOCABULARY LI.

تازه	*tāza*	Fresh.
مړی	*maray*	Dead body.
مړی به وشو	*maray ba wosho*	One would die.
قبر	*qabar*	Grave.
اديره	*adira*	Graveyard.
سپړودل	*sparōdal*	To untie, open.
كفن	*kafan*	Shroud.
را ټول كول	*rā tōl kawal*	To collect, to undress.
كپړه	*kapra*	Cloth.
گذاره كول	*guzāra kawal*	To live on
گذران كول	*guzrān kawal*	

تنګ کیدل	*tang kédal*	To be oppressed.
پهٔ لاس ورتلل	*puh lās wartlal*	To come to hand, to find.
ګنړه	*ganra*	Otherwise.
اسمان	*asmān*	Sky.
ستوری	*stōray*	Star.
مرض	*maraz*	Illness.
زیاتیدل	*ziātédal*	To increase.
دارو	*dārū*	Medicine.
ک-دمه کیدل	*da-dama kédal*	To recover from illness.
وصیت کول	*wasiyat kawal*	To make a will.
وران کار	*vran kar*	Evil deed.
قیامت	*qayāmat*	The day of judgement
نیکی	*néki*	Goodness.
وجه	*waja*	Reason.
دعا کول	*duā kawal*	To pray for.
نیک کارونه	*nék kārūna*	Good deeds.
نتیجه	*natija*	Result.
عمل	*amal*	Act.
بخښل	*bakhal*	To forgive.
کسب	*kasab*	Occupation.
پهٔ غلا	*puh ghla*	Secretly.
اولنی	*awalanay*	The first one, the former.
جوړ	*jōr*	Accordingly.
وروستنی	*vrustonay*	The last one, the latter.

خدای دِ ئی وبخښي	*khudāi dé yé wo bakhee*	May God forgive him !
حیادار	*hayādār*	Modest.
شرمَول	*sharmawal*	To put to shame.
دَ وړستني پهٔ نیوو پسې شول.	*da vrūstoni puh niwo pasé shwal*	They were after arresting the latter.
(ته) دَ اسمان ستوري ښیل	*(ta) da asmān stōri khayal*	To punish severely, (lit. to show the stars of the sky).

Exercise 50.

یو سړی وه چهٔ تازه مړیَ به وشو نو دَ شپې به ورغیَ قبر
به ئی دَ دهٔ وسپړو دلو دَ مړيِ نه به ئی کفن راښول کړ کور ته به ئی
راوړ دا دَ کفن کپړه به ئی پهٔ یو بل خرڅوله او پهٔ دې به ئی ګذُران
کاوهٔ خلق ور نه ډیر تنګ شوُ مګر پهٔ لاس نهٔ ورتلو ګنړه دَ اسمان
ستوريِ به ئی ور ته ښیئليِ وُ یوه ورځ ناجوړَ شو مرض ئی ورځ
پهٔ ورځ زیاتیدهٔ پهٔ هیڅ دارو ئی ښه نهٔ کیده نو پوه شو چه اوس مِ
آخر وخت دیَ نو خپل ځوئ یې راوغوښتلو ورته ئی وصیت کاوهٔ ویل ئی
چهٔ ګوره بچیَّ ما ډیر وران وران کارونه کړيِ ديِ خدائې خبر چه
پهٔ قیامت کښې به څما څهٔ حال ويِ تهٔ خپل موُنځ اودس کوه
اوبد کاروُنه مهٔ کوه داسې کار کوه چه خلق درنه خوشحالَ شيِ-او
ستَا دنیکئ پهٔ وجه ماته هم دعا کويِ چه کفن کښ (*kakh*) مړ
شو نو ځوئ ئی پهٔ زړهٔکښې ووِ چه کهٔ زهٔ ډیر نیک کارونه کوم خو
نتیجه به ئیِ هم ماته رسیږيِ پلار ته به مِ څهٔ فائده ونه رسي څکه
چه هر سړیَ به پهٔ خپل عمل خلا صیږيِ جوړ ماله داسې کار کول
پکارديِ چه ور باندِ م پلار ته خلق دعا کويِ او خدائې ئی وبخښيِ

نو هاک هم دَپلار کسب شروع کړ چه مړےَ به وشو نو د شپې بهٔ
وزغیَ قبر به ئی دَ دهٔ وسپړود کفن به ئی تر راښکول کړ او بیا به ئی
وزنه پوزه او غوږونه. هم پرې ښکل خالقو چه داکار واید نو پیر خپه
شوُ ویل ئی، اولدَی کپن کښن (*kakh*) د خدايي وبخښې پیر
ښهٔ حیادار سړے وهٔ کفن به ئی یوړو. ولی مړےَ خو به ئی نهٔ
شرمَوُلو نو و ړبې کپن کښر (*kakh*) ته به ئی دعا کوله او دَ ورستني
پهٔ نیولو پسی شول—

MISCELLANEOUS COLLOQUIAL SENTENCES V.

When did you hear this news ?	*Dā khabara dé kala aurédalé dah?*
It is only a rumour that the Amir of Afghanistan is coming to Peshawar.	*Dā khāli yau awāza dah chi da Afghanistān Amir Pékhawar ta rāzee.*
The whole of our Regt. deserted from the field of battle.	*Da jang luh maidān na zamūng tōla paltan wo takhtédah.*
50 of them have been taken prisoners.	*Panzōs qaid shwal.*
We know nothing of the others. They may have gone towards the enemy.	*Da nōrō puh bāb ké hiss khabar nuh yū dushman ta ba takhtédali wi.*
Wire the Police and inform the Deputy Commissioner.	*Pūlas ta tār* war *kra aw dipty comishnar khabar kra.*
They all will be tried by Court Martial.	*Pa kōt marshal bāndé ba da dūi faisala kégee.*

Sign this agreement, write your name here.	*Pa dė iqrār nāma bāndė daskhat wō kra, dalta khpal nūm wo lika.*
Do you plead guilty or not guilty ?	*Tuh gunahgār yė kuh bėgunāh ?*
Do you want to produce witnesses in your defence ?	*Tuh khpalė safāi da pāra gawāhān pėsh kawal ghwārė ?*
Is this your signature ?	*Dā stā daskhat day ?*
Why don't you complain to Govt. against him ?	*Walė war bāndė sarkār ta shikāyat nuh kawė.*
I have seen it with my own eyes.	*Mā puh khpalo stargō lidalay day.*
What enmity is there between you and him?	*Stā aw da haghuh puh mianz kė suh dushmani dah ?*
Can he sing and dance?	*Hagha sandarė wayalay shi aw gadėday shi ?*
Tell the truth and nothing but the truth.	*Rikhtiā rikhtiā khabara kawa.*
This village is of very bad repute.	*Dā kalay dėr bad nām day.*
The Regt. will head the list.	*Paltan awal lambar ba shi.*
You will get two months furlough after the grand parade.	*Da lōi parait na pas dar ta da dwao miāshto razā ba milāo shee.*
It is a very disgraceful thing.	*Da dėra da sharam khabara dah.*

First take a good aim and then shoot.	*Awal khuh zéray wo lagawa aw biā yé wola.*
Challenge them first and then shoot.	*Awal war bāndé awāz wo kra aw biā yé wola.*
We stood our ground for the whole day.	*Tōla vraz mūnga muqābila wo kra.*
The ascent is difficult on that side, one cannot climb that way.	*Puh haghe taraf charāi grāna dah aw saray war bāndé khatalay nuh shee.*
It is all descent from Cherat right down to Pabbi.	*Luh chirat na ain tar pabō pōré utrāi dah.*
My double barrelled gun has been stolen. I suspect my servant.	*Zamā dwa naliz tōpak puh ghlā talay day puh khpal naukar bāndé zamā gumān day.*
We surrounded the fort and blocked all the approaches to it.	*Mūnga kalā géra kra aw tōlé lāré mo war ta bandé kré.*
I am very glad to see you, Sahib.	*Sahiba? Zuh stā puh lidalō dér khushāl yam.*
You only recently came to Peshawar so I thought I should come to pay my respects to you.	*Tuh ōs ōs Pékhawar ta rāghalay yé no fikar mé wo kar chi pakār di chi zuh stā salām wo kram.*
I am feeling very cold.	*Zama déra yakhni kégee.*

It is a pity that you did not tell me this before.	*Dā da afsōs khabara dah chi dā hāl tā mā ta awal wo nuh wayalo.*
Owing to the Mohmand expedition, no harvesters can be found as they all work as labourers.	*Dā Mohmando da lām puh sabab laugari mūndal grān kār day, zaka chi tōl mazdūri kawee.*
I cannot drive a tonga as I have never tried.	*Zuh tānga nuh sham chalawalay zaka chi hicharé mé kōshash nuh day karay.*
He is a great miser and will pay up with great difficulty.	*Hagha dér shūm day aw puh déra mushkela sara ba pésé war kree.*
This will be settled later on when the sahib comes back from tour.	*Vrosto ba dā faisala shee kala chi sāhib luh dauré na biarta rāshee.*
Where were you born?	*Tuh puh kum zāi ké paida shway wé?*
How long has your Regt been in this Station?	*Stā paltan pa dé chāwnrai ké kala rāsé dah?*
Do you own any land? what revenue do you pay to the Govt?	*Stā suh zmaka shta? sōmra mālia sarkār ta war kawé?*
Wake me just at 7 if I am still asleep.	*Jukht puh owuh bajé mé wikh kra kuh puh hagha wakht zuh ūduh yam.*
Bring my breakfast while I am in bed.	*Kala chi zuh puh kat ké yam, no zamā hāzéri rāwra.*

Take the horse for exercise and saddle it at 5 p. m.	*Ass rōl da pāra bōza aw puh pinzuh bajé māzdigar yé zin kra.*
Do not be late.	*Nāwakhta kawa ma.*
Why did not you bring me some hot water as I told you?	*Chi dar ta mé wo wayal no walé dé suh garmé obuh rā nuh wré?*
All the towels in the house are dirty.	*Puh kōr ké tōl taulyāgān khiran di.*
Bring any one you like.	*Sōk chi dé khwakh wi hagha rāwala.*
Wind this watch as it will stop.	*Dé garai la kunji war kra zaka chi banda ba shi.*
Pump the cycle up I think it is punctured.	*Bāisekal la bād war kra, zamā puh kheyāl ké panchar day.*
Tighten the screws of the wheel.	*Da pāyé dibrai sakhté kra.*
Take the measurement of my foot.	*Zamā da khpé nāp wākhla.*
The leather must be soft.	*Pakār di chi sarman narma wi.*
This room is full of mosquitoes, flit the whole room.	*Dā kamra da māshō na daka dah puh tōla kamra ké da māsko tél charqāo kra.*
I shall dismiss you if you don't prove it.	*Kuh dā khabara sābéta nuh kré, no zuh ba dé nūm kat kram.*
Is there any fishing obtainable here now?	*Oss dalta suh da kabānō khkār mūndalay shi kuh na.*

When the water is clear the fiishermen will come with their nets from Lalpura.	*Kala chi obuh ranré shee no machi mārān ba luh lāl pūré na sara da jālūno rāshee.*
The sky is very clear today.	*Nan asmān bilkul* or *tak shin day.*
It is getting cooler day by day.	*Vraz puh vraz yakhni kégee.*
It is cloudy and cold today, it is drizzling.	*Nan woriaz dah aw yakhni dah, sāskay dāy.*
The rain has stopped now, let us go to the city.	*Oss bārān walār day, rāza chi khahar ta lārshoo.*
Why did your pony put its foot into the hole?	*Walé stā da ass khpa puh grubi ké lāra.*
Because it was dark and he could see nothing.	*Zaka chi tyāruh wah aw hiss yé lidalay nuh shwal.*
The tiger made a will in favour of his son.	*Zmari khpal zōı ta wasiat wo kro.*
Tell your local officer to keep a watch along the river and other places so that the tribesmen may not join the disturbance.	*Da khpal qām masharāno ta waya chi da sind ghāré aw nor zāyūno ta khyāl kawee chi da qām khalq puh dé jagara ké shāmel nuh shi.*
A weaver had climbed up the tree and could not get down.	*Jōla puh wana ké khatalay woh aw biā ra kūzédalay nuh sho.*
How did the people bring him down?	*Khalqo sanga ra kūz kar?*

They had made a permanent residence on the top of the hill.	*Hagho da ghar puh sar bāndé khpal dà osédo zāi jōr karay woh.*

VOCABULARY LII.

وړوکی غونډی	*warūké ghundai*	Low ridge.
غونډی	*ghundai*	Hillock.
لوړه ژوره	*lwarā jhawara*	Low undulation.
ختل	*khatal*	Ascend.
کوزيدل	*kūzédal*	To descend.
تنګه تنګی	*tanga tangai*	Narrow defile.
قريب قريب	*qarib qarib*	Practically.
حد-بريد	*had, brid*	Limit.
دره	*dara*	Valley.
معمولی	*māmūli*	Precarious kind.
بيا هم	*biā hum*	Even then.
عين تر-پورې	*ain tar-pōré*	Right down till.
لائيق	*lāiéq*	Fit, worthy, capable.
اباد	*abād*	Cultivated or populated.
ابادي	*abādi*	Cultivation or population.
کلپ	*kalp*	Steep.
اوبهٔ خور	*obuh khwar*	Irrigation.
تل	*tal*	Bed (of the river or well.)
تلی	*talay*	Palm of hand, Sole of foot.

پټ	*pat*	Stealthily.
ګڼ ځنګل	*ganr zangal*	Dense Jungle
لوښه	*lūkha*	Reeds.
لوی لوی واښه	*lōi lōi wākhuh*	High grass.
املي	*imli*	Tamarind.
تر اوس پوری	*tar osa pōré*	Still.
غریب خلق	*gharib khalq*	Miserable inhabitant.
ژور	*jhawar*	Deep.
پلن	*plan*	Broad.
اوبهٔ ترزنګون زنګون پوری دي	*obuh tar zangūn zangūn pōré di*	The water is knee deep.
ګرزیدل	*garzédal*	To walk, to turn.
وران	*vrān*	Ruined.
زنګون یا ګوډه	*zangūn* or *gōda*	Knee.

EXERCISE 51.

The road now leads over the low ridge on the left, and going over some low undulations, descends to the river through a narrow defile between low hills. This pass is practically the limit of the cultivation of the Mashhad valley; for though there is a little bcyond, it is of the most precarious kind. The villagers exist in constant fear from Turkoman raiders; yet under a strong government the whole valley of this river right down to Akdarhand, is capable of being kept in the highest state of cultivation, as there is abundance of water in the river, of which banks are low enough to admit of its being distributed for irrigation. The road now goes along the bed of the river, which is covered with a dense jungle of tamarind and high grass and one mile and a half further on passes the old Fort of Nazarian, where there are still a few miserable inhabitants. It then crosses the river which is here only two and a half feet deep and thirty feet broad, then turns to the left and ascends the right bank to a ruined fort. It then passes over an undulation and descends again to the bed of the river at Inayatabad.

VOCABULARY LIII.

قارغه	*qārghuh*	Crow.
پۀ امان	*puh amān*	Peacefully.
سلامتی	*salāmati*	Safety.
سلامت	*salmat*	Safe.
فارسی خوان	*fārsi khwān*	Persian (man.)
پاي	*pāi*	Foot } Persian.
دست	*dast*	Hand } Persian.
يا دست مرد يا پاي مرد	*yā dasté mard* *yā pāi mard*	Either make use of your hands or feet. (you should fight otherwise run away to save yourself.)

مقابله کول	*muqābéla kawal*	To witnstand.
دا بهتره دَه	*dā behtara dah*	It is better.
خود	*khud*	Certainly.
تښتيدل	*takhtédal*	To flee.
تېښته	*tékhta*	Flight.
ادميان	*admian*	Men.
بزُدل	*buzdil*	Coward.
بزدلي	*buzdili*	Cowardice.
دين	*din*	Religion.
مذهب	*mazhab*	Religion.
روا يا حلال	*rawā*, or *halāl*	Lawful.
خصوصاً	*khusūsan*	Especiallv.
هر کله	*har kala*	When ever.
ټيټ کيدل	*tit kédal*	To bend down.
لوټه يا غونډه	*lūta* or *ghunda*	Clod of earth.
اوچتول	*ūchatawal*	To pick up, lift up.
لستونړی	*lastōnray*	Sleeve.
لهٔ لری نه	*luh laré na*	From a distance.
لهٔ ورايه	*luh vrāyā*	From a distance.
سيل کول	*sail kawal*	To fly about.
خواه مخواه	*khwāh makhwāh*	Some how or other.

EXERCISE 52.

يو قارغهٔ خپل ځوي ته نصيحت کاوهٔ ويل ئی چه ويره لهٔ هرڅيز
نه ښه دَهٔ هر څوک چه ويريږي نو مدام به پهٔ امان او سلامت وي

فارسي خوان وائي يا دست مرد يا پاي مرد او ځمونږ دَ خلقو
خو دَ مقابلې طاقت خود نشته نو دا بهتره دَه چه دشمن ته ميدان
پرېږدو او وتښتو ترنه او فرض کړه چه موږ مقابله هم وکړو نو خوا
مخواه به مو يا لاس مات شي يا پښه نو پۀ جنګ کښې څۀ خير دَی؟
نو بچي ځما نصيحت واوره هر يو ځناور چه ورته تيغ شي نو تښتيدَه تر
دي تيښتي ته آدميان بزدلي وائي ځکه ځمونږ پۀ مذهب کښې
روا دَه خصوصاً لۀ سړي نه ډير ويرېدل پکار دي هر کله چه دی زمکې
ته ټيټ شي نو سمدستي تر الوځه څکه چه دا لۀ زمکې نه کاڼي يا
لوټه را اوچتوي بچي ورته پۀ جواب کښې وو چه بابا؟ کۀ دغه
سړي پۀ لستوڼي کښې پټ دَ ځان سره کاڼي راوړي وي نو زۀ
بۀ ئې څۀ وکړم دابۀ ښۀ وي چه سړي لۀ لري نه و وينم نو به تر والوځم
پلار ورته وِ شاباش؟ تۀ لۀ ما نه هوښيار ئې ورځه سيل کوه هر چرته
چه ځي سلامت بۀ ئې—

VOCABULARY LIV.

ټټو	*tatu*	Pony.
روان کېدل	*rawān kédal*	To set out.
نور خاتۀ	*nwar khātuh*	Day break.
اوبۀ ډکول	*obuh dakawal*	To draw water.
ګيره	*gira*	Beard, whiskers.
بريت	*brét*	Moustache.
ګڼړل	*ganral*	To consider.
اوتر	*autar*	Alarmed.
پس لۀ هغه	*pas luh hagha*	Afterwards.
پېرَی	*péray*	Genie.
خاپېرۍ	*khāpérai*	Fairy.

EXERCISE 53.

I arrived with the Regiment I was attached to all safe at Agra where I bought a pony for eleven rupees and in company with four or five other sepoys, who had got leave also, I set out for my village. I reached my home early one morning before it was light and waited outside till day break. When my mother came out to draw (fill) water, I called to her, but she did not recognise me in the least, for during the four or five years I had been absent, I had grown from a boy into a man. I had also whiskers and a moustache and considered myself a handsome sepoy. My mother seemed so alarmed when I spoke to her, that I also became frightened, but afterwards my father told me that my uncle had written home to say that I had been killed so my mother thought at first that I was a genie.

VOCABULARY LV.

اعتبار	*itĕbār*	Trust.
محتاج	*muhtāj*	Needy.
شتهٔ من	*shtuh man*	Rich.
دا یوه عامه خبره ده	*dā yawa āma khabara dah*	This is a common thing.
پردی	*praday*	Stranger.

خلق ور ته نهٔ شيِ کتَی	*khalq war ta nuh shi katay*	The people cannot bear to see him.
شرميدل	*sharmédal*	To be ashamed.
حاکم	*hākam*	Ruler.
سپک کول	*spak kawal*	To insult.
برباد کول یا تالاکول نړوَل	*barbād kawal* or *tālā kawal* or *narawal*	To ruin.
کهٔ داسی نهٔ شيِ کيدیَ	*kuh dāsé nuh shi kéday*	If this is impossible.
کوهیَ	*kūhay*	Well (of water.)
ور گذار کول	*war gūzār kawal*	To throw down.
گُذار	*gūzar*	A blow.
خير	*khér*	Well.
دَ پهٔ سر	*da puh sar*	Against.
مُخبر	*mukhber*	Informer.
سرهٔ زر	*sruh zar*	Gold.
سپين زر	*spin zar*	Silver.
زيړ	*ziar*	Brass.
تانبه	*tānba*	Copper.
موړ	*mōr*	Rich, replete.
ماړهٔ	*māruh*	Rich, replete (Plural.)
جوړ	*jōr*	Accordingly.
اندر پايه	*andrapāya*	Ladder.
گُټ	*gut*	Corner.
پهره	*péhra*	Sentry go.

سنتري اودرول	*sentri ōdrawal*	To post a sentry.
پهٔ ډاګ کښې اچول	*puh dāg ké achawal*	To post (a letter).
پهٔ باندې لاس پورې کول	*puh bāndé lās pōré kawal*	To start. commence.
کالي	*kāli*	Ornaments.
نغدې روپئ	*naghdé rupai*	Cash.
پنډ	*pand*	Parcel, bundle.
مالګه	*mālga*	Salt
اوچت پاڅیدل	*ūchat pāsédāl*	Get up straight.
نمک حلال	*namak halāl*	Loyal.
نمک حرام	*namak harām*	Disloyal.
نمک	*namak*	Salt (Urdu.)
اوړیدل	*aurédal*	To cross over.

EXERCISE 54.

دَ خلیلو پهٔ علاقهٔ کښې پهٔ یو کلي کښې یو دولتمند زمیندار وهٔ چه
خلقو وِ بانده دَ ډیر لوئي دولت اعتبار کاوهٔ ډیر ښهٔ سړی وهٔ د خدائي
پهٔ نامه به ئي غریبانو او محتاجانو له ډیر څهٔ ورکول مګر دغه یوه
ګناه ئې وَه چه شتهٔ من وهٔ نو ورځ پهٔ ورځ به ئې پهٔ کلي کښې
دشمنان زیاتیدل او دا یوه عامه خبره دَه چه دَ پښتنو پهٔ وطن کښې
څوک دولتمند شي او خدائ پاک ورله عزت ورکړي نو دَ خپلو پردو
بدي شي او ورته نهٔ شي کتی او دَ هر یو داخوښه وي چه دَی
خوار شوی بد نام شوی وشرمیدی نو یاخو یې دَ علاقې پهٔ حاکمانو
سپکوی لو برباد وي ئې او که دا نهٔ شي کیدی نو پټ پله ورته څهٔ
ناځهٔ دوهی وکړي پهٔ کښې ئې ورګډاږ کړي خیر دَ دې دولتمند

زمیندار پهٔ سر ږیری مُخبرئ غیر علاقی ته لاړی چه کهٔ داړه
پِروکړئ نو پهٔ سرو سپینو به ماړهٔ شئ جوړ یوه شپه دَ پنځهٔ ویشتو
اپریدو یوه داړه چه ورسره دَ کلي بدمعاشان هم یو ځائی شول پهٔ
نیمه شپه پهٔ کلي راننوته اندر پائی یی وتړلی او سم دَ دی زمیندار پهٔ
کور ورواوړیدل اول خوئی دَ کور ټول سړيِ او ځوکیدار وتړلو او بیا ئی
دَ کور ښځی یو خواته وشړلی او پهره ئی پرِ ودَروله چه شور ونهٔ کړیِ
او بیا ئی پهٔ لوټ لاس پوری کړ ټول کالي جامی او نغدی روپئی ئی
راجمع کړلی پنډونه ئی ترِ وتړل چه روانیدل نو یو په کښی وو چه داده
روپئی راځئی چه ویئ خوروٗ جوړ ټول راجمع شول روپئ ئی
وخوړه پهدی کښی یو مشروٗه اوچت پاځید ویل ئی راځئ چه
خوٗ چه دَ دی کور نمک مو وخوړ نو غلا ئی نهٔ کووٗ آخر موٗږ. کښی خو
هم ځهٔ پُښتو شته لاړل پنډوونه ئی پهٔ ځائ پریښودل—

VOCABULARY LVI.

میدان	*maidān*	Open ground, plain
خوشَی	*khushay*	Deserted, useless.
خالی	*khāli*	Empty.
کوچ	*kōch*	March.
شګه	*shaga*	Sand.
څاڅکَی	*sāskay*	A drop.
موسمی باران	*mōsami bārān*	Periodical rain.
تلاوٗ	*talāw*	Tank.
اوچ	*och*	Dry.
سفر	*safar*	Journey.
زرَی	*zaray*	Guide.
زیرَی	*zéray*	Good news.

پاؤ باندِ یو میل	*pāw bāndé yau mil*	1¼ mile.
تالاش	*tālāsh*	Search.
کنودل	*kanōdal*	To dig.
مشک	*mashk*	Mussak.
دَ مخ کښې ضرورت	*da makh ké zarūrat*	Future necessity.

EXERCISE 55.

After leaving this place we proceeded twenty three miles and encamped near a well on a piece of open ground in the jungle. Many deserted (empty) villages were met with on the march and the road was, for the most part, over heavy sand, (there was much sand on many parts of the road) without a drop of water near. Periodical rains had failed in this part of the country, the tanks and wells had mostly dried up, which rendered the heat and length of our journey that day all the more distressing. Luckily the guide whom we had brought with us and who had frequently travelled along this road, informed us that at about a mile and quarter distant were a few huts, the inhabitants of which were supplied with water from a spring. We set out immediately in search of it and our great joy found it was not dried up (When we found that it was not dried up we were very much pleased) and on digging up a little in the sand an abundance of water flowed out, from which we drank ourselves and watered our horses and camels and made the bhisties fill their mussacks for future necessities.

VOCABULARY LVII

ملاقات	*mulāqāt*	Interview, visit.
لنډ	*land*	Short.
لنډه خلاصول	*landa khlāsawal*	To cut short.
خبره داده	*khabara dā dah*	The true fact is.
عام	*ām*	Common.
ګوته	*guta*	Finger.
بر خلاف	*barkhélāf*	Against.
بر ناحقه	*barnāhaqa*	Without any cause or reason.
نو څۀ چل وشي	*no suh chal woshee*	Then what happens.
لخته	*lakhta*	Stick, cane, power.

EXERCISE 56.

یو زمیندار د ډپټی کمشنر صاحب ملاقات د پاره تلی ؤ چه وئی
غوښتو نو په ملاقات کښې تر نه صاحب پښتنه وکړه چه ماته د پښتنو ټول
حال ووایه چه داغځه خلق دي دی سړي ورته وِ چه صاحب
د پښتنو قصی خو ډیری او لوئی لوئی دي نو لنډه ئی خلاصه کړم او
بۀ دا اورېدی قصی درته راشروع کړم صاحب ورته و لنډه ئی ووایه ځکه
چه ماته دومره وخت چرته دی چه داسی لوئی لوئی قصی واورم

دهٔ ورته وِ صاحبَ ؟ خبره دَ اده چه پهٔ پښتنو کښې يو سړىَ لهٔ
عامو خلقو نه يوه ګوته اوچت شيِ نو خلق ئى خوا مخواه برخلاف شيِ
او چه دوه ګوتى اوچت شيِ نو خلق ئى بر ناحقه دشمنان شيِ
او چه درى ګوتى اوچت شيِ نو بيا يى وژنيِ نهٔ ني پريږدى په
دى باندِ صاحب پيرِ وخندل او تپوس ئى ترِ وکړ چه کهٔ خلوو ګوتى
اوچت شيِ نو بيا خهٔ چل وشى زميندارو بيا سلامت شيِ دا
خاورمه ګوته ستاسو لخته دَه چه چاله ئى پهٔ لاس ورکړئى نو طاقت ئى
پيدا شيِ او خپل خان پر بچولىَ شيِ—

VOCABULARY LVIII.

پهٔ باندِ بحث کول	*puh bāndé bahas kawal* or *khabaré ataré kawal*	To discuss.
خبرِے اترِي کول		
فيصله کول	*faisala kawal*	To decide, to settle.
ټُکړه	*tukra*	Piece.
دَ حق شفعى دعوىَ کول	*da haq shufé dawa kawal*	To claim a right ? of pre-emption.
جګړه	*jagara*	Quarrel.
شريعت	*shariāt*	Mohammedan Law.
کهٔ داسى نهٔ کويِ	*kuh dāsé nuh kawi*	If they refuse to do so.
پهٔ-باندِ لښکر کول	*puh-bāndé lakhkar kawal*	To raise an army against.
پهٔ-باندِ پهٔ زور کول	*puh-bāndé puh zōr kawal*	To compel.
قبضه	*qabza*	Possession.

پښتو	*pukhtu*	Pathan honour.
عرضی	*arzi*	Petition.
پهٔ پښتو کښې دا کارِ نهٔ دیَ پکار	*puh pukhtu ké* *dā kār nuh* *day pakār*	The Pathan honour forbids this.
لو کول	*law kawal*	To harvest.
څهٔ خاص کار	*suh khās kār*	Particular business.
کهٔ دی کښں ورتهٔ څهٔ خیر وِی	*kuh dé ké war* *ta suh kher wi*	Should it be made worth their while.

Exercise 57.

The matter was discussed at a full Jirga of all tribes. It will be remembered that the Mondo Khel purchased and forcibly took possession of a piece of land over which the Takhli Khel claimed a right of pre-emption. It was decided that the Mondo Khel should be offered an opportunity of deciding the dispute according to the Mohammadan Law and that if they refused to do so the united tribes should raise an army to compel them. The Mondo Khel said that if they had known that there would have been all this trouble, they would never have taken the land but as they have actually got possession, Pathan honour forbade them withdrawing then. They accordingly sent an application to three tribes asking for their assistance. Had it been worth their while, these tribes would certainly have joined in, as they had finished cutting their crops and at that time had no particular business of their own to attend to.

VOCABULARY LIX.

لټ	*lat*	Slothful.
ناراستي	*nārāsti*	Laziness.
خوزيدل	*khwazédal*	To move, (intransitive.)
نور	*nwar*	Sunshine.
لاروی	*lāraway*	Traveller.
لوکوټي	*lūkūti*	Little.
مونږ سوري ته کړي	*mūng sōri tā krai*	Take us into the shade
بعضې	*bazé*	Some.
ساده	*sāda*	Simple.
خوار	*khwār*	Poor, helpless.
راکوزيدل	*rā kūzédal*	To come down, dismount.
خداي دِ و بخښه	*khudāi dé wo bakha*	May God forgive you !
ثواب	*sawāb*	Reward from God.
ثواب به دِ وشي	*sawāb ba dé wo shee*	You will get reward from God.
بينت	*baint*	Cane, stick.
بې غيرته	*bé ghairata*	Oh, you shameless one !
دومره نهٔ شرميږې	*dōmra nuh sharmégé*	Have you not so much shame ?
روغ موټ	*rōgh mōt*	Safe and sound.

بچوٗ	*bachū*	My son! (in a sarcastic manner.)
ازار	*āzār*	Curse.
بیره	*bera*	A wild plum.
غلیَ	*ghalay*	Silent.
ځان دِ کوٗنړ کړ	*zān dé kūnr kar*	You pretended to be deaf.
حد	*had*	Limit.
دهٔ له حدَ وویسته	*duh luh hada wo wista*	He has gone beyond the limit.
کم بخت	*kam bakht*	Unlucky.
کوری شه	*kuré sha*	Get out you beast. (driving away a dog)
له دهٔ نه به څوک څهٔ خیر و ړیِ	*la duh na ba sōk suh khér vree*	What good is he to people?
حکومت کول	*hukūmat kawal*	To rule.

EXERCISE 58.

پهٔ یو ځائ کښې دَ یوی ونی لاندِ دری لگان پراتهٔ وُو - ناراستیِ
ئی دی حد ته رسیدلی وَه - چه دَ ځای نهٔ خوزَیدل - چه نور به
پرِ راغیَ نو دَ لاری لاروٗ ته به ئی ووِ چه لوکوټیِ خو موٗږ سوری ته
کړیٔ - بعضی به چه ساده خلق وُو نو دوی به ئی سوری ته کړل
یقین به ئی وشو چه خواران به ناجوړ ویِ - ښکه لهٔ ځایَ نهٔ شیِ
خوزیدیَ - او چا به ور پوریِ و خندل ترِ به تیر شو یوه ورځ وربانډِ
یو سور راغیَ - چه دَ دوئی خوا ته را نیږدی شو نو یو ورته اواز وکړ -
چه ځوانَ لوکوټیِ دَ دی اسَ را کوٗز شه او لږی اوبهٔ راکړه - خدای
دِ وبخښه - ثواب به د وشیِ - سور چه دا خبره واوریده نو ورته ډیر

په قهر شو ورغی او یو ښو بیننتونه ئی پرِ واچول او وئی ویل چه بی
غیرتَ دومره نهٔ شرمیږی چه ما دَ اسَ، را کوزَ وی او ته پخپله روغ
مونږ ئی دَ ښای نهٔ پا ښی چه اوبهٔ وسکی ـ هغه بل ور باندِ
اواز وکړ ویل یی بچوٗ ښځه؟ ښما ازار ووهای که نه ـ هغه بله ورځ
مِ درته واز وکړ چه لوکوټیِ راشه دا بیړه راته پهٔ خولهٔ کښں واچوه
نو ښځه دِ ښان غلیَ کړ ـ هغه دریم دی سورته اواز وکړ ویل ئی
صاحبَ یو ښوئی نورهم ووهه دَ ناراستيِ خو هم یو حد ویِ ـ دهٔ لهٔ
حدَ وویسته ـ هغه بله ورځ یو سپیَ راغیَ ښما مخ ئی ښکولو ـ
دی کم بختِ ورته دَ ناراستئي نه دومره نهٔ ویل چه کوری شه ـ لهٔ
دهٔ نه به ښوک ښهٔ خیر وړیِ ـ سور چه دَ دی بل لیښ دا خبره
واوریده نو اول خو حیران شهٔ او بیائي ډیر وخندل ـ او وئي ویل
چه کهٔ دا حال ويِ نو ښځه به دَ هندوستان خلق پهٔ خپل ملک
باندِ حکومت وکړی ـ

VOCABULARY LX.

خاندان	*khānadān*	Family.
ملا	*mulā*	Priest.
بهادري	*bahādari*	Adventure, bravery.
تکړه ژوندون	*takra jhwandūn*	Active life.
هغه به لار نیوله	*haghuh ba lār niwala*	He took to the road.
مشهور	*mashhūr*	Famous.
داسی چل وشو	*dāsé chal wo sho*	It so happened.
فرض یا کار	*farz* or *kār*	Duty.
پسی کیدل	*pasé kédal*	To hunt down.

نیول	*nıwal*	To capture.
مفرور	*mafrūr*	Outlaw.
انعام	*inām*	Prize or reward.
نوی اودریدلی	*nawé odrédalé*	Newly raised (regt.)
د گائد پلټن	*da gāid paltan*	The Guides Regt.
کوشش کول	*kōshash kawal*	To try.
تنبو یا خیمه	*tanbū* or *khéma*	Tent.
خیال	*kheyāl*	Thought.
خیال کول	*kheyāl kawal*	To think.
لار	*lār*	Path, road.
خوړ	*khwar*	Nullah, ravine.
دره	*dara*	Valley.
غاښی	*ghākhay*	Pass (on the top of the hill).
دا خاص د گائیډ د پاره لائق دی	*dā khās da gāid da pāra lāiéq day*	He is just the man for the Guides.
چټي یا خط	*chitai* or *khat*	Letter, note.
راغوښتل	*rāghukhtal*	To invite.
پړاو	*parāw*	Camp.
معامله	*māmela*	Matter, affair.
په دې معامله کښې خبرې اترې کول	*pa dé māmela ké khabaré ataré kawal*	To talk this over.
د پهٔ سر روپئی (یا پیسي) منل یا ورکول	*da-puh sar rupai* (or *pesé*) *manal* or *warkawal*	To put a price on someone's head.

دَ خبره منل	*da khabara manal*	To accept invitation.
رسوخ-اعتبار	*rusūkh* or *itébār*	Reputation.
عزت	*izzat*	Honour.
سرکار	*sarkār*	British govt
لرل	*laral*	To possess, have.
گوره	*gōra*	Look here !
زوړند کول	*zwarand kawal*	To hang.
دَ خلقو دَ وړاندِ	*da khalqo da vrāndé*	Publicly.

EXERCISE 59.

Delawar Khan was a Khatak of good family. He was brought up as a priest, but his love of adventure let him to a more active life. He took to the road and in time he became the most famous robber in the whole of Yusafzai. It happened that one of Sir Harry Lumsden's duties was to hunt down and capture Delawar Khan, who was now an outlaw with a price of two thousand rupees on his head. Many a time did Lumsden and his newly raised 'Corps of Guides' try, but they could not capture Delawar. One day sitting in his tent Sir Harry Lumsden thought that this man must know every path, nullah and pass in the District. He is just the man for the Guides. I will send him a note. A letter was therefore sent to Delawar Khan inviting him to come into the Camp to talk this matter over. One day Delawar Khan in answer to this letter, came up to Lumsden. This man, with a price on his head, accepted the invitation. It says much for the reputation for honour which the British possessed in borderland. Lumsden said to him, " Look here, Delawar, you are a fine fellow, but one day I will catch you and hang you publicly on a tree".

VOCABULARY LXI.

د پهٔ ستر‌ګو ګوتی منډل	*da-puh stargo gōté mandal*	To blame (lit. to push fingers into some one's eyes).
شاړ	*shār*	Barren (land), uncouth, uneducated (person).
وينځه	*winza*	Slave girl.
بی بی	*bi bi*	Wife, mistress.
چاودل	*chāwdal*	To split or burst (Intrans).
چاودی	*chāwday*	Burst (past part.)
مولی	*maulā*	God.
شادولا	*shādaula*	Saint (lit. small headed).
پهٔ زور کلي نهٔ کیږي	*puh zōr kali nuh kégi*	It cannot be done by force.

پهٔ سبق کینول	*puh sabaq kénawal*	To send to school.
مندرسه	*mandrasa*	School.
کینول	*kénawal*	To make to sit.
نهٔ دَ دین شو او نهٔ دَسادین شو	*nuh da din sho aw nuh da sādin shō*	He became useless for this world and the next.
زکه پکه	*zaka paka*	The last brass farthing.
باج کول یا داؤکول	*bāj kawal* or *dāw kawal*	To spend uselessly.
تل ټوکړه	*tal tūkra*	Land.
صبر	*sabar*	Patience.
(ته) خولهٔ چینګول	*(ta) khula chingawal*	To ask for help (lit to grin).
پهٔ باندِ زړه کول	*puh-bāndé zruh kawal*	To want to ask but hardly daring to.
(سره) لاس کول	*(sara) lās kawal*	To give a helping hand to.
دَ فکر پهٔ تال زنګیدل	*da fikar pūh tāl zangédal*	To be undecided.
زنګل یا زنګیدل	*zangal* or *zangédal*	To swing, (intrans.)
تش لاس	*tash lās*	Empty handedness
کهٔ رشتیا راباندِ وائې	*kuh rishtiā rā bāndé wāyé*	If I tell you the truth.
کته	*kata*	Pack saddle.
تبخې	*tabakhay*	Chapati cooking pan (Urdu Tawā.)
کټورې	*katōray*	Copper cup (Urdu Katōra)

کنډول	*kandōl*	Earthen cup.
ښلیَ	*salay*	Heap, grave-mound.
نقل	*naqal*	Copy.
ننګ	*nang*	Modesty.
پخوا	*pakhwā*	Formerly.
ګډوریَ	*gadūray*	Lamb.
پریوتل	*prèwatal*	To fall.
(ته) لاس ورکول	*(ta) lās war kawal*	To shake hands with, help.
ځانَ خپلَ ځانَ	*zāna khpala zāna*	Every one for himself.
ګنړه	*ganra*	Otherwise.
هیندکیَ	*hindkay*	Indian (i. e. non-Pathan.)
یادَول	*yādawal*	To mention, to talk about.
ټل ته کول	*tal ta kawal*	To defeat.
اغزیَ	*aghzay*	Thorn.
موټیَ	*mūtay*	Fist.
ټینګول	*tingawal*	To hold firmly.
کهٔ خبره پهٔ ځوی واچوی	*kuh khabara pūh zōi wāchawé*	If you talk about the son…
دَ پوزې سرئې غونډ شو	*da pōzé sar yé ghund sho*	He grew up (lit. the tip of his nose became round.)
تهٔ څوک او زهٔ څوک	*tuh sōk aw zuh sōk*	What do I care for you !

پهٔ باندې تانړه کیدل	*puh bāndé tānra kédal*	To be quartered on some one (exceeding laws of hospitality.)

EXERCISE 60.
(IDIOMATIC)

سړیَ هر سړیَ راځيِ او ښما پهٔ سترګو ګوتی منډيِ چه ښامن دړ
نه شاړ شوُ دَ وینڅی مات سر وینيِ او دَ بیِ بیِ چاودیَ زړهٔ ښوک
نهٔ وینيِ با با ؟ پهٔ زور خو کلیِ نهٔ کیږیِ دَ جماعت پهٔ سبقږ کینول
دَمنډرسی پهٔ سبقږ کینول چه نهٔ کويِ مولیِ نو ښهٔ به وکړیِ شادولا مشهوره
خبره دَه چه نهٔ ښی وابه دِخلم چه نهٔ خوری ښهٔ به دِکړم نهٔ دَ دِین شوُ
او نهٔ دَ سادین شوُ ښما خو چه ښهٔ زکه پکهٔوَه هغه م وربانډِ باج کړه اوس
دَخلقو زړهٔ دیَ چه دا ټل ټوکړهٔ م دَه دام هم وربانډِ داوُ کړیَ ولی
زهٔ ښهٔ وکړم کهٔ ګوشت ګران نو صبر ارزان آخر زهٔ خو هم پښتوُن یم
پُښتودَه راکښی چاته خو خولهٔ نهٔ شم چینګولیَ او کهٔ پهٔ چا بانډِ زړهٔ
وهم کړم نو چه ویی غواړم په دی خولی نو خورم بدیی پهٔ کومه خولی
آخر کهٔ ښوک چاسره ښهٔ لاس وکړیِ نو خوراکيِ خو یی نهٔ شی ټوله ورځ
دَ فکر پهٔ ټال زانګم چه تشه لاسَ تهٔمِ دشمن ئی او کهٔ رِښتیا راباندِ
وئی نو ښما خو هم دغه دَ کتی او دَ تبخيِ خبره دَه اوس خوداسی
وخت راغلیَ دیَ چه که کټوریَ ورکوی نو کنډول به پرِ ښوکَ دز نهٔ کړیِ
پهٔ پُښتنو لاړل خلیِ جوړ شول او نقلوُ نهٔ ئی پاتی شول نن خو
پُښتو دَ پښتوُنَ لاړه او ننګ دَ ٠غلَ لاړ پخوا به پښتوُن پهٔ پښتون سر
ایښو او اوس چه ښموُنږ مغرور یاغستانِ ته ورشیِ نو دَ سلو روپو
ګډوریَ شيِ پخوا به چه ښوک پریوتو نو چا خو به لاس ورکړو اوس
خو خانَ خپِلَ ښانَ کهٔ ویِ درسخه خو خورهِ ګنړهٔ مره خلقو به
هندکیان یادول اوس ئی هغویِ ټال ته کړیِ دیِ او کهٔ رشتیا درته

ووايم نو دَ دې زماني خامن څۀ دی که دا دَ دشمن سترګه کښې
اغزی نۀ وی نو چاله څۀ کوی بس چه دَ موټې دَ ټبرګولوشي
نو ځي دړ نه چرګ خو يو مارغۀ دی چه چا ونيوۀ دَهغۀ دی دَمور
زړۀ پۀ ځوی او دَځوی زړۀ پۀ اوچ ديوال پۀ دنيا کښې هم يو
پلار دی چه زړه ئی غواړې چۀ ځوی رانه اوچت شوی او کۀ خبره
پۀ ځوی واچوی نو دَليدو نه ئی پۀ نۀ ليدو خوشحال وي تر هغه
دِځوی وي چه لا ئی چرګورې بانګ نۀ وي ويلی خو چه دَپوزې
سرئی غوړې شي نو بس تۀ څوک او زۀ څوک داخو لا پريږده چه
ورارۀ مِ هم راغلی دی پۀ ما تاڼه دی—

Section 13.

The student is advised to learn the following idiomatic sentences carefully before going up for his Examination :—

1. Since I came to this place.	*Kala rāsé chī zuh dé zāi ta rāghalay yam.*
2. Until this is satisfactorily settled, the tribāl allowances as well as your own are stopped.	*Tar sō pōré chi da dé puh khuh shān sara faisala wō nuh shee, da qām mājėb aw stā khpal dwāra ba band wee.*
3. The ducks are swimming in the water.	*Hilai puh ōbō ké garzı.*
4. Tell the syce to cut some grass for the horse.	*Sāis ta wo wāya chi da āss da pāra suh wākhuh wo kree.*

5. We were cutting wood when they attacked us and carried off all our cattle.	*Mūng largee wahal chi rā bāndé yé hamla wō kra aw tōl zamūng māl yé bōtlo.*
6. I have nothing to do with him.	*Zamā war sara hiss gharaz nishta.*
7. I owe him five rupees.	*Da haghuh rā bāndé pinzuh rūpai dee.*
8. Yesterday you said he owes you some money.	*Parūn khō tā wo wé chi zama puh haghuh bāndé suh rupai dee.*
9. Yes, he owes me five rupees.	*Ho zamā war bāndé pinzuh rūpai dee.*
10. I can't help it, I will have to send you back to your own country.	*Pa dé ké zuh gram nuh yam, zuh ba tā khwā makhwā khpal watan ta biārtā légam.*
11. I will try my best to keep you as my own orderly but I do not know whether the colonel will be willing to allow this.	*Sōmrā chi mé da wasa kégee, dōmra kōshash ba wo kram chi tā da zān ardali kram, magar zuh khabar nuh yam chī karnail sāhib ba pa dé rāzee shi kuh na.*
12. I tried my best to send him to my own regt. but the Colonel did not agree.	*Sōmra chi da wasa mé kédalo, dōmrā kōshash mé wō kar chi zuh yé khpalé paltané ta wo légam, magar karnail sāhib wo na manala.*
13. This man says you have beaten him, what have you to say for yourself ?	*Dā saray wāyee chi zuh dé wahalay yam, puh dé ké stā suh jawāb day ?*

14. How far is it to the Mess ?	*Miskōt sōmra laré day?*
15. What is that firing?	*Hagha dazé da suh dee?*
16. What is that noise ?	*Dagha shōr da suh day ?*
17. I will write a letter when I have eaten food.	*Chi rōtai wo khuram nō chitai ba wō likam.*
18. When I had arrived in Kohat I met an old man.	*Kala chi zuh Kohāt ta wo rasédalam nō yau spin giray puh makha rāghlo.*
19. I saw him before he saw me.	*Hagha lā zuh lidalay nuh wam, chi mā hagha wōlid.*
20. If he had killed me he would have been as sorry as I should have been if I had killed him.	*Kuh zuh yé wajhalay way, nō haghuh ba dōmra afsōs karay woh, laka chi da haghuh puh wajhalo* (or *marg*) *mā ba karay woh.*
21. I wish I had gone to Kabul.	*Armān day chi zuh Kobāl ta talay way.*
22. I wish I had been married.	*Armān day chi mā wāduh karay way.*
23. I wish I had come before four.	*Armān day chi zuh luh salōrō bajo na awal rāghalay way.*
24. He not only beat me with a stick but if you had not come he would have certainly killed me.	*Zuh yé nuh seraf puh largee bāndé wo wahalam, balké kuh tuh rāghalay nuh way no zuh ba yé wajhalay wam.*

25. What do you do with your pay?	*Tuh khpal talab suh kawé?*
26. Let alone English I can not speak my own language well.	*Angrézi kho prégda chi zuh khpala jhaba hum kha nuh sham wayalay.*
27. See if my book is on the table.	*Gōra chi zamā kitāb puh méz bāndé kho nishta.*
28. See if the sahib is coming.	*Gōra chi sāhib kho nuh rāzee.*
29. The doctor advised him to drink two seers of milk every day.	*Daktar war ta wo wé chi da vrazé dwà séra pai ska.*
30. Come to my house every day and bring me some flowers.	*Mudām zamā kōr ta rāza aw rā la suh gulūna rāwra.*
31. Every kind of shooting can be had in this country.	*Pa dé watan ké har rang khkār mundalay shee.*
32. My only brother committed a serious crime and became an outlaw.	*Zamā khāli yau vrōr woh aw haghuh hum yau sakht juram wō kar aw mafrūr sho.*
33. This is the very man whom I wanted to see.	*Dā hum hagha saray day chi mā wayal zuh ba yé gōram.*
34. We started on the very moment and reached Kabul the same day.	*Hum puh hagha sāat mūng rawān shoo aw Kābal ta amrōza wo rasédoo.*
35. The thanadar laughed at the old woman	*Thānra dār būdai pōré wo khandal aw yé wo*

and said "This is the way with you people".	*wayal chi dā stāso da khalqō lār dah.*
36. Why did you laugh at him ?	*Walé dé war pōré wo khandal ?*
37. The dog began to bark but no one stirred.	*Spay puh ghapā sho magar hésōk wo nuh khwazéd.*
38. The sahib is about to come. Just wait he will be here in a moment if you want to see him.	*Sāhib rātlūnkay day* (or) *puh rātlo ké day puh yaw sāat ké ba rāshee kuh yé gōré.*
39. I suppose you consider yourself wiser than I am.	*Zamā khyal day chi tuh khpal zān luh mā na hukhyār ganré.*
40. A little more than three years later this city was again attacked by Aurangzéb.	*Luh dréo kālō na lag suh ziāt pas, puh dé khahar bāndé Aurangzéb biā hamla wo kra.*
41. He himself did not stay there any longer but left his Sardars to complete the work.	*Pakhpala kho dér halta pāté nuh sho magar khpal sardārān yé da kār pūra kawalo da pāra halta prékhōdal.*
42. Take either this or that.	*Yā dā wākhla yā hagha wākhla.*
43. I will take neither.	*Zuh yau hum nuh akhlam.*
44. Give them five annas each.	*War ta pinzuh pinzuh ané war kra.*
45. I must have seen this man but I cannot remember now.	*Dā saray ba mé lidalay wi, kho os rā ta yād nuh di.*

46. Remind me when I go to the Office.	*Chi daftar ta lārsham no rā ta yād kra.*
47. I threw a stone at him.	*Mā hagha puh kānrī wo wishtalo.*
48. When did you meet him ?	*Kala puh makha daraghay ?*
49. I met an old man whom a little boy was leading by the hand.	*Yau spin giray puh makha rāghlo chi yau warūki halak luh lās na biwalo.*
50. I was just missed otherwise my sight would have been destroyed for ever.	*Zuh ila bach shwam ganra da ūmar da pāra ba me nazar barbād shaway woh.*
51. The old man who had only one eye was telling stories to the boys in the Hujra.	*Spin girai chi puh yawa starga kānray woh, halakāno ta puh hūjra ké qesé yé wayalé.*
52. The old man's evidence should be accepted as he said he had read the marriage service.	*Da spin giri gawāhi dé manzūra shi chi wāyee chi mā yé nikāh taralay day.*
53. On the further side of the plain a river had to be crossed twice.	*Da mairé puh bala khwā luh yau sind na dwa zala poréwatal woo.*
54. He has to go to the office.	*Hagha khwā makhwāh daftar ta ba zee.*
55. My dog got a thorn stuck in his foot, went lame and would not work.	*Zamā da spi puh khpa ké aghzay māt sho. gud sho aw kār yé nuh sho kawalay.*

56. I shall pay him out when he comes back.	*Chi biarta rāshee no ba war sara poh sham.*
57. He was very disconcerted when the stolen property was found in his pocket.	*Chi da ghlā māl yé luh jéb na barāmad sho, no dér kacha sho.*
58. Needless to say he himself was convinced of his bad habit.	*Puh dé ké shak nishta chi hagha pakhpala hum puh khpal bad ādat qāil woh.*
59. I had many misfires but even then I shot 125 head of game.	*Dér zala mé tōpak ghal sho, kho biā hum mé pinzuh da pāsa shpag shalé marghān wo wishtal.*
60. I would have shot many more, but my cartridges were beginning to get wet and would not go off.	*Nōr dér ba mé hum wishtali wōo khō kārtūsāna mé puh laundédo rāghlal aw nuh khlāsédal.*
61. I have caught cold.	*Zuh yakhnai wahalay yam.*
62. Who has caught fever?	*Sōk tabé niwalay day?*
63. The villagers have small pox.	*Puh kali wālo bāndé nanakai khatali di.*
64. My servant has plague.	*Zamā puh naukar bāndé tāūn lagédalay day.*
65. After I came back from the office I had to go to the city.	*Luh daftar rātlo na pas zuh khwā makhwah khahar ta lāram.*

66. After I finish my work I will have to go to the cantt.	*Chi kār khlās kram nō khwā makhwāh ba chawnrai ta zam.*
67. Don't fire unless you are fired at.	*Kuh dar bāndé daz wo nuh shi no tuh daz muh kawa.*
68. Don't fire unless it is absolutely necessary.	*Kuh bilkul zarūrat pékh nuh shi no daz muh kawa.*
69. Don't allow him to go unless he has a proper pass.	*Kuh war sakha barābar pāss nuh wi no tlo ta yé muh prégda (*or *muh yé prégda chi lārshee).*
70. If I were or had been there I would not have let you do this work.	*Kuh zuh halta way, no mā ba tuh dé kār kawalo ta prekhay nuh wé.*
71. If he is there I shall certainly produce him before the Magistrate.	*Kuh hagha halta wi no zarūr ba yé zuh majestarait ta pésh kram.*
72. He abused me vilely but I said nothing.	*Rā ta yé dér (*or *bad bad) kanzal wo kral, kho mā hiss wo nuh wayal.*
73. The tribe gave 10 hostages and deposited 15 Snider rifles as security.	*Qām las tana yarghamal war kralo aw pinzalas kuniz topak yé da zamānat pa taur war kral.*
74. Formerly this land had no means of irrigation except rain fall.	*Puh khwā zamāna ké dā zamaka bārāni (*or *lalma) wah.*

75. Wait here until I come back from the city.	*Tar sō pōré chi zuh luh khahar na biarta rā nuh sham dalé isār sha.*
76. I sold my horse to him for 50 rupees.	*Mā khpal ass puh haghuh bāndé puh panzōs rūpai khars kar.*
77. Never mind I will engage a barrister and prosecute him in the law court.	*Hess bāk nishta yau wakil ba wōnisam aw war bāndé ba puh adālat ké dawa wo kram.*
78. I have engaged a mali, who really knows his job.	*Yau māli mé sātalay day chi waqi puh khpal kār khuh pōhégee.*
79. Challenge him first and then shoot.	*Awal war bāndé awāz wo kra aw biā yé wola.*
80. Will you call out to my servant?	*Lūkūti zamā naukar ta khō awaz wo kra?*
81. My village was raided on the 15th of last month.	*Da téré miāshté puh pinzalasam tārīkh zamā puh kali bāndé dāra préwata.*
82. If the stolen property is not found the tribes will be heavily fined.	*Kuh da ghlā māl wo nuh mūndalay shi no pa qām bāndé ba lōi jurum préwozi.*
83. Button your coat.	*Da kōt batanūna dé wāchawa.*
84. Tie on your putties.	*Patai dé wo tara* (or *tāw kra)*
85. Put on your turban.	*Patkay dé puh sar kra* or *wo waha.*

86. Put on your shoes.	*Panré dé puh khpo kra.*
87. If you like to start so early you will have to put on your gloves.	*Kuh dāsé wākhtī rāwānégé nō khwā makhwāh ba dastāné puh lās kawé.*
88. Do not be angry with me.	*Luh mā na muh khapa kéga.*
89. I am sorry I did not notice you until you passed on.	*Zuh afsōs kawam chi tar hagha wakhta mé wo nuh lidé chi tér shwé.*
90. Open your mouth, you must take this medicine at once, otherwise the fever will recur.	*Khuluh wāza kra, dā dārū dar la samdasti skal pakār di, kuh nuh wi nō taba ba darbāndé biā rāshee.*
91. Shut your mouth after drinking medicine.	*Luh dāro skalo na pas khuluh dé piché kra.*
92. Open your eyes and look towards me.	*Stargé wō gharawa aw zamā taraf ta wo gōra.*
93. Shut your eyes and don't open them till I speak to you.	*Stargé paté kra aw muh yé gharawa tar sō pōré chi zuh dar sara khabaré wo nuh kram.*
94. Open your book and start from where we had got up to	*Kitāb dé wo ghwarawa aw tar kuma zāia pōré chi mō lawastay day, luh hagha zāi na shūrū kra.*
95. Listen to me.	*Ghwag kégda,*
96. Do you hear?	*Ghwag dé day?*
97 I know what you mean.	*Sta puh matlab zuh pōhégam.*

98. I asked him what village he came from.	*Ma war na tapōs wo kar chi da kum kali yé.*
99. I have nothing to do with him.	*Zamā war sara hiss gharaz nishta.*
100. Can not you write with a pencil ?	*Tuh puh pensan nuh shé likalay ?*
101. I cannot give him any more.	*War ta nōr nuh sham warkawalay.*
102. In spite of all his good evidence the magistrate had to punish him.	*Sara da haghuh da khé gawāhai majestarait war ta khwā makhwāh sazā war kra.*
103. I will let you off if you tell me the whole truth.	*Kuh tōla khabara rā ta rishtiā rishtiā wō kré no pré ba dé gdam.*
104. Let us go to that large village and arrange for grass for our horses.	*Rāza chi hagha lōi kali ta lār shōo aw da khpalo asūno da wākho da pāra bandūbast wo kroo.*
105. Sahib, I have suffered much injustice.	Sā*hiba puh mā bāndé déra be insāfi shawé dah.*
106. He must come himself and bring all the books with him.	*Pakār di chi pakhpala rāshee aw tōl kitābūna da zān sara rāwree.*
107. After three days we found out that the ropes of the tents were missing.	*Dré vrazé pas mūng khabar shoo chi da tambwānō rasai vraké di.*
108. Put it.	*Ké yé gda.*
109. Give it to me	*Rā yé kra.*

110. He has two sons, one takes after his mother and the other takes after his father.	*Dwa zāman yé di, yau mōr ta talay day aw bal plār ta talay day.*
111. I would rather sit in the veranda than out in the field.	*Da bahar pati na kho zamā khwakha dah chi puh baranda hé kénam.*
112. He lives next door to me.	*Hagha rā sara déwāl puh déwāl osee.*
113. Next door but one there lives a gambler.	*Puh drem kōr ké yau jawārgar osee.*
114. Last year the Malik's wife eloped with a Peshawari barber.	*Parosakal da malak khaza yau pekhawri nāi sara lāra* or *matiza shwa.*
115. I saw him passing by my door.	*Mā hagha wo lidalo chi zamā puh darwāza térédo.*
116. You ought to have gone yesterday.	*Tā la parūn tlal pakār woo* (or) *pakar woo chi tuh parūn talay way.*
117. I must write to the General about the deficiency of rations.	*Da rasan da kami pa bāb ké pakār di chi zuh jarnail sāhib ta wo likam.*
118. Wind the watch otherwise it will stop.	*Garai la kunji war kra ganra wo ba drégi.*
119. May God make you the king of this country !	*Khudāi dé da dé mulk bādshāh kra !*
120. This made me think that my regt.	*Pa dé khābara mé fikar wo kar chi bala*

would move on the next day.	*vraz ba paltan mé rawānégee.*
121. Wind your turban round my gun.	*Patkay dé zamā luh tōpak na tāw kra.*
122. I saw him coming.	*Hagha mé wo lido chi rātlo.*
123. I shot him dead with a revolver.	*Hagha mé puh tamācha wo wishto au mar mé kro.*
124. A scorpion stung my toe.	*Yau laram da khpé puh gōta wo chichalam.*
125. He fired at me and hit my finger.	*Rā bāndé yé daz wo kar aw puh gōta yé wo wishtam.*
126. Have my watch repaired.	*Garai mé puh chā muramata kra.*
127. Come on this day week.	*Puh nananai vraz rāsha.*
128. Learn your yesterday's lesson.	*Parūnay sabaq dé yād kra.*
129. Take care not to come by this road again.	*Paham kawa chi biā pa dé lār rā nuh shé.*
130. He may come.	*Gundé hagha rāshee.*